Barbara & Marvin,

Never give up.
Never give in

Stay RIGHT always!

Gil @ the Tygrrrr Express

TYGRRRR EXPRESS

IDEOLOGICAL VIOLENCE

A politically conservative and morally liberal Hebrew alpha male hunts jihadists, peace activists, and other violent leftists and shoves the American flag up their (redacted).

By eric aka the Tygrrrr Express

iUniverse, Inc.
New York   Bloomington

IDEOLOGICAL VIOLENCE
A politically conservative and morally liberal Hebrew alpha male hunts jihadists, peace activists, and other violent leftists and shoves the American flag up their (redacted)

iUniverse books may be ordered through booksellers or by contacting:

iUniverse
1663 Liberty Drive
Bloomington, IN 47403
www.iuniverse.com
1-800-Authors (1-800-288-4677)

Because of the dynamic nature of the Internet, any Web addresses or links contained in this book may have changed since publication and may no longer be valid.

ISBN: 978-1-4502-1486-5 (sc)
ISBN: 978-1-4502-1488-9 (dj)
ISBN: 978-1-4502-1487-2 (ebk)

Printed in the United States of America

iUniverse rev. date: 3/11/2010

Eric is the brilliance (and lowest common denominator) behind the Tygrrrr Express, the 2007 Bloggers Choice Award for Most Passionate Fan Base.

He is also the author of the books "Ideological Bigotry" and "Ideological Idiocy."

"The Tygrrrr Express" has been published in the Washington Times, Jewish Journal, RealClearPolitics Online, Commentary Magazine Online, and on the Web sites of Hugh Hewitt, Mark Steyn, Michelle Malkin, and Andrew Breitbart's "Big Hollywood."

A sought after public speaker, he has addressed many chapters of the Republican Women's Federated. He enjoys talking to the ladies because the men are sissies and the women feed him better than his exes. He has also spoken to College Republicans, Young Republicans, and the Republican Jewish Coalition. Occasionally those meals are not bad.

A radio host since 1992, his radio beginning was a sophomoric hard rock music program entitled "Hard as a Rock." Maturation settled in (barely), and serious radio interviews with top politicos and other notables ensued. On the flip side of the microphone, the Tygrrrr Express has been a radio guest of Hugh Hewitt, Dennis Miller, and Armstrong Williams, in addition to being a frequent guest of Frank and Shane of "Political Vindication" on Blog Talk Radio.

The Tygrrrr Express has conducted print interviews of virtually every top politician, although the Secret Service still will not allow a warm hug of President George W. Bush or Vice President Cheney.

Honors and privileges include sleeping for an entire week in a sports bar with full access to the beverages and pizza, in addition to meeting Miss Wilmington, North Carolina.

Often referred to as a "typical white person," the Tygrrrr Express in the future will be editor of the yet to be created "Boring Dull Whitey Monthly."

Rumors of his spending quiet evenings alone dreaming about passionate nights with Barbara Bush are not entirely true. Rumors of the Secret Service investigating whether he means the granddaughter or the grandmother are somewhat untrue.

About: The Tygrrrr Express is me. I am Brooklyn born, Strong Island raised, and currently living the good life in Los Angeles as a stockbrokerage and oil professional.

While Wall Street is forever in my blood, I am now on the speaking circuit full-time.

I like politics, the National Football League, '80s hard rock music, the stock market, and red meat. Blogging is a shameless ploy to get what I really want, which is to be sandwiched between a pair of Republican Jewish brunettes, and impregnate at least one of them. There will be a ceremony several months beforehand since my parents are NRA members.

The only political issue more important than killing taxes is killing terrorists. I do not sing "Kumbaya" with Islamofascists or leftists. Scorched Earth is my approach, with the grace and subtlety of a battering ram. The events of 9/11 fuel my emotions every day. Civilization must defeat barbarism, and my generation is up the challenge. We will win the War on Terror, because we are Americans.

eric, aka the Tygrrrr Express

To my future son: Although you have yet to be born, my generation's fight to the death against third-world genocidal Islamists is so that you can live in a peaceful world. For the good of civilization, I pray that you end up with my last name and your mother's everything else.

Warning: This book was written between March of 2007 and December 31st, 2009. It was written under the assumption that Islamofascists did not blow up the world on January 1, 2010. If they did, you have bigger problems than this book not being up to date.

Contents

Chapter 0:
A Combative from the Get-go Foreword

When I wrote my first book, I expressed that those wishing to learn all about me could buy my second book. Consider this my third book. If you are already monitoring me, you have seen me sit for hours on end watching ESPN and Fox News. You have witnessed me railing against bad referees and all liberals. If watching me in this way excites you, then you need to be reported to the cast of *Law and Order: Special Victims Unit*. You are most likely some sort of stalker or predator.

My family consists of intensely private people. They did not ask about you, and won't answer your questions. They don't even answer mine. Then again, I mind my own business and don't ask anything.

Besides that, I am so unbelievably important that you should know who I am already. Sorry about that remark. I briefly became a liberal college professor screaming at an imaginary police officer. The flashback is over.

The world is going to heck in a hand-basket. Conservatives are busy trying to save the world. Liberals are trying to figure out whether we should ask the bad guys to be nicer, apologize for inconveniencing them, or both.

Without love and laughter, there is no life. Nothing I do will change the world, but if I get a stiff person to lighten up and smile, I am pleased.

So whether your favorite charity is Enemas for Mullahs or Nuke the Libyan Baby Seals, the political spectrum of life has space for you.

Relax, have an artificially flavored beverage and red meat derivative, and enjoy what I have to say. You already bought the book, so you might as well read it.

This book is a compilation of columns ranging from the angry to the lighthearted. This was done so that if what I am saying enrages you, in two or three pages I will be on to something to make you more enraged and forget the first offending remark. For those that abhor salaciousness and scandal, skip chapter seven. For those that want to avoid anything that may expand the mind, skip the first six chapters.

So get on board and ride the Tygrrrr's back to the finish line of this book. You'll be glad you did. Welcome to the 2007 Bloggers Choice Awards Winner for Most Passionate Fan Base. Welcome to the Tygrrrr Express.

eric

P.S. I sign my name with a lowercase "e." If this bothers you, take a pen and correct your own copy.

Chapter 1:
Ideological Violence

Liberals like to declare every conservative on the planet to be either evil or stupid. This book is about their declaration of our unadulterated evil. This is ideological violence. Ideological violence is the frothing, pathological desire of liberals to resort to any anti-social means necessary to hurt conservatives for merely being alive and having a pulse. Such actions would include hate crimes except that crimes cannot be committed against conservative, white male oppressors. Liberals are angry when they wake up in the morning and enraged when they go to bed at night. They will not stop the violence on their own. When dealing with any jihadist, war is the answer.

Ideological Bigotry Part VIII–Search and Destroy

The ends now justify the means. For the sake of the common good, it is permissible to lie in the name of a higher truth. Slander and libel are necessary if it leads to a better world.

I have not become a liberal. I just borrowed page one from their life playbook. The next time one of them stands up and demands that the politics of personal destruction come to an end, I will simply reply, "You are a liberal. You are the politics of personal destruction."

To hell with comity. It doesn't work. It's pointless. Liberals despise conservatives with a ferocity that conservatives reserve for al-Qaeda.

I have disagreed with many liberals, but I never despised them. I want to defeat them at the ballot box, not destroy them personally. This is where we differ. For those who complain that indicting all liberals is unfair, my challenge is that the good ones stay silent. Silence is acquiescence. Edmund Burke himself said that evil prevails "when good people do nothing."[1] The left in this country is divided between practitioners of hatred and quiet enablers. Several victims have been targeted simply for being conservative and existing.

Bill O'Reilly was labeled a racist for being a white conservative who discussed race. Many people in this country dislike Bill O'Reilly. He has been described as bombastic, pugnacious, obnoxious, overbearing, and other friendly adjectives. Every single one of those descriptions is completely within the bounds of conversation. Labeling someone a racist is not. There is only one legitimate reason to label somebody a preacher of hatred. The description must be truthful. There is no evidence that Bill O'Reilly has ever made racist remarks. If he was a racist, he would not be on television. Bill O'Reilly was slandered. No "greater good" justifies this.

Rush Limbaugh was also targeted. He once commented about people who pretended to serve in the military. He referred to those exaggerating or outright lying about their service as "phony soldiers."[2] The left screeched that Limbaugh derided all soldiers who were against the Iraq War. They were all unpatriotic, phony soldiers.

This was an outright lie. Rush Limbaugh is in the public arena. His comments are absolutely fair game for legitimate criticism. Manipulating his words to completely change the meaning of what he says is disgusting. Those repeatedly doing this know that their charges are false. Mr. Limbaugh has over two decades of stating his respect for soldiers. He does not question the patriotism of people just because they disagree with him. It was majority loser Harry Reid who called Limbaugh unpatriotic.[3]

Another person slandered by Harry Reid and Hillary Clinton is General David Petraeus. They called him a liar. They did not use the actual word, preferring to fall back on gutless similes such as "misled," "strains credibility," and, "defies belief."[4] In plain English, the general was told that his pants were on fire. Moveon.org referred to him as "General Betray Us"[5] because he disagreed with their assessment of the war. The basis of his disagreement appears to stem from his having had boots on the ground in Iraq. Militarily, he is an intellectual titan. His critics are intellectual ants.

Some say that Bill O'Reilly, Rush Limbaugh and General David Petraeus deserve this treatment. O'Reilly and Limbaugh regularly skewer progressives on their show. The general is leading a war they despise. These men got off easy compared to one of the most brutal character assassinations in American history. Brutal slander and libel was directed at U.S. Supreme Court Justice Clarence Thomas.

Justice Thomas is an American success story. He has never hosted a radio show or led an unpopular war. All he did was rise out of abject poverty to become a respected professional in the legal field. At the eleventh hour, when liberals failed to defeat the conservative nominee on merit, Anita Hill came forward with sexual harassment charges that to this day have never been proven. It was "the seriousness of the charges"[6] that led to the delay. Apparently the same standard was not given to Bill Clinton. Ted Kennedy of all people got to sit on a panel and offer judgment on the moral fitness of Clarence Thomas to be a judge. The bloated, besotted senator was not known for expertise in morality or fitness.

Some might ask why Judge Thomas is not hailed as an America hero given his incredible rise in society. The mediocre Sonia Sotomayor was celebrated for being a Latina liberal. White latte liberals publicly adore Latina liberals, even if they privately would never deign to associate with them. Justice Thomas is a black conservative. His true story getting out could still galvanize blacks. While not automatically voting Republican, at least there is a chance blacks would listen to what conservatives had to say.

Judge Thomas properly described his confirmation hearings as a "disgrace," and a "high tech lynching for uppity blacks."[7] How else can one describe the viciousness with which this man was attacked?

Liberals could have attacked Justice Thomas on his qualifications. I was not convinced he was one of the finest legal minds when he was nominated. Given that he almost never asked questions, I found it tough to learn more about him. However, an interview he did showed an incredibly bright, thoughtful and kind human being. I have never heard a story of Justice Thomas being rude to anybody.

While Limbaugh and O'Reilly can be inviting targets, Justice Thomas seems to be an overwhelmingly gracious individual. Does fearing his willingness to overturn Roe vs. Wade justify lying about him and trying to destroy his honor?

Where does it end?

I supported the investigations of the Clintons, but was horrified at stories declaring Chelsea a product of rape, or that Hillary was a lesbian. I was one of the first people to stand up and say that Hillary and Bill loved each other, and that they raised a daughter who has blossomed into a successful young woman that any parent would be proud to call their own.

I disagree with almost every belief that Hillary and Bill stand for. I still want them to lead happy lives nowhere near 1600 Pennsylvania Avenue. I would invite Bill over to watch the NFL on Sundays as long as he focused on the games (the same rules apply for all guests who mistakenly think free speech exists in my home when watching football).

One lingering question that must be answered is…who cares? Why does this matter?

The first reason this matters is because the pendulum swings. Neither side has power forever. Both sides can argue over who started decimating opponents. Neither side is willing to unilaterally stop for fear of being seen as weak. Yet it must stop. If Hillary were to lead, how could she expect to be treated with grace when her path to power is scorched Earth? How can liberals talk about building bridges when they are burning them every chance they get?

The second reason this matters is because it is just plain wrong to lie. The ends do not justify the means. Ethicists do not even support the "therapeutic lie" concept, rejecting it en masse. Macbeth got to be king, but look at the price he paid. Without the moral authority to lead, everybody suffers. Those who tore down Bill Clinton should not have been shocked at what was done to George W. Bush. Those who tore down George W. Bush should not be shocked at what happens to Barack Obama. Some may say, "Well in our case it was justified. Look at his policies." These men are not Hitler, Stalin or Pol Pot. Smears and lies are not okay. When lies are uncovered, other good ideas the liars may have been proposing get scrapped. Whole ideas get invalidated. The backlash causes more harm to the one firing the slings and arrows. People who could possibly work together for a common good refuse to do so because the animosity runs too deep.

The third reason this matters is because unlike Limbaugh and O'Reilly, most Americans do not have a platform to repudiate baseless accusations and venom. Accusations stick. They scar, wound, and destroy. People have committed suicide over despair. Does a person have to take their own life before others realize that they inflicted part of the pain?

The fourth and last reason this matters is the life and death struggle civilization currently faces. Between al-Qaeda, Iran, Hamas, Hezbollah, Damascus, and other global evils, our elected leaders should be squarely focused on fighting terror. Republicans are. Democrats are not. Liberals brag about standing up to Bill O'Reilly, fighting back against Ann Coulter, taking on Rush Limbaugh, and other pursuits that bring zero positives to society.

Ann Coulter did not fly a plane into the towers. Bill O'Reilly did not murder three thousand New Yorkers. Rush Limbaugh does not fund homicide bombers. Clarence Thomas is not harboring plutonium to build nuclear bombs.

Rush Limbaugh has twenty million listeners. Even if every one of them agreed with him (totally not the case), two hundred-eighty million people are not listening to him. Bill O'Reilly peaked at seven million listeners. While Clarence Thomas makes important decisions, he interacts with eight other people. Not eight million…eight!

Rather than hold positions that affect 10-12 percent of the electorate, and then blaming Republicans for being racist, insensitive bigots, the left should start talking to everybody! Take the passion reserved for talk show hosts with no real, actual power, and direct it at people who wish to murder all Americans, liberal and conservative.

The left must argue policy, and they must do so honestly. Lying about words, deeds and data only makes it tougher for the accuser to be given the benefit of the doubt when it is their turn under the microscope.

The left must stop the search and destroy missions. America is worth saving. The enemy of Americans is not their fellow Americans. We can either have reasonable discussions at the dinner table or we can break the table in half and have our grandchildren ask us why we failed to act in time to protect their way of life.

If we fail, God help us all. We must succeed. Ideological bigotry must stop.

eric

Bush Derangement Syndrome—The Suicide of Logical Reasoning

"November 8, 2004 — Families of 9/11 victims yesterday reacted with shock, sympathy — and anger — after a Georgia man killed himself at Ground Zero on his 25th birthday because he was distraught over President Bush's re-election.

The suicide victim, Andrew Veal, was discovered on a concrete slab in the construction pit near the Church Street subway entrance Saturday morning. A bottle of Jack Daniel's was by his side, and a 12-gauge shotgun lay across his body.

Authorities believe that Veal, who was engaged to be married, killed himself sometime Friday — his birthday, friends said. Law-enforcement officials and friends said Veal, a project coordinator at the University of Georgia Research Center who also did political polling, had been depressed over the outcome of the election. Friends also said he may have killed himself to protest the war in Iraq.

'He cared about politics, people and the state of the world,' Mary Ann Mauney, his supervisor at the university, told the Athens Banner Herald. 'Andrew was definitely sending a message [with the suicide].' Certainly, it was a protest."[8]

Excerpts from that *New York Post* article are still relevant years later. That Mother's Day found one mother without her son. I am sure she didn't care about anything political that day. She misses her child. My heart goes out to her.

For those who suffer from Bush Derangement Syndrome, George W. Bush had nothing to do with this kid's death. President Bush never met him. The kid did not serve in any branch of the Armed Forces. This deeply troubled young man was consumed and swallowed up by life. As too many do, he took his own life.

I wonder how many liberals bothered to take the time to talk to this kid. He was one of them. Given how chic and trendy Bush hatred has become, one would think this kid was the darling of dinner parties. The problem with spreading hatred is that people are so busy talking and hating that they do not make time for listening and loving, even with people who agree with them.

I am absolutely not blaming liberals, liberalism or Democrats for this young man's demise. What I am saying is that a culture of hatred can lead to despair. When a political mob gets its youngest and most impressionable supporters to the brink of overload, perceived failure can lead to an irreversible downward spiral. Palesimian children are trained to be suicide bombers. Political warriors train young armies to engage in destruction. Too many children are taught to invest everything into some kind of cause. When everything activists believe in gets blown to kingdom come, the reaction of many is to end it all rather than go on.

How many Hollywood celebrities threatened to move to Canada or Europe if Bush was reelected? Why are they still here? They remain for the same reason that Osama Bin Laden and Yassir Arafat never personally flew plane into towers, put on a suicide vest, or had their families do so. Why fight for a fake cause when one can recruit innocent impressionable young minds, and mold them into true believers?

This young man was not born a Bush-hater. Somebody had to indoctrinate Bush Derangement Syndrome into his skull. Had people bothered to teach him that life is precious, he might still be living. Anyone can improve the world on any given day. He could have lived to see Nancy Pelosi become speaker of the house. That event disgusted me, but it would have made him smile.

Sometimes nothing truly can be done. Other times the signs were clearly marked. Kurt Cobain's last song was called "I Hate Myself and I Want to Die."[9] Four million people purchased that song. Had one of those people seen it was a cry for help, Cobain might be alive today. I disliked his music but still empathize that his daughter will never know her father. When a man is screaming that he wants to end it all, it might be wise to consider the possibility that he is sincere.

I was disgusted when Bill Clinton became president. My response was to become a member of the loyal opposition. Thanks to Newt Gingrich, Haley Barbour and Rush Limbaugh, America dragged Clinton rightward, and then gave us George W. Bush.

Perhaps it is an incredible mistake to offer rational explanations for irrational behavior such as suicide. Yet the coarsening of our culture is creating levels of rage, hostility, and seething resentment. Nothing positive comes out of this. What is the point of helping a candidate win an election if you lose your soul in the process? I fiercely disagree with liberals, but I do not hate their guts. If Hillary Clinton (God forbid) were to win the White House, I would be feeling negative thoughts and emotions that I hope I never have to describe. I would then go on trying to be a better person and making something of myself in this crazy world.

This young man was engaged to be married. If enough of the true believers around him had spent less time spreading poison and more time truly spreading peace and love, this kid might have survived the 2004 election.

Bush Derangement Syndrome has got to stop. Even the most powerful man in the world cannot directly make my life better or worse. I am my destiny.

I pray that his mother somehow manages to go on.

Perspective is so easy to lose. I am grateful that enough people around me are there to provide it for me.

I thank those who always gave me a sense of hope during my darkest hours. Knowing I can call them no matter how rough life gets is a life saver.

eric

January 20th, 2009–The Death of the Left

The left was on life support, and officially died on January 20th, 2009. This is because a new president took office.

It did not matter who won the White House. The left is done.

The Scott Beauchamp scandal was the final nail in the coffin. Without it, the left's demise would still be taking place. This scandal is only a symptom. The much larger disease is hatred.

The left has been reduced to rubble. They are simply a collection of angry, bitter, broken, hateful, spiteful individuals. I say this with zero glee. It is tragic.

Charles Krauthammer coined the term, "Bush Derangement Syndrome."[10] The left offers a multitude of examples that they consider legitimate reasons for hating George W. Bush. I will reject them all out of hand. There is no reason to despise him or any other mainstream American politician.

Adolf Hitler murdered members of my family. Hatred of Stalin, Pol Pot, and other despots whose lives are dedicated to mass murder is reasonable.

George W. Bush is only a cold-blooded murderer if one turns the world of right and wrong upside down. Why does this hatred occur?

The Clinton impeachment of 1998 and the close election of 2000 are the reasons for this. It has nothing to do with 9/11, the War in Iraq, abortion, or anything else. Republicans and conservatives were despised before George W. Bush ever began his campaign. George W. Bush himself was despised the moment he took office. The election was not stolen or fraudulent. It was simply close.

The left did not want to defeat President Bush legislatively. They wanted to humiliate him, grind him into dust, and haunt him for the rest of his life. That is what hatred does. It becomes an obsession. The problem with this is basic. George W. Bush left office on January 20th, 2009.

When Republicans win the White House again, the left will have to take all this hatred toward President Bush and direct it toward somebody new. They need to start despising potential conservative candidates now. Otherwise these people might be seen as human beings and not the evil cardboard cutouts that they need to be for the left to exist.

Winning the White House did not calm the left down. It actually made things worse for them. Republican victories had the left merely losing electorally. Democrats can win, but liberals cannot. When Democrats win, they face pressure by the moderates that put them into power to stay moderate. Even liberal sympathizers are unable to accommodate the left ideologically. Look at how many on the left booed Hillary Clinton.

This is not about elections. It is about humanity. I genuinely still fear for George W. Bush's life. I fear that some wacko on the left will abandon the democratic process. Conservatives routinely have their lawn signs stolen and their cars keyed. An act of unspeakable violence is certainly not out of the realm of possibility.

Many mainstream liberals may be horrified at such a scenario, but what are they doing to prevent it? If anyone thinks rhetoric does not lead to violence, ask somebody who bombed an animal testing lab or an oil factory. Look at the democracy of Israel. Yitzchak Rabin was assassinated by a Jewish citizen over a political issue.

Presidents have been killed before. I pray that the rage that has engulfed the left does not lead to more bloodshed. President Bush is called a murderer by many. He is compared to Hitler and called evil. It is totally reasonable to expect somebody to go over the edge and bring things to what they consider to be a logical and justified conclusion.

I even pray to God that the left somehow take collective deep breaths and realize that their existence does not have to depend on who is in the White House. I disagreed with Bill Clinton. It did not stop me from becoming a respected and productive member of American society.

Dissent is patriotic. Hatred is a poison. Look at the biggest suppliers of hate in the world. Syria and the Palesimians spread evil through Hamas and Hezbollah. What have they achieved that is positive? Nothing.

If you dehumanize your opponent and declare that opponent an enemy, is it no wonder that you will feel that your existence depends on your enemy ceasing to exist?

George W. Bush is a human being. Until the left finds a way to criticize his policies without hating his guts, they will remain lost and emotionally empty.

Emotional emptiness is what is forcing the left to lie so that their vision of George W. Bush fits their characterization of him as evil. An evil man would allow three thousand Americans to die in New York to boost his poll ratings. An evil man would invade a sovereign nation and kill millions for sport.

Those who speak the worst about the president have to therefore be telling the truth, no matter how much evidence refutes this. Scott Beauchamp lied about atrocities being committed by U.S. soldiers. A leftist magazine printed those lies. How could this have happened?

The lies spread because the truth did not matter. The story had to be told because it was powerful and bad for President Bush. This is how CBS can state that memos bashing President Bush are "fake but accurate."[11] This is how the *New York Times* can shred its reputation and become the "Jayson Blair" *Times* (*JBT*). The ends justify the means. People on the left are noble and righteous. People on the right are the enemy. It is acceptable to lie and cheat if one is doing so for noble reasons.

This is how liberals can tolerate one senator who drove off a bridge and killed a woman, and another that was a leader in the Ku Klux Klan. The ends justify the means.

Conservatives in this country were near death in the 1960s. We climbed out of the abyss by expressing principles and policies. We formed think tanks. We wrote position papers. We questioned everything we did, and built ourselves up again from scratch. Our ideas and principles led us to electoral success.

The left wants to get elected, and then have an argument about which way to direct the country. That is backwards. The rigorous, soul-tearing debates must come first. The Republicans got hammered in the 1964 election. The ensuing debate strengthened us in the long run. We did not sit around and despise LBJ. We licked our wounds and got back to work.

This is a moderately conservative country. We support the death penalty by an overwhelming margin. We think our government taxes and spends too much. We believe that free trade works, and that isolationism is impractical and unhelpful. We believe in God, and the right of people to pray without being harassed.

The left offers policies that are simply not what much of America wants at this time in history. Even Democrats winning the White House was due to a rejection of a particular Republican candidate, not an embrace of a liberal ideology.

Many on the left wanted to impeach President Bush, unable to comprehend that he was leaving office voluntarily long before the process would have finished. Some wanted to end the war immediately, because humiliating George W. Bush was more important than doing right by our soldiers. You cannot say you support the troops and then cut off their funding. A Democrat began leading them. Then what? The Iraq and Afghanistan wars are still going on. Is war now okay? The left is committing fratricide over this very issue that tore them to shreds in 1968.

Dissenters should have an alternative positive agenda. Republicans who sparred with Clinton offered the "Contract With America." Not everybody liked the plan, but at least a plan existed.

January 20th, 2009 came and went. I live my life. My happiness and existence is not determined by who wins elections. Some are still blaming President Bush for their miserable lots in life. Electoral victories will not fill the voids in their black hearts.

Those who offer only rejectionism, hatred and rage are spreading poison. When they win an election, they expect the right to then just make nice. Life does not work this way. I will not encourage payback, but I will not be able to stop it either.

I ask the left to please control its more volatile factions before something tragic happens. God forbid President Bush suffers a fate that no good man deserves. The entire left will be explaining why it does not have blood on its collective hands. Like Scott Beauchamp, these instigators will be lying.

May God bless and forever protect President Bush and his family from those who are perilously close to the edge. May they tone it down and see him as a human being. May they understand that he disagrees with them, but still cares about them. They are part of the family of America.

eric

Liberals Talk About Improving the World, Conservatives Actually Do It

Despite being hopelessly wrong on almost every significant issue, liberals are not my enemies. They are my political opponents. I do not hate them. I disagree with them. While some of them are disgustingly cynical (Harry Reid wanting America to lose in Iraq because it benefits Democrats at the polls, soldiers lives be d@mned), most liberals have generally noble intentions. They want to make the world a better place. The problem is that intentions are all liberals have. Conservatives bring results. Results are all that matter. Words are meaningless. Deeds change history.

Liberal environmentalists tell us that the planet is cooling, warming, and then just changing. Humans are causing this, humans can prevent it, and anyone disagreeing with this viewpoint is an imbecile. Conservatives understand that radical environmental regulations would cripple the global economy. The poorest nations would be hurt most.

On a small scale, I am less concerned about the spotted owl than I am about hundreds of families going hungry because timber workers are fired. We can help the owl and the timber worker, but the left simply values animal rights over human beings. Drilling in Alaska is a step toward reducing American dependence on foreign oil. That should be the overriding factor. Trees are not as important as human beings fighting a War on Terror.

On a large scale, liberals are wrong on trade. Free trade works. The positives to global trade deals far outweigh the negatives. We hear about outsourcing, but there is a significant amount of "insourcing." Protectionism has never worked. Wage and price controls don't work either.

Liberals want to raise taxes. Conservatives want to lower them. Those believing that governments do a better job than the private sector of anything (except the outstanding military, the one government entity liberals dislike) should ask the DMV, post office, or any other government service to help run their business. Government workers are not bad people. It's just that business is about reducing bureaucracy and encouraging innovation. Government by definition is a bureaucracy. Lower taxes help all income brackets. Tax cuts produce economic growth. JFK understood this. Democrats were not always liberals.

Liberals wanted peace between America and the Russians. Everything would be fine if we were just diplomatic with the Russians. Conservatives believed in the policy of containment (started by Harry Truman...back when Democrats were not liberals, they were allowed to be tough on foreign policy). When

Ronald Reagan said "Mr. Gorbachev, tear down this wall,"[12] he meant it. Reagan is beloved not just for his noble words, but for the resulting actions that took place.

Liberals spent years explaining why Iraq had nothing to do with the War on Terror. They remain utterly wrong. The Islamofascists trying to kill us said that it was the central front. A lot of good has come out of the Iraq War. Saddam is dead. So are his sons. Libya's Khadafi voluntarily gave up his weapons program. This was not because of years of negotiations. This is a total and direct result of Saddam being defeated, captured and killed. Often thought of as a lunatic, Khadafi turned out to be quite pragmatic. He saw what happened to Saddam and thought, "I don't need this hassle. Dubya has had it. I better take up golf or tennis instead." It is also worth noting that Khadafi slowed down severely after Reagan bombed his home in 1986.

Liberals complain that four thousand people died as a result of the Iraq War. I callously say that this is irrelevant. I honor the fallen soldiers. It sickens me to lose one American soldier. This is the price of freedom. We lost hundreds of thousands of soldiers in wars throughout our history. Should we have not fought at Gettysburg? What about World War II? Sometimes war is the answer. War is Hell. Losing all of civilization is worse.

Time after time, on issue after issue, well-intentioned liberals make great speeches that amount to nothing in terms of actual accomplishments. Barack Obama and John Edwards are brilliant speakers. My political resume is about as distinguished as theirs, and all I do is vote. Rudy Giuliani and John McCain are giants. They got things done.

Everyone wants to make the world a better place. Those on the left should come up with real solutions that are feasible and practical. A good start is implementing ideas without bankrupting the global economy or risking global security. Until then, liberals will continue to be seen as well-intentioned idealists that accomplish nothing. This is one step above making things worse, and two steps above praying for bad results globally to benefit themselves politically. Liberals could try another tack. They could actually do things…and do them right…and make a real difference…and benefit people everywhere. Then again, these people already exist. They are called conservatives.

eric

Why Not Just Kill All Conservatives?

Although I am a conservative, I have noticed that liberals in congress feel that the very existence of conservatives threatens this nation. Since it is the job of our current liberal leaders to protect Americans and keep us safe, why don't they just pass legislation to kill all conservatives?

I have not fallen off the cliff of sanity. I am following the logical train of thought.

Nazis felt that Jews were an enemy of Germany. Jews were subversives, an enemy within. As the son of a Holocaust survivor, I will be the first to attest to the pure evil of the Holocaust. At least the murderers followed a logical progression. They dehumanized Jews first. Once Jews were reduced to mere vermin or insects, treating them with the dignity that one treats human lives was unnecessary.

According to liberals in congress, conservatives are not human beings. They are a scourge. It makes perfect sense to just eliminate them forever.

This is not my decision. I am just listening to their words.

One Florida congressman decided to take over the role of leading bigoted lunatic in Florida now that Robert Wexler is leaving. His words were inspiring to anybody who found warmth in hatred.

"People who watch Fox News are collaborators with the enemies of America."[13]

Collaborators? I had no idea that people who watched Fox News favored putting my relatives into ovens.

For those who think that using the word "collaborators" is a reference to anything besides the Holocaust, separate your liberal head from your liberal hide. It is absolutely a Nazi reference.

Who are these enemies of America? Would that be al-Qaeda? Saddam Hussein? Khadafi Duck? Armageddonijad?

This cannot be. Fox News does not seem supportive of any of these men, based on what I have seen on the network.

I watch Fox News. Maybe he means me. Apparently I collaborate with enemies of America.

This could be true because I watch football with friends who also watch Fox News. At least now I know my fellow collaborators. I am still not sure what we are collaborating on. We can't even come together to agree on what to eat for dinner while watching the game.

The reference to conservatives as murderers and traitors to America is not new.

Al Gore, who almost stole a presidential election, said that George W. Bush "betrayed his country."[14]

Betraying America is treason, which is punishable by death.

Nancy Pelosi said that angry people at town halls reminded her of political murders that took place in the 1970s.[15] This is as disgusting as it is dishonest. George Moscone and Harvey Milk were both killed by fellow liberals. Conservatives do not wear t-shirts advocating President Obama's murder as liberal barbarians did with George W. Bush.

I look at George W. Bush and see a human being. I see a loving husband and father. Only after that do I see a president and a conservative Republican.

The media stayed silent when Al Gore's son got drunk and stoned and drove a car into a tree (The silence was appropriate, and it was a hybrid). Sarah and Bristol Palin were brutalized because Bristol brought a beautiful new life into this world. Liberals were bothered by this because it was a new conservative life (Bristol may not have been driven to the hospital in a hybrid). Like roaches, every new conservative makes it harder to eliminate them all.

Anybody thinking this is far-fetched should explain why hate crimes legislation applies to racial and ethnic bigotry but not to ideological bigotry. If Howard Dean finally snaps and kills some Republicans after one of his anti-Republican screaming rampages, isn't that a hate crime? The man said, "I hate Republicans and everything they stand for."[16] That sounds crystal clear to me.

Liberals in congress hate conservatives with the same ferocity that conservatives hate al-Qaeda. Some of these liberals accused George W. Bush of being behind 9/11. If this is true, wouldn't killing him be noble? Whoever planned 9/11 should be killed.

I am not advocating the murder of George W. Bush. I love the guy. I don't want anybody in our government to be killed. I wouldn't mind if some liberals in congress shut up, but I do not wish death on them or their families. I will never compare them to the people that murdered members of my family in 1940s Germany.

Yet again, if conservatives really are less than a noble opposition, and are truly evil, wouldn't it be patriotic if these liberals converted their verbal violence into actual violence?

I have been personally harassed by staff members of Henry Waxman simply for breathing while conservative. Staffers including Lisa Pinto, "collaborated" with Paul Reznik at the West LA Chamber of Commerce to make sure that I knew my place at the bottom of the humanity hierarchy.

Some liberals will complain that I am blaming them all for the sins of a few. Nonsense. Silence is acquiescence. They got indignant when a congressman accused (accurately, but still in bad form) President Obama of lying. They then stay silent when their own side compares conservatives to racists, bigots, sexists, and homophobes simply because we exist and breathe air.

Not all of them stay silent. Some of them quietly cheer. Some of them even loudly cheer.

Liberals saw the title of my column advocating the killing of conservatives. I am sure plenty of them chuckled and thought "Hey, that's not a bad idea."

They will say they were just joking and don't really mean it. What they mean is that they have to take a poll or convene a focus group first.

Until liberals in congress and their supporters can see conservatives as human beings made of blood, plasma, and water, they will continue to feel justified demonizing us.

For those still not convinced, enter a liberal synagogue and listen to the sermon. The Nazis were unpleasant chaps, but those conservatives in their navy blue suits are downright frightening.

In 1930s Germany, it started with dehumanizing people and ended in murder.

Don't think it can't happen here with any group, even if that group consists of guys wearing red and blue diagonal neckties.

I can understand why liberals would want to murder me. I watch Fox News and vote Republican. I am a collaborator. We know what happens to collaborators.

eric

Taking Ted to the (Wood) Shed

Ted is dead.

I honored a self-imposed twenty-four-hour grace period, which the left would never give to George W. Bush or any other conservative.

I was willing to leave Ted Kennedy alone and let his family mourn that day. One day later, it was time to tell the truth.

I will not sit back and let the media lionize his life.

It is time to take Ted to the (wood) shed.

He was more than a bad person. He managed to make everybody around him worse.

I will not let Chappaquiddick go. Liberals chanting "Bush lied, people died," apparently do not care that Ted Kennedy left a woman to die, and then lied about it. He put his political career over the life of a human being.

If KKK members build roads, that does not erase their Klan membership. Hamas builds schools. They are still terrorists who blow people up. A murderer who goes to prison and donates a kidney is as life neutral as the phonies who believe in carbon offsets.

Ted Kennedy did positive things. If I picked up an industrial strength magnifying glass, I might find something. That does not mitigate Chappaquiddick. He got drunk, drove a car off of a bridge, and left a woman to die. All the while he used his money and power to cover up the truth.

Long before taking a human life, he cheated at Harvard. His family used their money and power to reduce an automatic expulsion and lifetime ban to a one-year suspension. This was more than a disgrace for Ted Kennedy. This occurrence is part of a series of events over the past forty years that has led Harvard to decline from a first-rate institution to the Poison Ivy League joke it is today. University slots are finite. Bringing Ted back came at the expense of some random "little person" that nobody bothered to think about.

Supporters of Ted Kennedy have sunk to his level of worthlessness. The National Organization for Women remains a collection of hags and harpies that have zero interest in women's rights. Any organization that finds Ted Kennedy better for feminism than Sarah Palin is phony. Sarah Palin did not kill a woman. Sarah Palin is faithful to her spouse. Sarah Palin is cursed because she did not drive her daughter Bristol over a bridge to prevent a child from being born. Perhaps if Senator Kennedy had let his lover and child survive, he would be pilloried today.

George W. Bush used to drink. Unlike Ted Kennedy and Christopher Dodd, President Bush did not sexually assault his serving waitress.[17] Those criticizing George W. Bush for having succeeded due to his family name should look at Ted Kennedy with an honest lens. George W. Bush held real jobs in the private sector before and after his presidency. Ted Kennedy claimed to care about the working man. He never was one. Being a "hardworking senator" is not lifting a lunch pail and putting on a hard hat.

Ted Kennedy claimed to care about people. He was as phony on other policies as he was about women's issues. He claimed to be for renewable energy sources, but blocked a wind farm that obscured his pristine view from his Massachusetts home. He raised taxes for average Americans who could not afford the expensive tax attorneys and tax shelters that he utilized to evade the very laws he enacted.

He was phony to the end. He was concerned that if John Kerry was elected president (shudder) in 2004, Republican Governor Mitt Romney would appoint a Republican to Kerry's senate seat. Kennedy had the law changed to call for a special election in that scenario, removing the governor's power.

This in itself was not bad, even if the motives were impure. What reeked was his 2009 attempt to change the law back because he wanted ultra-liberal Governor Deval Patrick to appoint another liberal rather than risk a special election.

Personally, Ted Kennedy was a bully. His treatment of Robert Bork and Clarence Thomas was abusive. In an office setting, his behavior could have even been actionable. He took decent men and libeled them.

Worst of all, Ted Kennedy abused people who tried to reach across the aisle to him.

John McCain made the mistake of calling Ted Kennedy his friend. Ted Kennedy responded by lambasting him far beyond traditional politics during the 2008 election.

President George W. Bush worked with him on an education bill. He then turned around and called President Bush a liar. This is like the pot calling the kettle African-American.

Ted Kennedy personified the politics of personal destruction. His passing will hopefully lead to a more civil discourse in society. At the very least, the senate became nicer by a small percentage.

As I predicted, the leftist bullies tried to get a terrible health care bill passed in his honor. "Win one for Teddy" was used to tar opponents of the bad bill. Opponents were defiling the memory of a man who died of brain cancer. This fits in with the left's refusal to acknowledge that reasonable people can have principled disagreements.

Ted Kennedy did not just die of cancer, which I wish on nobody.

He was a cancer. He was pure poison. He destroyed innocent lives while holding himself up as a paragon of virtue. He wrecked reputations and lives for no other reason than pure power.

I wish no pain on his family, but I will not shed a single crocodile tear on his passing.

I cannot think of a better way to honor America than to defeat any bill that was his awful life's work.

eric

Chapter 2:
Jewish Ideological Violence

Too many rabbis skipped Jewish history in school. Somewhere along the line they heard the voice of God. Most people at that point just get carted away like John Denver. Rabbis get larger congregations instead.

Somewhere in heaven God is sending his chosen people a message. He doesn't care about trees or animals. If he wanted us to avoid eating animals he would not have created skillets or seasoned salt. As for trees, a medical procedure can help remove them from liberal hides. Only a wooden stick in the wrong place could make one that intolerably smug.

Ideological Bigotry Part III—Love Your Fellow Jew is Becoming a Hollow Slogan

"I'm pretty open-minded and usually end up with people that I didn't fit into a checklist."

That was written on her JDate profile. I contacted her with a very pleasant note. I also told her that she could check out my blog to see a picture of me posted. I woke up the next day to an e-mail reply.

"You seem like a really nice guy, but unfortunately, I can't stand Republicans and from your blog, I believe that you are one. It's probably the ONLY deal-breaker I have. Best of luck!"

Whether or not this woman is beyond hope is not my focus. I do hope that other people read comments like these and understand that…again…hatred of Republicans is no better than hatred of blacks, gays, women, etc…It is ideological bigotry, and is just as pernicious as racial or any other bigotry.

Actress Julia Roberts stated "If you look up the word Republican in the dictionary, it falls between repugnant and reptilian,"[18] I chalked that up to a Hollywood celebrity spouting nonsense (redundant, I know).

Congressman Charles Rangel labeled conservatives racists for simply being conservatives. "They used to wear white hoods and yell (insert the s-word for Hispanics and the n-word for blacks). Now they wear blue suits and red ties and say let's cut taxes." [19] I find it disgusting that economic theory can be connected to hatred of anyone. Supply-side economics cuts black people's taxes as well. Taxes are race-neutral. I can wash away Mr. Rangel's comments because he is a pandering politician (also redundant).

The JDate girl's bigotry is worse because she is Jewish. This does not make the contemptible comments by Julia Roberts or Charles Rangel acceptable. There are just so few Jewish people in this world. There are many people who want to kill us simply for being Jews. We should be united. This does not mean we have to agree on every issue. Anyone who has sat around a Jewish dinner table knows it is often a charged environment. However, it is one thing to disagree with people. It is another to say you can't stand them without having met them.

The woman admitted that I came across as a nice guy. She saw I was a Republican, and then automatically had to cancel her assessment. The rationale is simple. If a Republican could be a nice guy, then maybe Republican ideas are not evil. If a good person thinks things, then maybe those things are not as bad as initially suspected.

People are normally dynamic, not static. I am a clear thinking individual not beholden to pre-programmed rigid ideas. There are conservative Democrats and liberal Republicans.

I am not going to lose sleep over the fact that this woman and I will never meet. To quote rapper and actor ICE-T, "If you don't like my lifestyle, f*ck you."[20] What truly concerns me is that this woman represents a larger number of people than some would suspect. If a majority of Jews are liberal, to deduce a plurality might be afflicted with the cancer of ideological bigotry is not a large leap.

The Nazis in World War II did not discriminate between Jews who voted Democrat and Jews who voted Republican. Neither did the Islamofascists that killed us on 9/11 and then blamed us for it. With over 50 percent of young Jews not married, we really should not give in to the madness of limiting that pie even further. To quote an old Jewish summer camp song, "To love your fellow Jew…just the same as you…that's the basis of our Holy Torah."

The Torah does not tell Jews to hate Republicans. Orthodox Jews spend their whole lives reading the Torah, and 70 percent of them vote Republican.[21] They might be on to something. More importantly, they do practice what they preach. They love all people, including all Jews. They would even reach out to this JDate woman, and others like her.

Someone should reach out to these women. Somebody explain to them that six million of us did not die for them to be unable to stand their fellow Jews, Republican or otherwise.

Hineni. Here I am. Republican, Jewish and proud always…and tolerant of others.

eric

Ideological Bigotry Part IV–*The Cancer Eating Away at Liberal Jewish Souls*

The Jewish community has decided to cannibalize itself. The people that have been the victim of the worst evil known to humankind have decided to turn their fire inward. A conversation with a liberal Jewish woman was pleasant until she mentioned the big sign in her life that said, "Republicans need not apply." She is not an aberration. Her vitriol is now mainstream in the Jewish community.

Racists and other bigots are sometimes forced to change, either due to societal pressures or court orders. They might sit down with leaders of the communities they hurt. Reformed Neo-Nazis sit down with black church leaders and rabbis. Gay bashers sit down with gay leaders. While this does not always work, dialogue and outreach has led to positive changes in individuals. Even one individual giving up bigotry is a victory for good over evil.

Liberal Jews need to be confronted, shamed and humiliated into changing. Attempting to be nice is not working. Dialogue has failed. Outreach has improved nothing. For the umpteenth time, let me explain it to them.

Republicans are human beings. This phrase needs to be piped over a loudspeaker until it is drilled into their enlightened tolerant skulls. Republicans…are… human…beings.

Conservatives have different ideas from liberals on how to improve the world, but their intentions are just as noble.

Republicans are not evil. They have different beliefs. Different does not mean evil.

It may seem odd that I am explaining a concept that a six-year-old child can understand. Six-year-old children are too young to develop irrational hatred.

Liberals will say, "We can accept Republicans and even conservatives, provided they are not Bush supporters."

They still don't get it. You have to accept people for who they are. Exceptions can be made in extreme cases such as Hitler, Stalin, Saddam, Osama and Pol Pot. Any person putting any American political figure in this category needs a good beating. That is what they would get if they lived in any area under the rule of one of the above mentioned leaders. My father is a Holocaust survivor. I can guarantee you that if he were to wake up in the middle of the night screaming, it would not be because of pro-Israel President George W. Bush.

Jewish liberals complain that George W. Bush is pro-Israel because he wants to Christianize all the Jews. This is also bigotry. Christianity is apparently a religion, and a popular one at that. Hatred against Christians is bigotry. For those liberals who only object to Christians voting Republican, that is ideological bigotry.

Some liberal Jews have expressed to me that by fiercely criticizing my own people, I am giving credence to anti-Semitism. This bogus argument is used to justify bad behavior. Many blacks are critical of Bill Cosby for airing black America's dirty laundry. Cleaning a community is not pretty, but it is vital. Liberals were overjoyed when Democrats won congress in 2006. The Bush administration finally had some "oversight." Jews need some oversight right now. Too many Jews are afflicted with a cancer that is eating away at the soul of the community.

I am not indicting Jews for merely being liberal. I am criticizing the many Jews that have an intolerance toward anyone that is not liberal.

I use the term "ideological bigotry" because it stings. It is one thing to tell people that they are insensitive. Calling them bigots gets their hackles up. It is a powerful term. It forces one to either reject the claim outright (which should be done if the claim is false), or take an introspective look inside oneself, and confront possible internal ugliness.

I will not stop battering the liberal Jewish community until all forms of hatred are loudly condemned. Liberal Jews worry about Darfur even though they have never met these people. The nation of Sudan has never shown an inkling of caring about anything Jewish. Liberal Jews worry about racism against black people. Black leaders such as Al Sharpton and Jesse Jackson respond with anti-Semitic comments. Liberal Jews must confront the fact that hatred of conservatives and Republicans, especially Jewish ones, is destructive.

Absolutely nothing in Judaism mandates a person to be politically liberal. Using the Torah to justify liberalism is as valid as Islamists using the Koran to justify jihad. I am not comparing liberals to terrorists. The comparison fails in terms of deeds. In terms of self-destructive and corrosive words, it is highly analogous. Whenever any group of people gets dehumanized, the results are dangerous and often violent.

Conservatives do not key liberals' cars, shout down liberal speakers, or throw objects at them. It is often stated that while all Arabs are not terrorists, most terrorists are Arabs. Many liberals are not ideological thuggish bigots, but most ideological thuggish bigots absolutely are liberals. They are Jewish in an amount disproportionate to their percentage of people in society.

Ideological bigotry is a cancer eating away at Jewish souls. The Jewish community has a 52 percent intermarriage rate. This is not the fault of George W. Bush, Dick Cheney, Karl Rove, Rush Limbaugh, Sean Hannity, or anybody else that causes liberals to foam at the mouth like rabid dogs.

Somewhere along the line, good little Jewish children forgot the lessons of history. When children and grandchildren of Holocaust survivors are preaching hatred, we are immolating ourselves. Many cultures from Germans to Arabs have tried to kill us. We respond by trying to kill our own.

Many Jewish liberals go to synagogue on Yom Kippur, the Jewish Day of Atonement. I wonder how many of them apologize for all the things they say about George W. Bush, Dick Cheney, and Republicans and conservatives everywhere. I doubt they silently apologize to the evangelical Christian brothers who support us (Lord knows why. We don't deserve it the way we treat them. The only people who like us…we spit on them).

I am the first person to fight anti-Semitism and other bigotry from outside cultures. I will keep my integrity by fiercely defending Republicans from ideological bigotry, especially from within the Jewish community.

Hineni. Here I am. Conservative, Republican, Bush and Cheney supporting, and proud, ready to combat the cancer of ideological bigotry until every liberal Jew is cured.

eric

Ideological Bigotry Part VI–Liberal Jews vs. John Roberts

In typical fashion, the *Jewish* (Liberal) *Journal*, or *JLJ* for short, has decided to publish fringe commentary from a Jewish leftist. It is ironic that the same people screaming at the top of their lungs that Jesus was not a Republican seem to have no problem declaring Moses a Democrat. The *JLJ* will publish an article by conservative Dennis Prager every once in awhile. In their minds tokenism equals diversity.

For the many that have still not been effectively clubbed over the head, I again state the obvious. Liberalism is a political philosophy and ideology. Judaism is a religion. The two have nothing to do with each other. Any overlap is either coincidental or the result of indoctrination. It is not fact or text-based. There is nothing in the Torah that commands one to be politically liberal. Social justice, the argument frequently used, is code for socialism. It is not connected to any religion. The highest form of charity in Judaism is helping one help themselves, a politically conservative message.

Another practitioner of ideological bigotry is the American Jewish Committee. The *JLJ* quotes the AJC's legal counsel Jeff Sinensky as follows: "Looking forward, it's likely that the majority, now headed by Justice John Roberts and with Justice Samuel Alito coming on the court, have a fundamentally different perspective than the Jewish community."[22]

Do liberal Jews have any spokespeople at all that are not arrogant gasbags? Who is this Jewish community that he claims to speak for? My Republican Jewish friends and I would like to know.

If these Jewish liberals had any intellectual and emotional honesty (we know they do not), they would state the following: "We run a liberal organization. The court is conservative. That is a threat to our liberal beliefs." There is no need to bring Judaism into the mix, unless one is trying to use religion to advance a political agenda. How can one attack conservative Christians and then turn around and behave in the exact way that conservative Christians are being slandered about?

Some liberal Jews at this point will say that if I love Christians so much, I should just become one. This is equivalent to the elementary school children on the playground saying, "If you love it so much, why don't you marry it?" I do not need to be a Christian to respect them. I will continue to fix the problems in my own community.

I will speak up when Temple Valley Beth Shalom on Hanukkah has a rabbi who states during a holiday speech, "Forget your stressful day. Picture a calm peaceful existence, a world without problems and war, a world without negativity…a world without Donald Rumsfeld being in the news."[23] The liberal Jewish audience chortled. I pictured a world where VBS loses its tax-exempt status.

I will speak up when Sinai Temple, on Memorial Day, has liberal activist Ruth Messinger give an antiwar speech laced with references to Darfur. Darfur aside, would it have killed Sinai Temple to reserve Memorial Day for positive references to the soldiers instead of bringing in perhaps the only woman too liberal to be elected in New York City?

Getting back to the Roberts Court, what were the cases that had the so-called Jewish community up in arms?

One was an abortion case. The last time I checked, abortion involved a medical procedure. First a liberal activist Supreme Court invents a right to privacy, and now liberal Jews try to find a religious reason to be pro-choice. This would be less than hypocritical if they would stop criticizing evangelicals for also having a contradictory religious belief.

Another case involved a time limit on pay discrimination cases. A third case involved a school busing issue, which I think relates more to the black community in the 1960s than the Jewish community. Jews never had to ride in the back of any bus in America.

The last case ruled that activists cannot challenge faith-based programs in court, since they were not personally injured. Somebody has to be actually wronged rather than theoretically wronged to have the ability to ask the court for redress. This is a bizarre concept for non-thinkers. Even more troubling was the fact that while Christian groups embraced President Bush's faith-based initiatives, liberal Jews fought him.

If liberal Jews do not want more money to help their communities, just donate it to Christians so it will not be wasted. Faith-based initiatives are not a way of forcing God upon children (although the fear of God would solve many societal ills). They are a way of helping priests, rabbis, ministers and imams aid people. In the same way more money for community policing helps reduce crime, more money for those who feed, clothe and protect the poor is a positive development for everybody except those who prefer lip service to actual results. Come to think of it, that defines liberalism perfectly.

Buried deep in the article is commentary by Orthodox Jewish organizations that are quite satisfied with the Roberts Court. They actually wished the court went even further in support of faith-based programs. Given that Orthodox people spend their whole lives reading and studying Torah, I am willing to trust their version of it as opposed to the evolving Torah that secular liberal Jews have created as an ugly kid sister to their evolving constitution.

The Anti-Defamation League also laments the Roberts Court based on the same cases. Did the Roberts Court pass a constitutional amendment declaring Zionism equal to racism? That was the liberal-loving bastion of uselessness, the United Nations.

Did the Roberts Court ban Judaism? Did it sanction pogroms, mandate America fund Hamas or Hezbollah, say Israel should not exist, or ban the right of Jews to pray in synagogues? What did the court do that in any way attacks the right of Jews to practice Judaism? Nothing!

It boggles my mind how Jews, long known for being the educated "people of the book," can have such fierce hostility toward John Roberts. He is one of the finest legal minds America has ever seen. He gained his knowledge through thorough readings of the required books. John Roberts may not be qualified to argue the Talmud or other Jewish texts (with his brilliance he might be), but his liberal Jewish critics do not have anywhere near his knowledge of American legal texts.

Jewish entities such as the ADL, AJC and *JLJ* have to put aside their phony commitments to diversity and justice unless they are willing to defend everybody, including conservatives. I have never been the victim of a pogrom, or of bigotry by any devout Christian. Many devout Muslims have been fabulous to me. Yet try being a Jewish Republican attending a Jewish dinner party, and see how pervasive the hostility is by enlightened, tolerant, liberal Jews. It is frightening.

Liberal Jewish groups should simply state that they are liberal first and Jewish second. Otherwise, why reflexively follow a liberal agenda?

Liberal Jews have every right to battle with a court that they see as conservative. That is debate. It makes for a vibrant healthy nation. What they do not have the right to do is claim that Judaism is liberalism. If this were true, does that mean that the many Orthodox Jews that vote Republican and are politically and culturally conservative are not practicing Judaism? I do not want to witness that potential bloodbath.

Liberal Jews are constantly accusing the Orthodox community of being intolerant toward them. Perhaps liberal Jews might wish to look in the mirror. Perhaps they might wish to use Yom Kippur to apologize for all the vicious things they have said about President Bush, and conservatives in general.

Perhaps they might wish to drop the hostility against John Roberts. His only "sin" is being the Chief Justice of a Supreme Court that wants to give rabbis more money to strengthen synagogues so that congregations may have richer Jewish experiences.

eric

Ideological Bigotry Part XII–Stephen S. (Not So) Wise

Another Friday night dinner party at a synagogue was tarnished by left-wing activism.

This time Stephen S. (not so) Wise is the place in desperate need of having its tax-exempt status revoked.

Jews have to be broken from the stranglehold that liberalism has over them. There is nothing…repeat nothing…let me again say nothing…that requires Jews to be liberal.

There is nothing in the Torah that forces one to be a Democrat.

The concept of social justice is not found anywhere in any Hebrew book written by anybody with any credibility. *Social Justice* was the name of a 1940s magazine that was anti-Semitic in nature. This makes sense. Liberal Jews respond to those who kick them in the teeth by thanking them and asking for more. This explains the Eliot Spitzer scandal. Liberal Jews are masochists.

I entered the synagogue hoping to hear what Jews should hear in synagogue… Judaism. As political as I am, a Friday night service is a way to unwind after a long work week. It is about reducing the stresses of life, which include the stock market, war, and politics.

I am asked if I would feel the same way if the message were Republican. I respond by saying that if that were to ever happen, I could let people know. My integrity runs deep, so it would still be inappropriate.

The speech at Stephen S. Witless was about vegetarianism. According to some liberal fellow that was either a rabbi or just a guy speaking, Jews should become vegetarians. He also wanted to make it clear that he was not a vegetarian himself. This fits perfectly into the "Do as I say, not as I do" stereotype of liberals that is one part hypocrisy, one part self-righteousness, and several helpings of smugness.

Apparently, hunting is wrong. Eating most animals is immoral. At least the rabbi did not start chanting "meat is murder." Maybe that happened after I left the room in disgust. Before that occurred, the lowlight of his speech was about how wrong it was to eat veal.

The only reason some people have a problem with veal is because they are baby cows. Baby animals are adorable. There is nothing in any theology that gives cute animals special treatment that average-looking animals can only dream about. This is not junior high school. There is a place for ugly animals.

Some would say that I should have known better than to have gone to a liberal synagogue. No, no, no. This is backward thinking. I was there for a dinner party and a Jewish experience, not a political rally. I suspect that the only reason this synagogue did not violate the Sabbath by passing around a collection plate was because the rabbis could not decide whether to ram their heads up the hides of Hillary Clinton or Barack Obama.

The only connection between Judaism and food is the issue of which animals are kosher to eat. Cows are kosher. Beef is legal to eat according to all Jewish doctrines, provided that the animal is slaughtered humanely. To imply that Judaism should encourage giving up eating animals is to confuse Judaism with liberal activism.

One reason I keep saying that liberal Jews need cranial-glutial extraction surgery is because they cannot seem to figure out what truly matters. Islamofascists are trying to kill every Jew on Earth. They are trying to do what Hitler failed to do over sixty years ago. For those liberal Jews who don't get it, when I say Hitler, I mean a German genocidal lunatic, not a pro-Israel Republican president. Only liberal Jews could have trouble making the distinction, hence my clarification.

Instead of talking about this, liberal Jews take synagogues hostage so they can talk about what they consider real threats, like veal.

Veal is not a threat to anyone but the cows. If a person wants to give up meat, fine. Just don't spend close to an hour telling me why I should, especially when you don't!

Some claim that meat is bad for the environment because of cows and methane gas. Try fighting through the noxious stench of a liberal rabbi gasbag trying to indoctrinate young minds with everything but actual real Judaism.

I want to relax in temple. It is tough to relax when I am rabid with rage, and fighting the urge to tell a rabbi "Shut up. Just shut the (redacted) up. Take your liberal activism and just shut up. I am here to learn about my religion. If you are not going to educate me specifically about my religion, then for the love of the Hebrew God I worship, shut up."

I am sure that the people running this sinkhole of a place of worship will offer some pabulum about how we should hear other perspectives. They might even babble about how they have actually allowed a token conservative speaker at some point, such as Dennis Prager. Actually, he was just there to do a Torah study.

Some will argue that places of worship have always been political. That does not make this occurrence acceptable.

I left the dinner party early when that unctuous rabbi (or whatever he was) came to the table I was at and made a joke about whether or not we were enjoying the veal. He then chortled at his own wit, because somebody had to do so. Smug people laughing about how smug they are is just delightful.

I ignored him, since trying to educate a man at that age is like trying to teach a pig to sing. It wastes time and annoys the pig.

I then announced to my friends at the table that I liked my veal the way I liked my Cappuccinos…that there was nothing tastier than a double half calf.

Of course I am not that heartless. After all, I hate coffee.

This rabbi was less harmful than the head of Reform Judaism, who seems to think that opposition to the War in Iraq has anything at all to do with any Jewish text written anywhere. His lack of a good speaking voice prevented too many people from being hypnotized, unless boredom hypnotizes.

Politics in temples is a cancer. Until enough of these institutions get their tax-exempt statuses revoked, there is no other form of radiation treatment.

Some liberal rabbis will complain that such threats are an attempt to silence them, which would threaten their freedom of speech. Good. A little fear would be healthy for them. The argument that I could just walk out as I did is not valid. I have to worship somewhere. My consenting to attend a dinner party with friends my age does not in any way imply that I am consenting to have an appendage of the Democratic National Committee talk down to me.

I do not expect Stephen S. Wise to learn from this experience. They are liberal. Asking liberal rabbis to learn class and tact is like asking Mahmoud Armageddonijad to learn and embrace Hebrew. At some point people are indoctrinated too deeply to change. In some ways the liberal rabbis are worse. Unlike Armageddonijad, they actually believe what they are saying.

Temples are bully pulpits. They should not be occupied by bullies.

The Jewish holiday of Passover tells the story of four sons. One of the sons is wise, and one is wicked.

Perhaps Stephen S. Wise should change its name to Stephen S. Wicked until it bothers to alter its sermons to include Republican Jews. We are human beings, contrary to what some liberal rabbis believe.

Hineni. Here I am. I am a proud Jewish Republican. I will not rest until synagogues are cleansed and scrubbed of every ounce of liberalism so that I may worship in peace.

eric

Chapter 3:
Pacifist Violence

The only thing more dangerous than a violent jihadist is a violent peace activist. I was minding my own business when one member of congress decided to try and bully the wrong person. I have now downgraded Henry Waxman to Waxboy. He hides behind his equally thuggish staff, which proves my theory that you should never send a liberal to do a man's job.

Worse Than Henry Waxman

On August 27th, 2009, I went to a health care "forum" featuring Henry Waxman that was definitely not a town hall. The event was a sham on so many levels. I will deal with that soon enough.

An event occurred at the event that was absolutely chilling. I initially had no evidence that Congressman Waxman was responsible for this negative incident, nor am I stating with certainty that he was.

My motives for attending this function were to have a story to blog about. My dream scenario would be Congressman Waxman putting his foot in his mouth, and giving me ammunition. He obliged. I will not make up a story. I am not Dan Rather, Mary Mapes, or the *JBT*. My integrity supersedes the story.

I do not act in an unruly manner. My life is dedicated toward trying to force the left into being more civilized in terms of their discourse. I am therefore very mindful of my discourse. I do not hold offensive signs, shout hateful epithets, or engage in any other similar behavior.

The event was a luncheon at the Luxe Hotel in Brentwood. The event was kept secret, and tickets cost $50. Supporters of Mr. Waxman were given preferential treatment. This was a tightly controlled campaign rally, not a real town hall. My main criticism involved a thug that works for the Luxe Hotel.

I have been to this hotel several times. The functions I attended probably featured more Republicans than Democrats, but they were non-partisan events. Many of these events were pro-Israel events, which simply is a bigger issue in terms of passion among conservatives. I do not recall ever attending a partisan political event there. I did sleep at the hotel once, because I had a coupon for a free night. It was a pleasant stay (obvious reasons–redacted), and I would have stayed there again had the hotel not been five minutes from my home.

Normally people just drive up with no interference. This time, a pair of men stopped me as I pulled up. They asked what I was coming to the hotel for. I explained to them that I was there to see the congressman, and gave them my name. They saw I was on the list, and let me through. I figured that was it.

I took my Republican Jewish Coalition tote bag, emptied the contents, and put them in my National Football League tote bag. This was before I exited my car. I simply wanted to avoid controversy. I entered the luncheon room, began to eat my salad, and was then accosted by a vice president of the Hotel, Seth Horowitz.

I had never met Seth Horowitz before. He told me that he knew who I was, and that if I had any intention of making a disturbance, I should leave immediately.

I was stunned by this. I was using my fork correctly. I told him I had no idea what he was talking about, and he emphasized that he wanted to make sure I did not cause any problems.

This was mind-boggling to me. There is nothing in my background to suggest I would do anything improper.

He actually threatened me. If I were anything other than a white male, I would probably have had a pretty decent civil rights claim. He told me that he would refund my money if I wanted, and that if I was not satisfied, he could have the police escort me out.

I asked him flat out why he was even approaching me. He would not say. He kept saying over and over that he did explain it to me. All he did was repeatedly say that he wanted to avoid problems.

(Only after insisting that I was there for peaceful purposes did he leave me alone.)

I never got an answer to a basic fundamental question.

Why did he think I would be a problem? What behavior triggered his reaction?

For those wondering why this matters, think about some basic things.

Everybody who registered for the event gave their name. This Seth Horowitz fellow, based on something, "knew about me."

What did he know? Were guests investigated? Did the valet people see the political tote bag, which I carefully turned around, before giving them my car?

If somebody were to research my name, it would take them several pages to find something. A jazz musician who plays saxophone and lives in San Francisco gets most of the attention. I am fine with this. To find something about me would take some serious time and effort.

More importantly, was this mere overzealousness by a hotel employee making sure his esteemed guest was happy? If so, why all the secrecy and evasiveness by Mr. Horowitz? He did not seem to be harassing most people. He was beyond rude. Another Republican in the room had somebody looking over his shoulder the entire time, checking out what the fellow was doing with his Blackberry.

For those who think I am being paranoid, explain to me how an unassuming guy minding his own business can be targeted without explanation.

Mr. Horowitz was willing to have me "taken care of," which could mean anything from being asked to leave to something more violent. He is a physically imposing guy, and got right in my face. This was assault.

I cannot imagine that Mr. Horowitz acted alone. Either Mr. Horowitz acted on direct orders, or he is a liberal activist. How would he know my views?

I am going to repeat over and over again that I have never at any time in my life engaged in any political behavior that could be considered dangerous or threatening to anyone. My conversations with Congressman Waxman were cordial. He is my opponent, not my enemy.

Seth Horowitz might be the second coming of Rahm Emanuel, at least from a tactical standpoint.

I wanted answers. Why was I targeted? What did he mean when he said that he "knew about me?" What does that mean? Whatever he "found out," through what means did he find out?

I have never given a political speech at the Luxe Hotel. None of my political speeches had ever been videotaped. I have never had an event occur at the Luxe Hotel that would be considered remotely controversial.

This was not a random targeting. This man had a beef with me, and was not offering an explanation.

Seth Horowitz was a bully on a power trip. The only thing bullies respect is force. I considered contacting every organization I have friends with, and pleading with them to boycott the Luxe Hotel.

This is America. Every citizen has the right to peacefully assemble.

Congressman Waxman's people may have had nothing to do with this, but that theory defies logic.

The whole situation stank to high heaven.

Seth Horowitz had to be held accountable for his behavior.

Otherwise, when he targets you, I will not be there to speak up.

Later on, Seth Horowitz called me and was very belligerent. He insisted that Congressman Waxman did not give the order to target me. When I asked if Congressman Waxman's people gave the order, he clammed up. He said he did it based on my behavior. I asked him "what behavior?" He would not answer. He hid behind his lawyers, after accusing me of trying to sue the hotel.

I called back and emphasized to the very pleasant woman in the executive suite offices that I had zero interest in suing the hotel. I simply wanted an apology and an explanation. I also called Waxman's office to find out more. While I suspect he may have an overzealous staffer or two, I still did not have any evidence at the time that Congressman Waxman was directly involved.

eric

Henry Waxman's Office

I was thankful for the deluge of support I received over my unfortunate experience at a Henry Waxman luncheon.

I began thinking a lot more about politics from an analytical sense than I usually do. Most of blogging is descriptive. "X" happened. Very rarely is the "Y," also known as "why" something matters, discussed in depth. Sometimes the why is self-evident.

I knew that I was accosted by Luxe Hotel employee Seth Horowitz at a function for Henry Waxman that required registration in advance. Mr. Horowitz told me that he "knew all about me," and that "if I was planning to cause any trouble or be disruptive," I would be arrested.

What I tried to find out is why this happened. I have said over and over to myself that I am not an "activist."

This is when I began what some would describe as deep thinking and others would describe as navel gazing. I will split the difference and declare it deep gazing.

I have come to the conclusion that I have a negative perception of what an activist is.

This is the second time I can think of where a mental block over a word affected me. I was terrible as a salesman because I had a negative view of what a salesman is. Salespeople bother other people and try to talk them into buying things. No matter how many times I was told that "everybody sells," it was still tough.

When selling my book, I prefer it when I give a speech and people voluntarily come up to me and offer to buy it. This happens frequently enough. Many people have bought my book because they liked my presentation. I still hate selling.

Being an activist is a label that bothers me. I associate activists, especially liberal ones, with grungers. I picture unshaven, foaming at the mouth lunatics, also known as the great unwashed.

Barbara Boxer even complained that certain Republican activists could not be real because they were dressed too neatly. This only feeds into the stereotype. I personally have viewed activists as the people in the town square rambling about stuff with barely more coherence than most homeless people and drug addicts.

I was wrong. While crazy people do exist, I have met many conservative activists. They are not crazy. They really are concerned citizens that do not like where their country is headed.

I have often said that I do not have time to protest because I have a job. That was arrogance on my part. Many of these senior citizens are worried that if things go to heck in a hand-basket, I will not have a job. They are trying to help me. They deserve my appreciation, not scorn.

I still believe that what I have seen from liberal activists is much closer to lunacy and further away from civility than the actions I witnessed from conservative activists. I am willing to take a closer look.

Even though I attend many political functions, I still do not see myself as an activist.

To me, activists are people that hold up signs.

I am definitely a football fanatic. I go to games, hold up signs, yell, and scream. I just have never done that with politics. I did go to one tea party, but the sign I held up was to make people laugh. It read "I dislike taxes, but I really hate tea. Death to Mint Medley. Death to Earl Gray. Death to Tetley."

I go to lectures to hear speakers, but that is so I have stuff to write about on my blog.

This is not to imply that I am indifferent to issues. I am just not angry.

There is nothing wrong with being angry if it is justified, but I cannot fake anger. I am not politically enraged. I am quietly concerned. Others are more vocal than me.

This is why the situation involving Henry Waxman and Seth Horowitz bothered me so much. I really was a quiet concerned citizen minding his own business. I was drawn into a battle I did not want. I was being sucked into the world of activism, which is foreign to me. Yet activism is better than passivism, which means rolling over and letting bullies hurt me. I am a reluctant warrior.

I called Waxman's Los Angeles Director Lisa Pinto three times, and the call was not returned. So I drove to the office, which was five minutes from my home.

I was not looking for a fight. I also did not even expect to see Congressman Waxman. I figured he was in Washington, DC, not Los Angeles. I wanted to speak to Ms. Pinto. She was at the Luxe Hotel, and could answer my questions about who targeted me and why I was targeted.

Congressman Waxman's Los Angeles office is 8436 West 3rd St in Beverly Hills.

Given that Beverly Hills is a wealthy area, I was surprised at how ordinary the building was. It was actually unimpressive. This is not a criticism. If anything, it deflects the charge that Congressman Waxman spends lavishly. Having a modest office is smart on his part. Perhaps his personal office is fit for a king, but the building was nothing extravagant.

One sad aspect is that when one walks in, the receptionist sits behind bullet proof glass.

I am also not going to criticize Congressman Waxman for this. It is a reflection of the world we live in. It is a difficult balance to maintain personal safety while not being isolated from voters.

I asked the receptionist, a very pleasant and polite individual, to see Ms. Pinto. She was on a conference call and unavailable. The receptionist asked me to e-mail her to make an appointment. I explained that I had already called her, but he explicitly stated that she scheduled her appointments through e-mail. I sent her a polite e-mail requesting a meeting with her.

I was sure I would now be labeled a danger to the congressman and be put on some sort of watch list. This may sound paranoid, but minding my own business got me accosted. I could only imagine what actually showing up to his office would do.

The complete truth is that I was in the office for less than five minutes. I was polite and friendly. I accepted the business card of Ms. Pinto, wished the receptionist a pleasant day, and left.

If the congressman sees anybody questioning anything he ever does as being a threat to democracy, then the fault is with him, not me.

Until the luncheon, I did not even know that his office was five minutes from my home. I had no reason to interact with him. My entire behavior toward him was voting against him every two years and then seeing him reelected. I have never gone to any other forum he has ever held. Given his reluctance to be around the voters, perhaps he never did any.

Ms. Pinto did call back. She did a football move that I refer to as the "Pinto Punt." Because I am a blogger, correspondence must go through the Washington, DC, communications director. They actually tried to call me on a conference call, and I accidentally left the phone off. I was sitting right there and missed the call. In all fairness, his staff initially appeared professional about the matter.

As for me, I am forcing myself to learn more and get more involved.

I have never sent any politician a letter. I certainly had never gone to their office before. I only e-mail members of congress to get interviews for my blog. I have never contacted a politician for anything else.

Dianne Feinstein works around the block from me in plain sight. Even had I known, I cannot imagine why I would go there.

The hilarious movie *PCU* (*Politically Correct University*) has students chanting, "We're not gonna protest" over and over.[24] Nevertheless, I am going to try and be more tolerant of protesters. This is provided that they act civilized.

I will respect their right to be upset.

I just hope they respect my right to voice my opinion in a calmer manner from behind a keyboard. This is less confrontational for me.

When the dust settled, and the evidence reflected my non-controversial existence, I still hoped to get the answers I was searching for.

Seth Horowitz accosted me. He implied that Waxman's staff put him up to it.

If this is how private citizens minding their own business get treated, I can only begin to imagine what happens to activists.

eric

Henry Waxman—Getting Much Closer to the Truth

One week after the incident, Seth Horowitz stated that he was not ordered to harass me on direct orders from the congressman. He tacitly admitted that the congressional staff was not so innocent.

The truth was slowly coming out.

I dropped by the office the prior day after three phone calls went unanswered.

When Lisa Pinto did call me back, she apologized for not being able to see me since she was on a conference call. I wanted the conversation to be cordial, so I immediately responded positively.

"Ms. Pinto, no need to apologize. I dropped by uninvited. I had every right to expect you to be busy doing your job. There was no harm done at all."

She responded pleasantly enough before proving most unhelpful. What little she blurted out inadvertently helped me connect several dots, before dumb luck helped me really tie this together.

She explained to me that she could not speak to me about the matter because I was a member of the media. All media inquiries or issues had to go through the communications director in Washington, DC.

I explained that I was not a member of the media, and that I had no idea where she got that notion. I told her that I was a stockbrokerage professional and private citizen that knew nothing about the entertainment industry.

She said that perhaps there was a mistake. Maybe she had been given wrong information. She was sure I was a professional blogger who blogged on other people's sites.

At this point the light went off. I was not willing to lie. Getting to the truth through lying does not work for me. I explained that I was a professional finance guy, but not a professional journalist. I did blog on other sites from time to time. I blogged mainly on my own site, with no compensation.

She stated that any blogging makes me a member of the media, which means that only the communications director can talk to me with regards to a meeting.

I told her that if she could discuss the issue with me on the telephone for three to five minutes, that would save us all some time of having to set up a meeting. She said she could not speak about the situation.

I then asked her if she could just listen and not say anything. She said she could not do that. Everything had to flow through DC.

Football fans, welcome to the "Pinto Punt."

I told her that even though I disagreed with Congressman Waxman on issues, I wanted to handle this matter quickly and quietly. I was not interested in getting him in trouble, especially if he was innocent. Some people wanted me to push this issue and try to make it a campaign issue.

That is not who I am or what I am about. I just wanted the truth. I offered to make any conversation off the record. Anybody who knows me knows that if somebody asks me to go off the record, I honor that.

All I asked is that I not be lied to or jerked around.

Seth Horowitz initially told me that he "knew all about me." I had no idea what he meant.

Yet one week later, Lisa Pinto expressed her concern at my being a blogger.

I never told her I was one. How did she know this?

Since the event required registration, a background check could be run on each attendee.

Yet I do not blog under my real name. I go by the Tygrrrr Express.

I also pointed out to people that if my name was typed in on Yahoo or Google, I would not turn up for pages and pages. This was because of the San Francisco saxophonist, or so I thought.

In the past, a Google search of me turned up nothing on the first few pages. Somebody suggested I Google myself again, since I had not done so recently. To my astonishment, I came up before the saxophone player.

My stint writing for Andrew Breitbart on his site "Big Hollywood" was under my real name. Mr. Breitbart required this.

Another person at the event that was harassed was Ari David. Ari David was actually running against Henry Waxman, but most likely Waxman would not know this. He has a safe seat, and ignores potential opponents. However, Ari David does write for "Big Hollywood" as well.

Andrew Breitbart has been a fierce critic of Henry Waxman. It does tie together.

I was never a passionate critic of the congressman. I voted against him every two years, but never blogged about him. I was focused on the presidential race.

I told Lisa Pinto that I wanted this resolved peaceably, but it had to be resolved. She offered to put me in touch with the DC communications director, or she could contact her directly.

I told her that if she gave me her word she would follow up, I would be fine with that. She did call me herself, even if it took a visit to the office to see some movement. If she lied, I could just call back. She gave me her word that she would contact me within a short amount of time.

I told her that I am Jewish, and that I know Congressman Waxman is as well. I wanted this resolved by Rosh Hashanah (September 19th, 2009) so that we could both start the year fresh. She laughed, and said that this was an interesting deadline. I told her that I did not want a quarrel with a fellow Jew, even one I disagreed with. My beef with the congressman has always been political, never personal.

She promised that I would be contacted well before then.

Seth Horowitz did not act in a vacuum. As soon as the owner of the Luxe Hotel got back in town, I sought a polite conversation with him. I had already e-mailed him. I also prepared a letter to the West LA Chamber of Commerce, who hosted the event and has Mr. Horowitz as a member.

Mr. Horowitz had no reason to act alone. Harassing hotel patrons is bad for business. He all but overtly admitted that Henry Waxman's staff started this chain of events. Lisa Pinto knew I was a blogger. The event required registration.

In legal terms, this was a case with strong circumstantial evidence.

What did Henry Waxman know, and when did he know it? Did he give the order?

If not, who on his staff needed to be reined in or fired for convincing a hotel thug to violate my civil rights and civil liberties?

Drip by drip, droplet by droplet, the levee of lies was slowly starting to collapse.

I was going to get to the truth. Count on it.

eric

Henry Waxman's Town Hall Sham

Lost in the furor over the Waxman event were his actual remarks.

For those offering support who wanted to call or e-mail the Luxe Hotel or Congressman Waxman's office, I implored that they be polite. I strongly disagreed with Waxman, but it was not personal.

I do have a problem with his refusal to do real town hall events. Because he gets millions from Hollywood celebrities, he has no reason to be responsive to the rest of the voters. He has a safe seat. In 2008 he ran unopposed.

Adam Schiff held an outdoor town hall and faced the music. Henry Waxman instead held his $50 private lunch with advance registration and background checks on all attendees. The goal was to intimidate anyone at the event who would be considered a political agitator. This meant that registered Republicans, including myself, were targeted for harassment.

Questioners were allowed thirty seconds. After that, a woman sitting at my table would hold up a large sign letting the moderator know that time was up. The moderator would then instantly cut off the questioner. This prevented manifestos, but it also cut off legitimate questions as well.

There were no name tags, but the moderator called mostly on friendly questioners. He accidentally slipped and called one of them by her first name. Liberal plants at this event were not so shocking.

Because I kept waving my hand, the moderator had no choice but to call on me after pretending not to see me the whole time.

Yet Henry Waxman's main problem is what he says, not what others ask.

He began by pointing out that while he thought the world of veteran Michigan Congressman John Dingell, it was time for a change of leadership in the energy committee. Waxman pointed out that Dingell had been in congress for fifty years, and was eighty-three years old.

This was an astounding line of attack. He was saying that Dingell had been in congress too long, and had lost touch. This is Henry Waxman in a nutshell. He has also been in congress forever. While his tenure is less than that of Dingell, he has been around a very long time. It was insulting to hear him try and justify why he wanted to control the energy committee. John Dingell was not an eviromaniac, being from Michigan and all.

While the town hall itself was supposed to be about health care, only about one-third of the event dealt with that. Energy and other issues were part of his speech, although many of the questions were about health care.

Congressman Waxman insisted on spending time discussing environmental issues, which is his right. He spoke about the U.S. Climate Action Partnership. He referred to it as a good example of a partnership between business and environmental interests. I cannot comment either way.

He did point out that we are dependent on foreign oil, but he refuses to support drilling. Leftists point out that drilling will not solve all of the problems. This is a phony argument. Conservatives are not saying that drilling is the only solution. It should just not be ruled out as one of several.

An odd statement he made was that as a California congressman, he does not spend time being concerned that the "Midwest is crying over the job losses they had."

He blamed George W. Bush, as any liberal would. "For eight years he denied science and censored research."

This has nothing to do with liberals refusing to support drilling.

He did address the important issue of unilateral disarmament with regards to cap-and-trade. Conservatives have a valid point when they say that if we adopt tough standards but China and India do not, then jobs will be lost to those nations. Congressman Waxman was correct when he pointed out that they can claim that they will not act until we act. With everybody waiting on everybody else, it becomes like "kindergarten."

This argument is not baseless, but where it falls apart is at the original premise stage that doing nothing is worse than taking the risk. I do not believe that the Earth is about to explode in a matter of milliseconds. I am fine with a cautious approach. In this case, a do-nothing approach is best. China and India feel the same way. There has been no evidence that any attempts to take the lead on such issues will lead to any support from our economic competitors.

He also came out in support of coal, but this is an example of Democrats talking without any concrete action to back up the words. The Democrats have the votes. Republicans would support them. It is laughable to think that Democrats support the coal industry.

"We can burn the coal and sequester the carbon without damaging the environment. We have an abundance of natural resources."

Fine. Offer a bill.

The speech then finally went into health care, where the obvious was touched upon.

"A lot of people are uneasy about government-run health care such as a single-payer system. They see big increases in taxes. It is not politically possible."

"Insurance companies should take everyone without increasing prices."

Has Henry Waxman ever run an insurance company? What he is suggesting is that businesses become charities. Businesses that do not make profits go out of business. Perhaps Congressman Waxman wants this. Insurance companies make fabulous bogeymen for people that never had their lives saved by a new drug that can only be researched and developed by a company with profits.

"Many people don't want to get insurance. They are young and invincible."

Forcing them to buy it is not going to happen. It can't. This is America. Should they? Yes. It is just not the responsibility of the government to make people more socially responsible. Some will argue that these people eventually cost taxpayers money in emergency rooms. That is a separate issue.

"Forty-six to fifty million Americans are uninsured."

Take out illegal aliens, and others that voluntarily refuse coverage, and the number drops precipitously. If people want to cover illegal aliens, then be honest about it. Let's have the discussion. Trying to inflate the figure only makes the opposition angrier because they feel they are being given a pack of lies.

"Deficits cannot be controlled without controlling health care costs."

This is a true statement that masks skyrocketing deficits caused by President Obama. Liberals hide behind George W. Bush, who was a deficit hawk by comparison. Until 2008, President Bush's deficits were caused by expenditures that actually mattered, not social engineering policies.

(Liberals who like to cherry pick conservative blogs will use that quote to avoid dealing with the actual topic, which is Waxman. I threw this line in deliberately to provoke such dishonesty.)

Congressman Waxman then spoke about how awful it was to compare Obama to Hitler. He failed to mention that the left compares every conservative to Hitler. All comparisons to Hitler are wrong.

"Rationing hasn't happened under Medicare. I can't imagine it will happen here either."

Notice that he failed to unequivocally say it will not happen. Rationing is a very real possibility. When one offers something free or at a reduced price, more people want it, and less of it exists. This is Economics 101.

Congressman Waxman then shifted blame from the house by pointing out that the senate is what is slowing everything up. It is true that the senate, since its creation by the founding fathers, has been where legislation goes to die. This does not mean that the house has been productive on this issue.

"The senate requires sixty votes to overcome a filibuster. The house wanted a bipartisan bill. Republicans don't want any Obama bill."

"We did not get bipartisanship on the stimulus bill. Economists on the left and right supported it."

Not true. Many clear thinking economists opposed it. We now know that the opposition was right.

"The stimulus bill is helping."

Who is it helping besides people who get paid to write legislation? At best it did not make things much worse.

"Arlen Specter left the Republican Party because he could not survive there any longer. Yet we still do not have sixty votes. Iowa Senator Chuck Grassley has threatened to block the bill. We lost Senator Kennedy. Senator Robert Byrd is very ill. He may not be able to vote."

One very honest questioner wanted to know why Democrats don't just ram the bill through using the reconciliation process. This would require only fifty-one votes, circumventing the filibuster.

"All of health care can't be in the reconciliation bill. It would have to be done piecemeal in that case. Also, the GOP may retaliate against reconciliation."

On this he is right. Play by the rules, or suffer the consequences when in the minority.

Another questioner wanted the Democrats to dare the GOP to filibuster. Congressman Waxman disagreed.

"Forcing a filibuster has been considered, but it is not the best alternative."

Another honest answer came when somebody brought up the fact that Obama outsourced the bill to Nancy Pelosi. I have personally stated that President Obama seems detached from doing the tough tedious work. Congressman Waxman stated that "Congress would have ignored an Obama bill." Congressional prerogative trumps loyalty to any president, even one of the same party. Robert Byrd took President Clinton to the Supreme Court and successfully had the federal line-item veto declared unconstitutional. Congress is supposed to write the bill.

I still see the president as disengaged, but the point has some merit.

"President Obama is willing to be a one-term president to get healthcare done."

I don't buy this. Let's see how he is in 2011. He is made out to be a saint. He really is just another politician. This is not an indictment. The notion that any president is such a true believer fails the cynicism test. Deliberately ramming through an agenda knowing it could prevent reelection is unprecedented. Talk of such nobility is hard to swallow.

One questioner wanted to know if Congressman Waxman would subject himself to the plan he wanted to pass. He declined to say that he would. He brazenly implied that the plan under discussion was a replica modeled after the congressional healthcare system. He actually was therefore subjecting himself to the same plan as his constituents. This claim would be laughable if it was not so upsetting. He simply lied.

Congressman Waxman was asked about excise taxes on food and beverages. He ducked the question by saying that "My committee is not involved with taxes. That is the Ways and Means Committee."

His answer to a question about mandates was mind-boggling in its brazenness.

"There is a requirement that everybody gets insurance. That is not a mandate. It is 'shared responsibility.' There will be a small tax on those who refuse."[25]

Don Corleone, meet Henry Waxman.

(I guess that makes Seth Horowitz the adopted Consigliore.)

Congressman Waxman was asked if he would be holding more open town halls where anybody could attend. He explained that his schedule was very busy, and that this might not be possible. He did state that he had already conducted several events. They were all tightly scripted.

One sycophant stated that she was "so happy for everything the government has done for our business."

(Perhaps she runs a brothel.)

My question for him used a trivial example, but was meant for a deeper and more serious point to be made. Given that Seth Horowitz was most likely nearby pounding his fists together like Rahm Emanuel, I did not want to take any chances.

"Congressman Waxman, my name is Eric. I am a Republican, but am moderate on some issues. There is a chance for some common ground. My question deals with your desire to see everybody covered. Aren't there people who maybe should not be covered, such as illegal aliens? What about Guantanamo Bay detainees relocated to America? Should they be given everything from healthcare coverage to gay marriage rights to everything else?

(the crowd laughed)

Congressman, in all seriousness, where do we draw the line?"

Congressman Waxman actually did answer the question. Whether or not he answered truthfully is a judgment call. He emphatically insisted that none of the proposed bills offered healthcare coverage for illegal aliens. He left no ambiguity. Illegal aliens would not be covered under the congressional plans. He did not use euphemisms such as "undocumented workers." He used the same terminology I did.

He then at the end of his answer stated that he had not heard of any proposal to give healthcare coverage or anything else to Gitmo detainees.

I wanted to leave illegal aliens out of it and just stick to Gitmo detainees. If I did that, the question would not be serious.

After the event, I approached Congressman Waxman. His handlers were trying to get him out of the room as quickly as possible. He was surrounded by his handlers and security people. He did turn around. I let him know that I was absolutely not implying that he or anybody else in congress supported healthcare for detainees. I was just using that as an extreme example to take the illegal alien issue one step further.

He asked me my name, and I told him. I also told him that while he was my political opponent, he was never my enemy. I told him that my father was a Holocaust survivor, and that if I saw anybody compare Barack Obama to Adolf Hitler (he mentioned signs at town halls reflecting such language), I would condemn it. He was appreciative. When I mentioned that it was also wrong for George W. Bush to be compared to Hitler, he did not respond. He was being pulled away at that point.

All I know is that Congressman Waxman would be a lot better off if he held real, honest town halls. His constituents would be as well.

The alternative is for him to stay isolated in a bubble. This does not serve democracy. It leads to paranoia, and results in ugly situations like the one I faced from Seth Horowitz.

Everybody deserves better.

eric

9/9/9—A Beautiful Day For a Congressional Cover-up

It was 9/9/9.

In mathematical terms, it was twenty-seven.

For those speaking German, a voice yelling "no, no, no" could be heard.

The day before the president spoke to children. This night he would be speaking to the rest of us as if we were children.

Yet 9/9/9 was about the ongoing congressional cover-up regarding my being accosted on August 27th. New information had emerged.

I participated on a conference call with Lisa Pinto and her DC counterpart, Karen Lightfoot. Her name of Lightfoot is highly appropriate. She is quite nimble.

A communications director's job is to appear cooperative while politely being confrontational. Ms. Lightfoot does her job well. Ms. Pinto explained that she was only following procedure, which is fine.

They stated how delighted they were that I attended the event. I knew this was not going to be a sincere conversation.

I wanted to know who gave Seth Horowitz the order to harass me.

Ms. Lightfoot claimed that the event was put on by the West Los Angeles Chamber of Commerce, and that the Waxman team had nothing to do with the event except for graciously showing up and attending.

I pointed out that it was Ms. Pinto herself who stated that my being a blogger was the reason for the incident. I made it clear that Ms. Pinto told me this. I wanted to know how they even knew I was a blogger.

Their version of events is that two days before the event, on August 25th, I published the upcoming event as a "healthcare town hall." Therefore, I misrepresented the event. It was a luncheon, not a town hall Climate change would be discussed, not just healthcare.

A concerned citizen came to them (Are you kidding me?) and let them know that a blog described the event incorrectly. They would not say the name of the person.

Ms. Lightfoot repeatedly passed the buck. She claimed that the West LA Chamber of Commerce was responsible for the event, with WLACC President Paul Reznik as the main point person. I did not recall ever meeting him before.

Ms. Lightfoot stated that Mr. Reznik handled every aspect of the event. It was communicated to him that he was to ensure that the event was "represented properly."

Ms. Lightfoot subsequently got very testy when I asked her a simple question.

What specific instructions were given to Mr. Reznik regarding me? What exact words were spoken to him regarding any action to be taken?

Ms. Lightfoot resorted to claiming that she "already answered me, we had gone around in circles," she "understood my frustration, but that there was nothing else to be said." She then started repeatedly talking over me, and raising her voice. She "understood" my desire to get to the truth, but she already told me everything.

No, she did not.

Somebody on Waxman's staff communicated to Paul Reznik. He then either directly or through somebody else went to Seth Horowitz.

I obviously hit a nerve with Ms. Lightfoot, especially since she said that she "wants all of us to put this behind us and move forward." This is what people who wish to obfuscate the truth do. They delay something long enough until it becomes old news, and boredom sets in.

She hung up the phone on me in a rude manner, specifically because I had the nerve to want a simple and truthful answer to a question lacking any complexity.

Ms. Lightfoot spent the entire conversation combatively explaining her cooperativeness.

As I said, she does her job well. It is a shame she has to sacrifice her integrity to protect her boss.

This is now officially a congressional cover-up.

Congressman Waxman himself could have had nothing to do with this. He does have overzealous staffers. This can now be declared a certainty. Maybe magic pixie dust was placed on their pillows by invisible unicorns ordering them to sanction abusive behavior that their sweet boss would never condone.

This is why so many people have so little faith in their government, and why so many capable people eschew public service.

Ms. Pinto and Ms. Lightfoot tried to deflect onto Mr. Reznik. He had no motive.

I was willing to hold back, provided I was being dealt with honestly.

At this point I had no choice but to go forward.

I was still going to get to the truth about Mr. Horowitz, despite Ms. Lightfoot's best efforts to suppress the truth under the phony guise of cooperation and transparency.

eric

Henry Waxman, Paul Reznik, and the West LA Chamber of Commerce

(Paul Reznik, Consortium Real Estate, Phone: (310) 948-0932, Fax: (818) 955-6503, prezrealtor@aol.com)

I had no interest in seeking a pound of flesh. I was willing to settle for an apology.

I had recently spoken to the owner of the Luxe Hotel, a Mr. Harkham. He was very gracious and apologetic. I politely explained to him that I had no interest in suing the hotel. I simply wanted an apology from Mr. Horowitz, and an explanation as to why this happened.

On September 10th, despite much belligerence prior to that, Seth Horowitz apologized.

"Dear Eric,

I apologize to you for the manner in which I approached you when you attended the event held by the West Los Angeles Chamber of Commerce for Congressman Waxman.

My intention was to ensure that the event would be held with 'decorum'. At no time was my intention to be in any way threatening to you.

The Chamber was made aware of your blog the day before the event. Your blog contained the Congressman's name and the event at the Luxe. Due to the nature of the dialogue around the country, and because your blog mentioned that the event at the Luxe was a 'Town Hall meeting regarding Healthcare', we were concerned that their might be some disturbance at the event.

Nothing you did while at the hotel was in any way a problem. You conducted yourself with 'decorum' and we thank you for that.

We pride ourselves at the Luxe Hotels as being committed active members of the community. We are more than tolerant of all points of view.

You are welcome to be a guest at the Luxe Hotel at any time. I look forward to meeting you again and hope to put this incident behind us.

Yours truly,

Seth Horowitz

Vice President of Hotel Operations

Luxe Hotels

General Manager

Luxe Hotel Sunset Boulevard

11461 Sunset Blvd., Los Angeles, CA 90049

Direct: 310.691.7513

Fax: 310.691.7533

Cell: 310.383.4449

www.luxehotels.com"

I sent Mr. Horowitz back an e-mail.

"Mr. Horowitz,

I genuinely appreciate the tenor, tone, and sincerity of your apology.

Apology accepted.

Please wish Mr. Harkham a Happy Rosh Hashanah and a peaceful Yom Kippur. If you are Jewish, I extend that to you as well.

Respectfully,

Eric

P.S. I still want to know exactly who gave you the instructions to approach me, and exactly what words were said to you. It seems that the Waxman team was behind this overreaction from the beginning. I do not blame the Luxe Hotel for their heavy-handedness. Nevertheless, the Luxe Hotel aspect of this situation is completely closed for me."

(The word "their," refers to the Waxman people, not the Luxe.)

Some may question the sincerity of the apology, but I do not care if it came through clenched teeth and a clenched fist. If I were the owner of a business and one of my subordinates caused a problem, and the victim had no interest in suing, I would want the matter put to bed immediately. Did Mr. Harkham put his steel toe in Mr. Horowitz's hide? I don't know or care. Rosh Hashanah was approaching. I accepted his apology at face value.

Does this close the matter?

Mr. Horowitz and the Luxe were in the past. Waxman's staff was absolutely not cleared.

I wanted to find out why this happened to begin with. Mr. Horowitz followed orders.

My conference call with Lisa Pinto and Karen Lightfoot showed Ms. Pinto to be a low-level person. Ms. Lightfoot controlled communications from DC. Ms. Lightfoot and Ms. Pinto explained exactly what Mr. Horowitz stated. My blog was the cause of concern.

Describing the event as a "health care town hall" and not a "luncheon" worried them.

This leaves a question for them.

Are you kidding me? Are you seriously that dishonest? Do you think that playing semantics changes the fact that you took an innocent guy and harassed him over nonsense because your congressman is so scared of the voters that he can't even handle his event being mentioned at all? Are the words "town hall" now dirty words?

That was several questions. They are all valid.

I wanted to know who gave the orders. They placed all of the blame on the West LA Chamber of Commerce. The WLACC was in charge of everything. All the congressman did was show up. He was merely an invited guest. WLACC President Paul Reznik coordinated security.

I left a message for Paul Reznik. He called back, and immediately got snippy.

I know that liberals hate it when I refer to certain behavior as being "typical liberal" behavior. The solution is to stop behaving this way, rather than lash out at me for properly pointing it out.

Examples of typical liberal behavior include smugness, condescension, and hostility toward conservatives for breathing.

Mr. Reznik is a typical liberal.

He told me that since I got my apology from Mr. Horowitz, I should be happy. He asked me what more I could possibly want. I told him I wanted the truth.

In the conversation he told me to "be a good little boy" and to "run along now."

He also said that he read my blog. He said he did not like that I was going after others such as Waxman. I pointed out that I was the victim in all of this. He then made an astoundingly arrogant comment, even for a liberal.

"The real victims are your readers. The readers of your blog are the victims."

Maybe Mr. Reznik should investigate whether any of my readers were accosted by me. The only accosting was done to me. Liberal smugness aside, Mr. Reznik was simply looking to humiliate a conservative. Unfortunately for him, I just get more emboldened when people like him act this way.

He actually tried to suggest that Mr. Horowitz acted on his own, a ludicrous assertion.

I pointed out to him that the Waxman campaign had already given him up. While Reznik was trying to throw Horowitz under the bus, the Waxman people were trying to do the same with Reznik.

While I had been completely right about most of this from the beginning, I did get one thing wrong. That led to another interesting development.

I figured that there was no way the WLACC would be liberal. Mr. Reznik asked me what I knew about the WLACC. I told him that as a branch of the national Chamber of Commerce, it most likely had moderate to conservative leanings, especially on business matters.

Mr. Reznik told me that I was completely wrong. He said…twice…to my amazement…that "The West LA Chamber of Commerce has a liberal bent on public policy."

This guy is the president of the group. He was emphatic that the group had a "liberal bent on public policy." He pointed out that the WLACC supported national health care and other liberal positions on social issues.

When the heck did the Chamber of Commerce turn into this? Then again, this is West Los Angeles.

(Other board members have since quit in disgust over Mr. Reznik. It was made clear to me that he has put his own liberal beliefs above the mission of the chamber. I was also told that the chamber had not taken a position on the bill. They might wish to investigate Mr. Reznik and his liberal proclamations.)

I initially figured that there was no way the chamber would sanction abusive behavior against a conservative. I thought they were a natural ally politically. I was wrong.

I then used Mr. Reznik's own proud admissions to point out that this gives him a motive to target me just as the Waxman people said.

He insisted that he did not give the order, but would not say who did.

He then got belligerent and insisted that the conversation was off the record.

Screw that! This typical liberal bully does not get to decide what is on and off the record. I explained to him that if he wanted it to be off the record, he should have stated in the very beginning that this was the case.

He then told me that he would monitor my blog closely to make sure I did not defame him. Good. Let him increase my readership. I have tons of things to say about him. Truth is an absolute defense. Let him sue me. I welcome making him the poster child for liberals gone wild.

I made him an offer at the end of the conversation, which he rejected. I told him I would allow the entire conversation to remain off the record if he gave me the name of the person who gave the orders to have me harassed.

The bottom line is that if Lisa Pinto, Karen Lightfoot, and Paul Reznik think that they are going to circle the wagons and cover this up, then they are off their abusive leftist rockers.

I was polite with all of them. Each one of them got nasty when I refused to just "let this matter go so we can all move on."

I will explain this in a way that even liberals engaging in a cover-up can understand.

I want the truth. I will get the truth.

Seth Horowitz did not stand in my way.

Neither will Paul Reznik. Neither will Lisa Pinto. Neither will Karen Lightfoot.

Neither will Henry Waxman.

You liberals tried to bully the wrong conservative.

I am just getting started.

For once in these peoples' ideologically bigoted lives, they are going to be held accountable.

eric

Chapter 4:
Palesimian Violence

Palestinians blow stuff up for the same reason the big kid takes the little kid's lunch money. He does it because he feels like it, and because the little kid does not yet have the training to take the big kid and burn his entire village. Palestinians will stop their behavior when they get indigestion from having Israeli Galils jammed up their homicidal hides.

Violence in Gaza–Oh, and Water is Wet

There is violence occurring in Gaza. In further news, a tree is falling in the forest somewhere. Like a third-tier presidential candidate, this story is gasping for air time. Let it die, along with the people there.

I said it. Humans are suffering. I am content to let them. I am Jewish, and the Torah I believe in does not ask me to pray for people that want to kill me. Jews are supposed to be fruitful and multiply. This is hard to do when living next door to genocidal lunatics.

Although I had grave misgivings about the Gaza pullout (I felt Israel should have taken more land), I trusted Ariel Sharon. It was difficult to watch Jews leave their homes, but once the Jews were gone, the Arabs (Palesimians are simply Arabs, and the worst of the lot at that) would have no excuses. They would either succeed as a civilization in Gaza or they would fail. Shockingly enough, they continued killing each other.

A dirty not so little secret about many Arab nations is that while they publicly hate Israel, they hate each other more. Does any sane person honestly believe Kuwait hates Israel more than Iraq? Does anyone honestly believe that Saudi Arabia worries about Israel more than they do Iran? Israel is the best thing that ever happened to the Arabs. It is the only thing that (most of the time) keeps Arab nations from firing their guns while standing in a circle.

Some commentators mentioned that without Israel controlling Gaza, the Palesimians would descend into a civil war. My only difficulty was trying to figure out what the down side of this equation was. Of course they were going to kill each other. They had to kill somebody. That is what killers do. The Roman Empire collapsed because it was founded on military victories. When Romans had nobody left to fight, they got bored and turned inward.

Forget the obligatory politically correct nonsense about the peace-loving Palesimians. For those claiming that the many are held hostage by a few renegades, turn on the television. There are no Jews left in Gaza. Palesimians are still killing each other. For what? I know not and care not. I suspect they are arguing about who would be best at killing Jews. This is just as worthy and noble a goal as fighting illiteracy, starvation and homelessness.

It is said about the Palesimians (and all Arabs) that they "never miss an opportunity to miss an opportunity."[26] At least they are consistent, hobgoblins of mindlessness that they are. Their billion Arab brothers want to help them against the Zionist infidels. This is if help is defined as leaving them to rot in their own misery.

Like a government civil service worker on lunch break, I am declaring this not my problem. I do not care. I encourage my fellow Americans to not care. If we must, we can act like liberals and pretend to care. We just say we care without actually doing anything. We can call this the "Darfur method" of problem solving. It involves making pious speeches, wearing ribbons, and then nothing. It is like an Obama speech, except even more pointless.

There is violence in Gaza because it is Gaza. Water is wet, the sun rises in the east, and Gangsta Rapper Old Dirty B@stard (rest his dirty soul) beat up his girlfriend. These things are the norm. The *JBT* may never get the story right or put important stories on page one, but every once in awhile they fail to put a non-story on page one as well. They are to journalism what Hamas and Fatah are to civilization.

If an eye for an eye makes the world blind, why not just flip this expression on its head and turn a blind eye? Not everything in life is worth fixing. The people leading Gaza have only two hobbies, killing Jews and killing each other. They will never give up the first hobby They are unwilling to learn a third nonviolent hobby, perhaps something safe and boring like golf or macramé. The second hobby is all that is left.

Let them kill each other or figure it out on their own. I have washed my hands of them. Unlike their hands, mine have no blood on them.

There are too many important things happening in this world to worry about dealing with these miscreants. It is no longer even news.

eric

U.S. Liberals and Palesimian Terrorists–Different Means, Same End

The politics of personal destruction is guided in America by warrior liberals (the only time liberals ever support war is against Republicans). Real destruction is taking place in the Middle East. Normally this would not be news. In this case it is significant because it is Fatah vs. Hamas. They are in a battle to see which genocidal lunatic faction can represent their darling people best. Liberals fail to acknowledge that what they are doing to their political enemies (what civilized people refer to as opponents) is not much better.

I am not referring to liberals as murderers. Even Ted Kennedy only committed negligent homicide, not murder. Some liberals may speak up and criticize me for painting a broad brush. They should condemn their own radical elements to have any credibility. Silence is acquiescence, hence the broad brush. The means of U.S. liberals and Palesimians are far different (words vs. bullets). The ends are equally destructive to the bomb-throwers and the targets.

It has been said that Palesimians (Arabs) would be ready for peace when they decided that they loved their own children more than they hated Jewish children.[27] This has yet to happen. Proof of this is Hamas fighting Fatah. The winner of this "Super Bowl of nutcases" gets to lead the charge against Israel. When two sides are fighting to represent a cause they completely agree on, you know they are far gone. Not since a television show in the 1980s satirized peace groups (One group was named WIMP, for "War Insane Make Peace." It led to a fight between the peace groups.) has such ridiculous dinner theatre been part of the news. Apparently Palesimians did not get the liberal memo about singing "Kumbaya" and starting a love train.

This brings us to our liberal friends (boy am I being generous). In 1992 they had all the levers of power. They fought amongst themselves, bringing Newt Gingrich and the next leg of the Reagan Revolution to power. Liberals were great at being revolutionaries themselves. They found governing was tougher. They simply did what liberals normally do when confronted with actually having to do things. They failed.

For the last several years the left has wasted time. For three years the Bush White House was harassed over covert *Vanity Fair* agent Valerie Plame and her husband Joe "sipping tea with despots" Wilson. Scooter Libby got dragged down. Why? Liberal vengeance. Paul Wolfowitz resigned from the World Bank. Why? Liberal vengeance. This had nothing to do with his job. He is a Neocon who pushed the Iraq War, so the left needed to punish him. Alberto Gonzales was admittedly not a spectacular public relations person, but he was an honorable public servant. He was being dragged through the mud for badly articulating why the president fired people he had every right to fire. This was liberal vengeance.

Liberals forgot long ago how to debate on issues of actual policy. Maybe they have no policies. Maybe they know most Americans disagree with them, so they hide their policies. A good example of this was their vow to never back down from President Bush regarding the troop withdrawal. The only withdrawal was meek liberals scurrying like rats to explain why the president kicked their hides that round. In plain language, he was right and they were wrong. Liberals learned the wrong lesson from this fiasco. Now they rarely ever announce policy initiatives or take stands on anything.

An immigration deal (I took no position. I am on the fence, no joke intended) could have gotten done. Two years were wasted with liberals trying to claim more scalps in the hope of getting President Bush removed from office. I then announced to liberals my brilliant plan to remove him from office. It was called term limits. On January 20th, 2009, he left. The left spent the last few months of his presidency ripping him to shreds. Why couldn't the left be for things...anything...rather than merely against him?

Liberals want vengeance because they believe Bill Clinton should not have been impeached (the whole rationale for Moveon.org before it became another irrational group), and that George W. Bush stole the 2000 election. Moveon never did move on. Bill Clinton's impeachment was legal. All proper procedural channels were followed. Rodney King asked if we could all get along, If he really wanted to improve the world, Bill Clinton could tell his fellow Democrats to stop the attacks and focus on positive change. The reason that George W. Bush was not found guilty of corruption is because he was not corrupt. He is a good decent man who enacted policies that some agreed with and some did not.

If liberals keep going down the Bush Derangement Syndrome road, they might find it an ugly place once the tables are turned. From Robert Bork to Clarence Thomas to George W. Bush, conservatives have had it. Telling Republicans not to retaliate will fall on deaf ears. I would not blame conservatives. We have had enough.

Liberals cannot burn down the village and expect it to be in one piece when they want to rule. Liberals should talk to their friends in Hamas and Fatah. Payback can be brutal...and unproductive.

It is time to work on actual policies. It is called governing. When liberals drop their jihad against Republicans and conservatives, they might wish to try this phenomenon of actually doing things. Meanwhile, liberals will continue griping. Conservatives do not have time. We have work to do, and work we will.

eric

Gilad Shalit—Another Israeli Surrender

For those who do not worship at the altar of Captain Obvious, let me state it plainly.

I am not a diplomat. I have a real job with actual responsibilities. Plus, I hate tea.

I am old enough at thirty-eight to remember when schools taught history. For the young generation, January 20th, 2009, is not what separates the Common Era from the BCE period.

The only lesson that needs to be learned from history can be summed up in two words.

Force works.

It has always worked. Force allowed Judah Maccabee, the predecessor to Paul Wolfowitz, to take down the Greeks. Hanukkah is not about dreidels and gelt. It is the Jewish July 4th.

The Roman Empire expanded by force. It was eventually conquered when it became complacent.

Ronald Reagan won the Cold War without firing a single shot. Make no mistake about it. The Russians surrendered because they knew they could not win. That is how wars end. One side looks in the mirror and says, "we can't win."

A chess match ends when the king sees his entire defense eviscerated. He surrenders to stay alive. The card game "war" ends when one player runs out of every single card. There is nothing left.

Very few world leaders ever seem to grasp this.

Alberto Fujimori got it. When leftist rebels took hostages in South America, he led a brilliant raid. He killed the rebels and rescued the hostages. He then added the exclamation point by putting his feet on the coffee table and lighting a cigar. He angered the leftists, the gun-control crowd, and the anti-smoking fringe. Sounds good to me.

Vladimir Putin got it. I know it is not politically correct to praise Putin, but has anybody noticed that rebel groups in Russia have taken up new hobbies? Does it seem interesting that Russian ships are not being hijacked by Somali pirates?

The pirates know better. They know that when rebels took over a school, Putin warned them that he would send his men in to kill everybody. Liberals declared that he would never let anything happen to the children. Putin knew that as awful as dead children look on the news, giving in to the terrorists would lead to many more dead children in the future. He may not be Harry Truman, but he certainly ended the conflict. Apparently Putin does not let CNN dictate his policy decisions.

Benjamin Netanyahu has the potential to be one of the great world leaders, along with Reagan, Margaret Thatcher, Winston Churchill, George W. Bush, and Ariel Sharon.

Bibi had that potential in 1996. He ran as an enforcer and turned into a deal-making pragmatist. I truly believe in Bibi, but I worry that the Gilad Shalit situation turned into a debacle.

The fictional invented creatures known as Palesimians have often been rewarded for their third-world genocidal lunacy. They blow up discos. Israel drops leaflets. They kill innocent civilians in pizza parlors. Israel drives Palesimian victims to the hospitals, which their relatives then try to blow up.

Palesimians release one or two Israelis, sometimes alive, sometimes dead. Israel releases hundreds of terrorists.

I cannot possibly know what Gilad Shalit's family is going through. I will never understand their pain. I wore the dog tags around my neck in solidarity. I took them off and threw them across my bedroom in disgust when I realized that two of the three kidnapped soldiers were murdered. There would be no justice for their killers.

The day an Israeli soldier is released, Palesimians fire guns in the air and plan the next round of kidnappings. The jihad continues.

There was another solution, but it is too late now for this round in the never-ending conflict.

When the next group of Israelis is kidnapped, and this will happen, Israel must take serious steps.

They must learn from Fujimori and Putin.

Force works. Two more words they must embrace: collateral damage. Finally, two more words: Scorched Earth.

God helps those who help themselves. Any people or nation that is unwilling to do anything and everything to defend itself will not be around for long. The Holocaust is proof of what can happen when evil goes unchecked.

This means burning every village, razing every field, slaughtering every goat (kosher-style of course) and sterilizing every prisoner so that they cannot reproduce a new generation of homicide bombers. Some say that Israel takes extra precautions because they value human life. If the Palesimians do not value human life, then that only provides extra justification for immediate and tough measures.

Time is running out. North Korea can kidnap a pair of American journalists and get rewarded with a photo op with a peripheral groveling ex-president. North Korea has nuclear weapons. China can make their 1989 crackdown seem like child's play tomorrow. The world will allow it because China also has nuclear weapons. What would President Obama do, something? Despots laugh the words "of course not."

Once the homicide bombers get the ultimate bomb, it will be too late. Israel has a few years left at most to take the Palesimians and break them physically, militarily, emotionally, and psychologically. Only when Palesimians are totally broken will they stop their madness. They may never stop. If they don't, they can also cease to exist. Rocket launchers are omni-directional.

I trust Mr. Netanyahu. There is no reason to ever trust the Palesimians. The only promise they have ever honored is their vow to try and destroy Israel.

Now is not the time to surrender.

Gilad Shalit may experience freedom. His parents will have their nightmare end. This is good. Yet the entire nation of Israel he fought to protect will once again be held hostage.

eric

More Palesimian and Iranian Madness Toward Israel and America

An Israel rally I attended brought me a flood of pictures and links.

A pair of critical occurrences pointed out by blogger Velvet Hammer took place around the time of the rally.

The first one involved Palesimians attacking children at a Christian concert. This did not happen in the Middle East. It happened in Charlotte, North Carolina.

The second one involved Iranian protesters in Tehran burning pictures of the president in effigy. This would be routine if it was George W. Bush. The universally beloved Barack Obama was burned.

These incidents must be made public to everybody in the civilized world. They should be used as crystal clear evidence that only the truly blind on the far left could ignore.

No amount of "dialogue" will solve this cancer. No amount of "restoring our position in the world"[28] will fix this. No amount of interfaith dinners will help.

Radical Islam has been terrorizing people for fourteen hundred years. In the seventh century, cutting off heads became a method of airing grievances.

This nonsense about "poor, suffering Palesimians" doesn't cut it in North Carolina. These Palesimians have a homeland. They are just as psychotically abusive as their murderous brethren in the Gaza Strip.

"When the youth group tried to enter the event, they were surrounded by a group of 'Palestinian' protesters against Israel. The protesters surrounded the American children, screamed profanity and called them horrible names such as 'baby murderers,' while waving signs of what was portrayed as 'mangled' children from 'Palestine.'"[29]

These Christian children had nothing to do with the Arab-Israeli conflict. They were the real innocent victims, not the poor, suffering Palesimians. Why does this happen? Why do Palesimian basket cases insist on trying to spread the Caliphate to North Carolina?

Basket cases is as basket cases does. It is self-evident. A = A. They are nuts.

Liberal hyper-tolerance only enables them. Such hyper-tolerance did wonders for Europistan. This either stops now, or the backlash may be so severe that the sequel to the crusades will occur. Some Muslims that then get murdered will truly be innocent victims.

Jews and Christians have had it. Jews keep quiet out of fear and our being small in numbers. Christians will not back down, nor should they.

The mother of one of the victimized Christian girls was at the end of her rope.

"Let's get this straight. The 'Palestinian' protesters were 'well within their rights' to detain, deter, harass, threaten and block a child's access to a peaceful act of worship in their religion? I imagine my complaint would have been addressed quite differently if the situation was reverse and it were Islamic children who were effected."

No level of grievance justifies the behavior of the savages known as Palesimians. If they want to be treated as human beings, they need to act like them. We all have grievances. Not everybody turns to violence. Palesimians do.

"It is true that the children of 'Palestine' are victims but it is not because of other countries like Israel and America that tries to protect its own children and their right to exist. It is also not because of other religions who don't agree with Islamic beliefs. It is because the very adults who are supposed to protect these children insist on making them targets in lieu of a treasure. These children are tragically forced into a dark world where their 'innocent' caretakers allow their schools to be used as launching grounds for terrorist rocket attacks and use Mickey Mouse-like characters to tell them at an early age how to kill Jews."

So what separates radical Islamic fundamentalism from Judaism and Christianity?

"It is not the policy of Christianity or Judaism to indoctrinate or involve their children in hate-filled political doctrine and attacks. However those rallying the 'Palestinian' battle-cry appear determined to reduce our children to political pawns as well. As the mainstream media gushes forth with prideful reports regarding the 'peaceful' protests on behalf of 'Palestinians' and police departments turn their heads, it appears that they are succeeding in their mission. This Wednesday night, I will be forced to explain the heartless political antics of the protest group to my own group of saddened and confused kids."

There are no peaceful Palesimian rallies. There are whitewashed rallies. The Palesimian kids that harassed the Christian children are well on their way to being future terrorists. Maybe they will not use bombs. Does anybody think their communities object to their thuggish behavior?

It is one thing for local governments to perfectly imitate ostriches. It is much worse for our federal government to cover its head in sand, when not having it trapped up its hide.

The election of Barack Obama was supposed to restore America's moral standing in the world. We were told George W. Bush was bad. We were not liked.

We elected a man whose middle name is Hussein. He offered nuanced platitudes about Israel. No longer were we going to be reflexively and blindly pro-Israel. He offered to close down Guantanamo Bay. The entire world was now going to finally like us.

Barack Obama was burned in effigy. At some point he might have shoes thrown at him. When these acts occur, I will condemn them for one reason.

Although I did not vote for him, Barack Obama is my president. When you burn my president in effigy, you burn everything that I hold dear. You are my enemy.

I am ready to shake the pacifists out of their coma, stupor, blindness, or whatever adjective is used to describe these people. They either fail to grasp the truth out of ignorance, or deliberately ignore it out of anti-west viciousness.

There is nothing America can do to be liked. Short of surrendering and being part of the Caliphate, we will always be hated. We can close Gitmo, apologize for inconveniencing terrorists, try our best to understand them, and continue to watch them murder us.

"Welcome to center stage Obama. Maybe President Bush could give you a few pointers on how to handle intense criticism with class. Heh That thin skin you had during the election had better thicken up real soon. Or your entire presidency will consist of whining. It was NOT Bush it IS America they hate. Kapish?"

President George W. Bush kept us safe. He did this by passing the Patriot Act. He had help from FISA Courts and from intelligence members willing to use coercive interrogation methods. We waterboarded three people, including Khalid Sheik Mohammed.

President George W. Bush made the hard choices. He took all the slings and arrows. He did not back down.

The Islamists cursed, spit, threw shoes, and burned him in effigy. The *JBT* did too, along with the Axis of Anti-Semitism of the *Daily Kos*, *Huffington Post*, and Moveon.org.

He was vilified.

He also was…and is…right.

Barack Obama has one obligation that trumps all else. He must keep America safe.

He said all the right things during the campaign. Iranians are still burning him in effigy. Palesimians are still terrorizing Christian children in North Carolina.

Barack Obama stated that he is a Christian and not a Muslim. I do not question this. He should therefore loudly condemn criminal attacks against his own faith.

He is an intelligent man, but book smarts do not equal street smarts. President Bush had something that Mr. Obama did not have. President Bush had the experience. He sat in the chair. He has seen the evil and made the impossible decisions.

Mr. Obama is exceptionally bright. He will learn. He must learn. He must see that it is not about America, Israel, a lack of hope, poverty, suffering, or any other "tragedy."

It is about a genocidal ideology that prefers a culture of death over one that values life.

Israel must smash the terrorists in the Gaza Strip. The United States must smash the terrorists in Iran and Syria. There will be collateral damage. Innocent Iranians, Syrians, and Gazans will die.

This unfortunate fact cannot be a deterrent. The madness must be stopped before it reaches our shores again. Another 9/11 must be prevented.

Nobody died in this North Carolina incident. Waiting until American Jewish and Christian children are killed trying to attend a church or synagogue service is not an option.

There can be no more dialogue with the madmen. They are future bombs. The clock, like any bomb, is now ticking.

eric

Chapter 5:
Media Violence

Our soldiers are fighting and dying to protect our freedoms. The *Jayson Blair Times* is doing everything it can to hasten a global world where American hegemony is replaced with multi-polarity. This is a fancy way of saying that the top brass at the *JBT* should be relocated to fancy new private offices in Sing-Sing.

The Collapse of the Jayson Blair Times, Palesimian Style

The *Jayson Blair Times* is on the verge of collapse. It is in free fall. It did not have to be this way. It seems that they followed the Palesimian business model for success.

For those wondering what the conflagration in the Gaza Strip has to do with a newspaper being printed in New York, the simplistic answer is bad decisions. What makes it worse is that these were bad avoidable decisions.

Let's start with the *JBT*. Everybody knows that the editorial pages are liberal. I have zero objections to this. They have every right to be liberal. I am a conservative. My column has a conservative bias. I freely admit this bias. The *JBT* denied its liberal bias to the point it was laughable. They did everything but run an editorial accusing George W. Bush of lighting puppies and kittens on fire and eating them. Like Palesimian leaders, the JBT editorial venom was almost pathological.

This alone would not be enough to destroy the paper, because the editorials are one or two pages. The rest of the paper was allegedly hard news. It was supposedly well-written. It got stories adequately right enough. Not anymore. Besides the crossword puzzle, which I am told is the best in the world, the *JBT* has become a tabloid. In fact, tabloids began scooping them. Matt Drudge broke the Bill Clinton affair with Monica Lewinsky.

Worse than being scooped, the *JBT* started letting bias infect its hard news columns. A major story was the day Iraqis voted. The *JBT* chose to run the Bush domestic wiretapping scandal story. A plot to blow up JFK airport was on page thirty-seven. Good news from Iraq was buried deep inside the paper. Worse than bias, the paper started getting stories wrong. It then buried those corrections, again far deep inside the paper.

Humans make mistakes. I wrote an article predicting the outcome of *The Apprentice*. My analysis was dead wrong. The next day I issued an equally prominent mea culpa. Credibility is all writers have. It is all anyone has. Without it, we are done. The *New York Times* forever became the *Jayson Blair Times* when they put their liberal ideological agenda ahead of quality writing and reporting. Jayson Blair was promoted because he was black. This perversion of affirmative action was an insult to white and black Americans that were qualified for a job that this man was given. He fabricated stories. That black eye to a once well-written paper has not subsided.

The *JBT* forgot to stick to the basics. Get the story first. Get the story right. Describe it with rhetorical flourish. They strayed from the core of what they were. This is described well in Laura Ingraham's book *Shut Up and Sing*.

Ellen Degeneres did not have her sitcom cancelled because she is a lesbian. She stopped being funny, and then blamed the network for declining ratings. Rosie O'Donnell is now known as a left-wing lunatic. When she was a VJ on VH1, she was very funny.

Everything comes down to likability. It is how we choose friends, lovers, presidential candidates, TV shows, and newspapers. The *JBT* became the Gore/Kerry of newspapers. They were smarter than everybody else, but the lower-class masses of ordinary people did not like them. The *New York Post* is a great read because they are like President Bush…simple, easy to understand, and downright likable. The paper can be lighthearted, but it is a fun read. When they make a mistake, they issue major retractions. Humility does help. The *Wall Street Journal* is brilliant. *WSJ* economics columns, unlike those of Paul Krugman at the *JBT*, are actually about economics. The *New York Post* and *Wall Street Journal* are conservative, but that is peripheral. They are well-written.

The *JBT* coasted on its reputation and good name. They also made a calculated decision to tilt further to the left and develop a core audience. Surely there were enough liberals in America to keep it afloat. They miscalculated there as well. Many Jews are liberals, and Jews do not want to read a paper that is almost as sympathetic to the Palesimians as Al Jazeera. The editorial pages occasionally border on anti-Semitism. This further reduced their readership, since many Jews are actually not self-hating.

It is the same reason *Air America* failed. It was not because they were liberal. It is because they were elitist, unprofessional, and occasionally anti-Semitic (Mel Gibson made anti-Semitic remarks. He starred in the movie *Air America*. Break out your conspiracy glasses). Worst of all, they were the biggest sin in any media form…boring. Rush Limbaugh has twenty million listeners. They are not all conservatives. Many people like him because he is funny. He entertains first. He is provocative, but never boring.

The *JBT* is bleeding dollars. The way out of this mess would be to improve the quality of the brand. Instead they are raising prices and lowering quality. This is a death spiral. Since their readers are liberal, they are actually giving liberals a delightfully ironic taste of their own philosophy with an ideological tax on liberals only. I wish the federal government would do this.

The *JBT* adopted the Palesimian business model. Divide people into groups. Those in your group are good. Everyone else is evil. When the Jews left Gaza, Palesimians had nothing to do but engage in fratricide. They cannibalized their own, and are dwindling in numbers by the day. If they ever decide to reach across the aisle, be open-minded, and expand their circle of people allowed to exist, they might find a receptive audience.

The *JBT* should (figuratively) blow itself up, start over, and rededicate itself first and foremost to being a well-written paper that many people would want to read. They might be taken off life support and breathe on their own. People will read well-written contra viewpoints. The other *JBT* option is to continue to narrow their audience to the few people who want to read something smug, arrogant, biased, poorly written, often wrong, and boring. The *JBT* seems to have chosen this option, placing themselves squarely along the lines of other failures, from *Air America* to Palesimian society.

eric

Ideological Bigotry Part XXIII–Bob Herbert's Racial Temper Tantrum

Bob Herbert of the *Jayson Blair Times* threw another one of his racial temper tantrums.

As usual, he is accusing a white Republican of being a racist. Bob Herbert is an expert on the subject. He may be the biggest race-baiter in the country not named reverend.

Talk about the pot calling the kettle African-American.

His screed is entitled "Fanning the flames of racial tensions."

I thought it was his autobiography, but apparently he does not own a mirror.

I never linked to the column because I do not link to garbage.

(This is a reflection of the column itself. I am not referring to Mr. Herbert himself as garbage. Actually, screw political correctness. I have changed my mind. I am referring to him, the column, and the *JBT*.)

What has Bob Herbert acting like himself again?

He is disappointed in Mayor Mike Bloomberg for fanning racial tensions.

He freely admits that on the overall issue of reduced racial tensions, Mayor Bloomberg has been very good. What changed? How could an entire two terms of being good on an issue be undone by one incident?

Did Mayor Bloomberg say something inappropriate? No.

Did he do something inappropriate? No.

He sat in a room where Rudy Giuliani spoke.

Rudy Giuliani stated that if Mike Bloomberg were to not be reelected, New York City would revert back to the way it was before Giuliani became mayor. Giuliani also said, "and you know what I mean."[30]

Bob Herbert is able to decode Giuliani's language using special racial grievance rabbit ears. It is the equivalent of a dog whistle. Only bigoted charlatans can hear the sounds that are non-existent to non-bigots.

Some people use vanilla extract instead of chocolate extract when baking a cake. This proves that nothing has changed since 1863. Selma, Alabama somehow applies. Let me again give America some basic facts about race. Please feel free to take notes.

Race is about a multi-syllabic word known as pigmentation. Pigmentation is a function of what scientists of all races call melanin content. Race is not an attitude, a feeling, or an experience. Going to the planetarium is an experience. Being black means being born to black people that at some point had intercourse. I know this is mind-boggling, but stay with me. It also works the same way for other races.

There is nothing in the racial composition of any human being that makes them inferior or superior to any other race. People of all races can therefore do a good or bad job at whatever they do professionally.

From 1989 to 1993, New York City was run by David Dinkins. He was a good, decent man and a terrible mayor. He was not tough enough for the job. He was lightly regarded. He once tried to calm racial tensions by picking up a megaphone and yelling "increase the peace" (a very decent gesture by a decent man). Somebody in the crowd threw a bottle at his head.

(Liberals only laugh when objects are thrown at Republicans. The bottle-thrower should have been beaten and arrested. The action was unacceptable. The lack of follow-up showed Dinkins's weakness. Nobody would have been dumb enough to throw a bottle at Giuliani.)

From 1993 to 2001, Rudy Giuliani turned New York City around. He was one of the best chief executives in the history of any government. He was that good. I know. I lived in New York during his first term.

At no time did it matter to me or most people that Dinkins was black and Giuliani was white. It matters to Bob Herbert. Black mayors have failed in New York City, Washington, DC, and Detroit. Bob Herbert is still blaming Ronald Reagan.

They did not fail because they were black. They failed because they were liberals.

This is not about race. It is about ideology.

Bob Herbert can't stand that a white Republican defeated a black liberal. Bob Herbert can't stand that all the bile in the world will not change the fact that a liberal did a lousy job running a city. A conservative came in and fixed it.

Rudy Giuliani cut taxes and cracked down on crime. That is what a mayor is supposed to do. David Dinkins failed to do this.

When Giuliani talks about New Yorkers not wanting to go back to the days before 1993, it is a reference to failed solutions that nearly destroyed the city. No amount of verbal bomb-throwing by the *JBT* will alter the fact that New Yorkers don't care about race. Like Americans everywhere, they want results.

Bob Herbert wants to party like it's 1989. For most New Yorkers, the city was dying. Rudy Giuliani revived Gotham City.

He cracked down on the squeegee guys. Some of them were black. Bob Herbert threw a tantrum. Fifteen years later, baby Bobby is still lobbing racial grenades. Nothing about a man with darker pigmentation guarantees electoral success. He can't accept this.

We are now in an era where a black man can become president. In the end, the only thing that matters is results.

Bob Herbert does not want equality. He wants lifelong employment for black politicians regardless of how dreadful their policies may be.

This is not justice or equality. It is an insult to every black person that succeeded in America not because of their skin, but because of this nation.

I would introduce Bob Herbert to Dr. Condoleezza Rice or Chairman Michael Steele, but then I would have to be in a room with Bob Herbert.

Sorry Bob. People like you (Yeah, "you people," that being racial grievance phonies) need to stop throwing racial temper tantrums.

Bob Herbert needs a timeout. Somebody get him a pacifier and some milk.

Make sure it is chocolate milk so he does not accuse me of racism.

eric

More Jewish Self-loathing From the Jayson Blair Times

The most self-hating people on Earth are liberal Jews. They beg Islamofascists to like them while despising themselves for not doing enough to bring world peace. They concurrently disparage evangelical Christians, who for some reason tolerate this.

The most anti-Semitic newspaper in the country is the *Jayson Blair Times*, run by self-hating Jew (to be fair, he did convert away from the faith) Arthur "Pinch" Sulzberger Jr.

The *JBT* thinks that Arabs are innocent victims of evil Jews. The *JBT* will offer a "balanced perspective." A Jewish voice is allowed in their paper provided that the Jew is an apologist that also blames Jews. Arabs do not have apologists. They shoot them.

Richard Cohen has a Jewish last name. I wish he understood that when Iran tries to form a Caliphate, he will not be spared.

His self-loathing screed came in the form of supporting victim Iran over aggressor Israel. His article came out during Passover. That was just icing on his anti-Israel chocolate digestive, or in his case, indigestive.

He accused Israel of "crying wolf" over Iran. That is a fancy way of calling Israel a liar.

His "evidence" is flimsy at best.

"Four years earlier, in 1992, he'd (Shimon Peres) predicted that Iran would have a nuclear bomb by 1999."

"You can't accuse the Israelis of not crying wolf. Ehud Barak, now defense minister, said in 1996 that Iran would be producing nuclear weapons by 2004."

I want to be more eloquent than simply referring to Mr. Cohen as a self-hating Jew and left-wing horse's hide. Yet equine anus is as equine anus does.

The issue is not whether the predictions were 100 percent accurate. The issue is whether the predictions were reasonable. Based on observed behavior, of course the predictions were reasonable.

Iran has not blown up Israel yet. They are trying to do so every waking moment.

This same idiotic logic says that Hamas and the Palesimians should be rewarded because homicide bombings are down. Homicide bombings are down because the Israeli Defense Forces are getting better. The Palesimians are as bloodthirsty as ever. They are just less successful.

Iran only needs to get it right once.

One school of thought that those on the left continue to spout is that Iran will not attack Israel because Israel would then obliterate them. This argument is beyond flawed.

The mullahs are not pragmatists. They are not afraid to die. They believe that the Caliphate will be spread when the twelfth Imam returns. This can only happen after a cataclysm.

There are one billion Muslims in existence. There are fourteen million Jews. If the Iranians sacrifice ten, twenty, or fifty people for every single Jew, they still win.

During the 1980-1988 Iran-Iraq War, the mullahs sacrificed women and children. Fourteen-year-old boys were sent to die. The mullahs do not care. Dying in battle is glorious. They have the people to sacrifice.

"Netanyahu also makes the grotesque claim that the terrible loss of life in the Iran-Iraq War (started by Iraq) 'didn't sear a terrible wound into the Iranian consciousness.' It did just that, which is why Iran's younger generation seeks reform but not upheaval; and why the country as a whole prizes stability over military adventure."

The young people have no say. They want to rise up and revolt within, but need U.S. support. Republican presidents did not finance this. A liberal president who speaks in soft professorial platitudes without carrying a stick would not even consider helping.

The Iran-Iraq War did not make the mullahs averse to war. It just made them determined to get better weapons.

The notion of prizing stability is imbecilic. Iran foments worldwide terrorism. They fund instability. Their leaders are unstable. Unstable people cause unstable situations. Even liberals should grasp this. If not, they can go to Amazon and buy a thesaurus.

In 2009, Benjamin Netanyahu referred to Iranian President and psychopath Armageddonijad as a "wide-eyed believer."[31] Roger Cohen saw a bigger threat that he described as only a smug liberal could.

"I must say when I read those words about 'the wide-eyed believer' my mind wandered to a recently departed 'decider.' But I'm not going there."

Liberals love to chortle at their own wit. This guy is practically French he needs rhinoplasty so bad.

What liberals pass as "dialogue" is advancing the idiotic notion that President George W. Bush is more dangerous than Armageddonijad.

I challenge Roger Cohen to take his liberal smugness to Iran and see how long he lasts. Nicolas Berg and Daniel Pearl were beheaded by Islamofascist zealots, not Republicans.

Let's see how funny Iran would find Cohen if he made remarks about Iranian leadership while living there. It is pretty easy to be brave when working for a morally bankrupt newspaper that exists because American soldiers protect and defend the paper's right to be hateful and wrong.

"I don't buy the view that, as Netanyahu told Goldberg, Iran is 'a fanatic regime that might put its zealotry above its self-interest.' Every scrap of evidence suggests that, on the contrary, self-interest and survival drive the mullahs."[32]

What scrap of evidence? I forgot. In *JBT* world, "fake but accurate" memos are considered evidence. In the real world, allowing your nation to receive economic sanctions puts fanaticism above self-interest. Refusing to allow western culture, including technological advances that could help with oil infrastructure, puts fanaticism above self-interest. Driving out Jews from your country despite the fact they bring economic value to every welcoming nation, is putting fanaticism above self-interest.

Murdering your own intellectuals and beating your own women while refusing to let them get educated is putting fanaticism above self-interest.

The mullahs are not pragmatists. They are prepared for Armageddon as soon as they get the tools to bring it to their enemies.

Self-loathing liberal newspapers are bad enough. They will soon be bankrupt financially, to accompany their moral and ethical bankruptcy.

Liberal Jewish apologists are more threatened by a Republican president reelected after liberating two nations than a nation run by murderous monsters. They need to have their heads examined.

It is not paranoia when they really are out to get you.

It is not crying wolf when the wolves really are there, with blood dripping from their Islamofascist fangs.

The mullahs want to kill Roger Cohen. He wants to blame Israel and Republicans.

Who or what could be so disgusting to tolerate such a useless human being?

This bile secretion boob is located in the bile secretion tube of fellow self-loathing Jewish apologist Arthur Sulzberger Jr. at the *Jayson Blair Times*.

eric

Chapter 6:
Financial Violence

In fantasyland, all corporations are evil. Regulators are white knights in shining armor. In the real world, crooked regulators with unchecked power wreak havoc on small businesses that lack the resources to hire an army of attorneys to fight the government behemoth. Corporations are not sympathetic figures. That is the precise reason we must stand up for them. The only other solution is to become land rats trying to subsist on tree bark and pine cones when every company goes out of business. Liberals call this sharing the wealth. I call it financial rape.

Dear Detroit: Drop Dead

Bob Herbert is a black man whose hobbies include hating whitey. He and the *Jayson Blair Times* exist solely to tell conservatives how evil they are.

One Baby Bobby Herbie screed was a self-righteous lecture on why Washington, DC, should rescue Detroit. There is nothing overtly racial about his column. There are absolutely racial undertones.

Send General David Petraeus in to level Detroit like Fallujah and start over. This waste of a city is beyond hope. Not one dollar of tax money should have been spent on General Motors, Ford, or Chrysler. I don't care if the Japanese take them over. "Buy American" should not be an excuse to support mediocrity. Mediocrity might be too generous for these failed businesses.

Herbert started out his liberal blustering by accusing conservative hardliners of "smug certainties." Liberal columnists at the *JBT* have no business using the word smug unless they are looking inward. Smug certainties are why the *JBT* keeps getting stories wrong.

"The ideological hard-liners have now cast their collectively jaundiced eye on Detroit's automakers. Their response to the very real danger that General Motors might crumble into bankruptcy is: C'est la vie."

That is too soft a response. A well-placed F-bomb between the words "go," and "yourself" would be a good start.

"I can agree that it's impossible to make a positive case for the backward, self-destructive practices of the auto industry over many years."

He then goes on to justify bad behavior, which is what liberal apologists do.

"But in the current environment, allowing one or more of the Big Three to go bankrupt would be like offering up your nose to Sweeney Todd to spite your face."

It would be offering up the bad companies' heads on a silver platter.

"The U.S. auto industry is the cornerstone of American manufacturing. It supports millions of jobs, directly or indirectly, in a vast array of businesses."

The U.S. automobile industry is the second most bloated, bureaucratic, and inefficient entity behind the federal government. Unions have destroyed the very workers they claim to care about, which is what unions do. Americans are not inferior to Japanese people when given a fair chance to compete. We do produce inferior products when we let unions and excessive regulations destroy our companies. For those who care about the environment, Toyota makes the Prius. While I detest that car, and occasionally fight the urge to savagely beat people who drive hybrids, the Japanese seem to be able to make better quality cars at lower prices. We deserve to lose and get swallowed up. I love America. I detest the fact idea Americans should settle for garbage.

"It's easy to demonize the American auto industry. It has behaved with the foresight of a crack addict for years. But even when people set their own houses on fire, we still dial 9-1-1, hoping to save lives, salvage what we can and protect the rest of the neighborhood."

We do not rebuild their house for free (not that Barney Frank and the Pelosiraptor haven't tried). We do not pay their medical bills or their rehab expenses. The rest of the neighborhood consists of the forty-nine states that are not as pathetic as Michigan.

"The government should craft a rescue plan that is both tough and very, very smart. That means dragging the industry (kicking and screaming, no doubt) into the twenty-first century by insisting on ironclad commitments to design and develop vehicles that make sense economically and that serve the nation's long-term energy security requirements."

Who enforces this? I say let these companies burn like Lehman Brothers and Bear Stearns. Smarter companies gobbled up these firms. Smarter automobile companies should take the dead charred remains of auto relics and recreate them lean and mean without an ounce of government help. The incentive would be profit. Propping up a failing firm is like trying to prop up a stock market with a disastrous bailout package. Coincidentally, our government did that. The market crashed anyway as expected, with General Motors leading the race to the bottom.

"Let the smartest minds design a bailout that sparks a creative revolution in the industry."[33]

They are in the private sector, Bob. They can do it without government help, which means it might actually get done right.

As for the racial aspect of an issue that does not seem to mention race at all, let's be brutally honest. The real reason Bob Herbert cares about Detroit is because Detroit is a black inner city. If the automakers would have been located in the whitest and most conservative parts of Utah or Idaho, Bob Herbert would be encouraging their demise. For those who disagree, read his past columns and pretend not to manipulate them.

To discuss Detroit without mentioning felon Mayor Kwame Kilpatrick is astounding. While he is not responsible for the pathetic Detroit Lions, he was the chief executive who allowed crime, drugs, and union thugs to continue the destruction of once-proud Motown. The Ford family owns of the Detroit

Lions. They run their football team the same way they run their automobile company...dreadfully.

The entire state of Michigan is a disaster from the top down. Governor Jennifer Granholm was born in Canada and should have stayed there. If there was ever a reason not to change the Constitution to allow foreigners to be president, this failed governor is it. Only a city held hostage to union bullies could reelect a failed executive. Why hire a pro-business conservative when a perfectly incompetent liberal is available?

Bob Herbert talks about cutting off noses to spite faces. That is what the *JBT* does. They would rather lose money and destroy their own paper rather than offer a fair, quality product that would appeal to the reasonable masses. That is what Detroit does. They allowed failed liberals to destroy a once-proud city rather than even attempt conservative solutions. Heaven forbid Detroit become New York City. Gotham was revitalized when conservative Rudy Giuliani turned around a mess his liberal predecessor left him.

Detroit is dying from high taxes, high regulations, and negative results.

Other cities in America, particularly located in red states, are succeeding. Low taxes and business friendly climates work.

Shut Detroit down. Not just the automakers. I mean the entire city. If Detroit was a corporation, the shareholders would have fired the entire board.

If the shareholders of Detroit choose to keep the same board of misdirectors, then they deserve to have the value of their investment crash.

When an illness breaks out, the infected people get quarantined so that the entire world does not get infected. Let Detroit burn. Let the rest of the nation go about our business. When the value of Detroit finally reaches absolute zero, an enterprising American can build it again at a profit. Otherwise, the city can just shut down permanently (During the rebuilding people can move to Flint and live in Michael Moore's mansion). Outside of the Red Wings, the country will be unaffected from a quality standpoint.

I have student loans. Until I get my bailout, Detroit needs to go down in flames.

The automakers need to drop dead. They deserve nothing.

The city of Detroit deserves even less for expecting the rest of America to clean up their failures.

eric

Ideological Bigotry Part XI: Another Activist Lunatic

Either December contains some left-wing ideological holiday, or the inmates in the political asylum were all released onto the streets at once. I was the victim of behavior that made San Francisco look like a city of functional people.

There are normal liberals in society. Being liberal does not automatically make one hateful, or a wack job. I am all about fighting ideological bigotry. Yet I was on the receiving end of behavior that should make even liberals embarrassed. I am a provocative person, but I know when lines of decency have been crossed.

The incident took place at work. Politics has no place in the workplace. Workplace rules set up by corrupt labor lawyers (redundant, I know) provide free speech for everybody except conservatives. Individuals of all political stripes should restrain their beliefs when dealing with customers. I have no idea what the political views are of my auto mechanic, doctor, or dry cleaner. I only care that my car, body, and clothing are in better condition after visiting them than before.

Many activists are separate from normal people. These activists cannot fathom that most people want to get through their day without being shouted at, preached to, or bombarded with leaflets. Maybe many of these people could afford clean shirts if they did not spend all their money on leaflets.

Anybody, even me, can generalize. Specific examples are now the public domain.

I was having a telephone conversation with a woman whose job was to mediate a dispute between a firm and a client. Mediation can be a vital tool in negotiations ranging from business disagreements to divorce settlements. A mediator must be calm, cool, and level-headed. Mediators have to take parties that may be at each other's throats, and keep the discussion rational.

This one mediator (I will anonymously call her Joan Protess, because the last name sounds like protest) may or may not be a disgrace to her profession. I do not like to base an entire career on one incident, but this incident was pretty hairy.

I have spoken with her several times. It is always a mind-numbing discussion. She spends the first twenty minutes reminding me of her credentials. I call this the "Harvard Syndrome." There was an episode of *Frasier* where series lead Kelsey Grammer mentioned his Harvard background. His boss replied, "I find it obnoxious that you have to mention that you went to Harvard in every sentence."[34] It is like listening to Hillary Clinton brag about her "solutions," and her "thirty-five years of experience."[35] General Colin Powell had thirty-five years of experience in the military. He does not spend his life boring people about it. He does what dignified people do. He goes about his business. Professionals do not have to announce how professional they are. They are work horses, not show horses.

Ms. Protess kept mentioning her sixteen-and-one-half years of experience, reminding me of a child that still celebrates half-birthdays. She kept mentioning her 92 percent success rate, which I had no way of corroborating at that moment. She is successful because she says so.

Without contrary evidence, I could just sleep through the twenty minutes where she tells me of her god-like status. Maybe she does not recognize my level of boredom. My main criteria for judging somebody is whether or not they get the job done. Effectiveness can render the rest forgiven. This is where all Hades broke loose on the telephone.

She made recommendations to me. I disagreed with her proposed resolution. I was not attacking her personally. I am sure she put some effort into her work. I was the customer. I simply felt that she was asking for more than I was willing to give. I politely let her know that despite her efforts, the two parties were far apart. Negotiations most likely had broken down.

I was not aware how personal this mediator valued her success rate. She did her work. I did not like the results. I decided to reject the proposed offer. Mediation is not binding. I thought I was engaging in my normal right to take an alternative approach.

She then went ballistic on the telephone. She violated more than one rule of professionalism.

She began spewing profanity at a rapid clip. She threw out words that rhymed with spit, luck, and rap. This is not an acceptable way for a professional to behave, especially one that is a mediator! She made it clear we would regret not taking her advice. If we ignored her, we ran the risk of facing financial consequences worse than what she was proposing. I "needed to understand this, and make my boss understands this as well."

I don't "need" to understand such simple concepts as settling or rolling the dice. I understand the concept of risk vs. reward. My analysis disagreed with hers in terms of the value of settling. The idea that I need to "explain" the situation to my boss implies that he is an imbecile who has not thought scenarios. I guess he was too busy building a successful business to think about things such as the value of a dollar today vs. two dollars tomorrow. I explained to her that my boss understood the situation and considered the advice, but decided to reject it. A professional can advise a client. At the end of the day, the client is the boss.

I again tried to explain to the mediator that we understood the risks of refusing to settle. We were completely prepared to accept the consequences. The mediator then went into a seven to ten minute profanity-laced tirade. I held the phone away from my ear and contemplated various thoughts, ranging from whether or not this hysterical woman needed medication to why my parents did not set me up with a trust fund (For the sake of ethics, I was most likely contemplating my navel. My middle shirt button was open from a defect in the material. A necktie hides this).

The mediator then completely went off the rails, screaming, "You can't take the 'my way or the highway attitude.' You can't be like George W. Bush going into Iraq hell bent on war without considering the ramifications of cowboy diplomacy guns blazing. You have to work with people."

I was stunned at this point. Not one aspect of this situation had anything to do with politics. This was a completely apolitical business dispute. This was again not the other party to the dispute. This was the mediator!

After literally waiting for her to stop speaking, I conducted myself in a professional manner. When not at work, I am perfectly comfortable taking verbal brickbats to liberal skulls. I do not have that luxury at work. I waited for her batteries to run out. Then I waited some more. Finally, I spoke.

"Ms. Protess, this is a very divided country. Before you start injecting your personal politics into this situation, in addition to your cursing at me, you should know that I am a rock-ribbed supporter of President Bush. I see no reason to continue this conversation."

She did briefly try to apologize before going back into her standard stump speech involving her credentials and why we should listen to her. I had to cut her off.

"I've heard what you had to say, quite clearly. I have made my decision. My firm will handle this as we see fit. Your left-wing politics should not have been brought up. I am leaving for the day. There is nothing left to discuss. I am off to drive home in my car containing my Bush-Cheney bumper sticker. Have a good day."

(I have no bumper stickers on my car because of women like this. I have encountered enough violent "peace" activists to avoid taking such a risk.)

Some will accuse me of cherry picking. They will say things like, "I agree with you. This lady is nuts, but it is not fair to paint a broad brush."

How many of these lunatics do I have to encounter before people on the far left realize that their rage is the norm, not an aberration?

How do I take these life forms and get them to become civilized human beings?

What do I have to do to get through a week without being exposed to the ugliness of those that let their ideological bigotry define them?

Those claiming that "both sides do it" are flat-out wrong. Conservatives behaving this way are statistical outliers, especially since labor laws ban conservatives from speaking to begin with.

At work, everybody should shut up. Receptionists should answer the switchboard. Salespeople should discuss what they are selling. Managers should focus on making sure things are running smoothly. Advisers should offer advice, but understand that the right to give advice does not imply or require consent.

Whether the organization manufactures widgets or offers high-tech widget consulting services, political activism at work ranges from unhelpful to detrimental.

My next decision was whether to let this matter go or file a formal professional complaint. I wrote a book instead.

Ms. Protess may wish to rethink her approach. Even old dogs can learn new tricks. Perhaps some additional training would be appropriate. I will resist the urge to make a remark about a female dog, even though what she said to me was much worse.

eric

Burn in Hell Eliot Spitzer

March 11th is a day that will live in American history. Then again, so will the other three hundred-sixty-four days.

March 11th, 2004…The Madrid bombing. We must win the War on Terror at all costs.

March 11th, 2007…The Tygrrrr Express entered the blogosphere. I thank every single person that contributed in any way, shape or form.

March 11th, 2008…Happy Anniversary to me, a sobering reminder of Madrid, and…skewering a man through song.

"I didn't know if it was day or night/I started screwing everything in sight/ When stung by a cop it was the end of the line/I lost my career/*Love Potion* Client *No. 9.*"[36]

One of the worst human beings to ever enter politics finally became burnt toast.

Like most liberals and women, he did not gracefully resign or surrender. He went kicking, screaming and browbeating to the poisonous end.

Burn in Hell, Eliot. I Spitzer on your political grave.

I am usually civil. This time the gloves had to come off. I want Eliot Spitzer destroyed and his insides ripped out.

This is not about liberal vs. conservative. It is about a horrible man destroying decent people just because he could. It is about a bully finally getting decked between the eyes and crying. Not since junior high school have I wanted to see a man get belted so ferociously.

Recall a scene from the 1980s gangster movie, "New Jack City." Ice-T played a cop. Wesley Snipes played a drug dealer. Ice finds out that Snipes's character Nino Brown randomly killed an innocent schoolteacher for sport. That was Ice's character's mother. Ice crashes through Brown's apartment with a motorcycle, shatters the glass, and punches Brown in the face repeatedly. When the shocked drug dealer cannot understand why business has gone bad, Ice responds, "F*ck business b*tch, this sh*t is personal!"[37]

I disagree with liberals. The differences are ideological. I am quite bothered by the Clintons. They offend me from a moral standpoint. With Eliot Spitzer, it is personal.

The man personally hurt me.

I am a creature of Wall Street. The opening bell of the stock market is like rocket fuel for me. I hear the sound, and in my best Mills Lane voice, yell,

"Let's get it on!" Whether up or down, every day is a new adventure. The smell of money is within reach.

On the trading floor, my friends and I had a creative strategy for making money. This strategy was utilized most effectively in a bear market. It was the closest thing to easy money I had ever made. I used to think that short-selling stocks was unpatriotic, because it meant placing bets against corporate America. I later realized that I was playing a fair game by the rules. If corporations did their jobs, made money, and proved me wrong, I would lose my bets.

Eliot Spitzer then came on the scene and waged a jihad against traders. The mutual fund timing scandal rocked Wall Street. Mr. Spitzer was having difficulty obtaining high-level white-collar convictions for his "perp walks" in front of the cameras. Instead of pursuing elephants, he went after mice with elephant clubs. He needed to look like he was doing something, anything, so he banned the trading strategy my friends and I were utilizing. The few hundred shares at a clip I traded were apparently a bigger threat than the billions flowing into mutual funds.

I walked in the office one day, and was told that my trading strategy was now illegal. I would have to find another strategy. That is a death sentence to many traders. Only the lucky few ever develop one winning strategy, much less two. I left the trading floor financially fine but emotionally angry.

Although I have built a great life for myself, it is tough to replicate the same joy and excitement that came from the trading floor. It is a past life. I am done.

Eliot Spitzer destroyed my trading career. I hope he forever burns.

Mr. Spitzer may be too old to know the fury of the music behind Guns n Roses, but lyrics from "Welcome to the Jungle" encapsulate my feelings.

"If you've a hunger for what you see/take it eventually/you can have anything you want/but you better not take it from me."[38]

Spitzer, don't ever…and I mean ever…mess with my family or my livelihood… and think I won't pray for vengeance. This was 2004. I still remember.

As the New York attorney general, he became the second coming of Eliot Ness from *The Untouchables*. He believed that he himself was untouchable. He harassed Wall Street like the liberal bully that he is. He banked on the fact that many liberals are so obsessed with class warfare that they would blindly accept that all corporations are corrupt, and that Wall Street was the root of all that evil. There is some corruption commensurate with any industry, but not on the massive scale he envisioned. He used blackmail and threats to force companies into settlements, knowing that fighting back would be a public relations death sentence.

He was the White Knight in shining liberal armor. He would get those big, bad, conservative, Republican, Wall Street bankers.

The king of regulation and indictments flirted with indictment himself, for taking part in a prostitution ring.

Although criminal sanctions and punishments involving sexual behavior are usually only directed at Republicans, this case almost became an exception. Bill Clinton was able to get away with it because few people expected any decency from him. Eliot Spitzer built his career destroying others for what he deemed to be immoral lifestyles. He got violently bucked off his own moral high horse. The moral concussion upon landing could not have happened to a worse guy.

His family means nothing to me. He did not care about mine.

It's the hypocrisy stupid.

Every liberal who ever criticized Joseph McCarthy should understand and accept why Eliot Spitzer deserves the emotional equivalent of being dragged through the town square. I think New York Senate Republican Majority Leader Joseph Bruno should have taken him away in handcuffs, a nice perp walk for the cameras. After all, Spitzer did use his office to try and trump up charges against Bruno.

Make Spitzer emotionally bleed.

He is nothing more than a left-wing crusader who tried to become president by trampling on the rights of innocent human beings trying to make a living. He babbled on about caring about the little guy. He should have made sure his own house was not rotting from the inside.

He blubbered in public about how he lost his honor. This is false. He never had any.

I then declared his way of living illegal.

New York got a new governor. Whether Democrat or Republican, they were better from a humanity standpoint because they are not Spitzer.

Hizzdishonor, let me again say to you what you said to me back in 2004.

Mr. Spitzer...you worthless bucket of scum...*Mr. Love Potion* Client *No. 9*...

YOU'RE FIRED!

Now get the f*ck out of my office. I am a taxpayer. It's my mansion, not yours.

eric

Ideological Bigotry Part IX–Shaved Legal Dice

I started blogging to combat the scourge of ideological bigotry. I hope that others continue to share their tales with me.

As far back as I can recall, there has been tension between the Republican Party and the liberal black leadership of America. The Republican Party did make some terrible mistakes. So what? Who hasn't? Two wrongs make a right only if the goal is vengeance instead of justice. Despite many decent black Americans truly wanting a better life for all Americans, the liberal black leadership in America today preaches division and racial animosity. Agitation is encouraged. Comity is considered weakness. Why offer an olive branch when one can act aggressively and be rewarded? Republicans, especially conservative ones, have been demonized. This is not for anything they do, but for being. Guilty white liberals are the cheerful accomplice enablers.

I worked in environments where politics was discussed. The discussions involved racial issues. I kept quiet. As a Republican, I was not in the mood to be called a Nazi, Fascist, racist, sexist pig. I remember one easygoing black man in his early thirties who, like me, always stayed silent. I asked him why he never got involved in the discussions. In his rich, deep voice, he replied, "Eric, here's my philosophy. The differences between black and white are nothing compared to the differences between men and women. If you're a man, no matter what color you are, there's a chance I can understand you."

Unfortunately, some people feel the need to not only take part in the conversation, but to dominate it. These people are often uninterested in facts. They delight in winning debate points by crushing whoever stands in their way, right or wrong. When an office bully wants to target you, no human resources department will stand in their way. Like Ted Kennedy going after Robert Bork and Clarence Thomas, facts get lost in a sea of poison and innuendo.

The way accusations work are simple. If a member of a protected group makes overt comments, those comments are rationalized away as the product of a rough childhood, tough background, or decades of injustice. If a member of an unprotected group makes a comment about the weather, and a protected member finds weather comments to be against their race or religion, grounds for a lawsuit exist.

Anybody thinking this case is overstated should talk to any man who has ever been railroaded. The deck is stacked when political correctness takes over.

Some believe in the legal system. No way. If I could give conservative Republicans advice, it would be to roll over and take it, or move to a red state.

There is no hope. Labor laws are set up to help those that have been oppressed in society. Wealthy, white, former oppressor Republicans deserve no mercy or benefit of the doubt. Labor lawyers by definition are activists. Their ability to be neutral arbiters can be compromised when the issues are political.

I know one guilty white liberal labor lawyer. I will secretly refer to him as David L. Moring (since Moring rhymes with whoring, the activity of screwing people). Mr. Moring "is not saying I am a racist, but I have racist tendencies." How does he know this? Did he ever ask me my opinions on anything? Of course not. He does not need to do so. I am a conservative Republican. I therefore cannot understand the subtle nuances behind racism. Labor lawyers like Mr. Moring shill for the ACLU, Legal Aid, and other organizations that spend their time coddling real criminals while productive citizens burn. Mr. Moring, who does pro bono "work" for the ACLU, was a part of a corrupt election involving dogs voting. These are the people enforcing ethics in America.

When an inherent bias prevents a lawyer from even asking the tough questions necessary to conduct a fair investigation, the honorable course of action is recusal. Honor is not known among liberals or lawyers. Combine the two, and it is unsurprising that real actual complaints disappear because people are afraid to speak up. Mr. Moring believes and preaches that the system works because it is his system. Racial or ethnic bigotry matters while ideological bigotry against conservatives gets celebrated.

The system is set up to do what is legal, not what is right. It is illegal to say bad things about protected groups. Race and religion are protected. Ideology is not protected. That means somebody could spend every day in an office explaining why they hate Republicans, and there is no recourse. A person could light a Republican pamphlet on fire, and that would be free expression. Try burning a Koran and see what happens. I am not advocating Koran burning. I am saying that those who would condemn Koran burning should not be so quick to want to burn anybody else's beliefs. I began blogging because a liberal woman expressed to me her hope that George W. Bush and his supporters were flammable. That is called lynching.

What does one do when the legal dice are shaved, and the labor laws are simply an appendage of the Democratic Party? Taking care of office militants is tough. For lawyers, there is recourse.

Lawyers can be disbarred. They can face reprimands and disciplinary hearings. They do not have absolute power. They do not have the right to retaliate against legitimate claims. They can sue for defamation if they are slandered. However, it is not difficult to prove bias. Labor lawyers love to explain how everybody else is biased. One doesn't become a left-wing ideologue without developing a certain amount of contempt for conservatives that borders on hubris.

In the same way college students need to strike back against corrupt liberal professors, conservatives should reject accusations of racism, even if the accuser has a law degree.

America in the twenty-first century is not Selma, Alabama. Most people just want to live their lives. I was not even born when Nixon developed the southern strategy that caused so many blacks to detest Republicans. Most black Americans are reasonable. It is the guilty white liberals that cannot be salvaged. They are a lost cause. All the labor lawyers in the world will not be able to protect them when conservatives start fighting back. You can only bully people for so long.

The legal dice are shaved. It is time to end this rigged game. This means exposing every person who promises to uphold the law and instead perverts it. Lawyers who let their own biases infect their ability to do their jobs must recuse themselves. Otherwise, concerned citizens can help the disciplinary committee do it for them. I hope that when they come for guilty white liberals like Mr. Moring, nobody will be willing to speak up.

eric

Dan Driscoll—Corruption at the NFA

In 1994 I became a proud member of the financial services industry. I was a stockbroker, a trader, and then a regulator. After spending over a decade with stockbrokers, I decided to join a commodity brokerage firm. Stockbrokers are regulated by FINRA (formerly NASD), the Financial Regulatory Authority. FINRA is a "rules based organization." The rules are clearly stated. Sanctions for violating rules are clearly spelled out.

Commodity brokers are regulated by the National Futures Association. The NFA is a "philosophy based organization." Many of the "rules" are guidelines. In other words, the organization makes stuff up as it goes along.

I would often receive memos saying, "NFA says this," or "NFA declares that." I kept pointing out silently that they should call themselves "the NFA." Adding the word "the" takes away their God complex.

There was corruption in the commodity brokerage industry, so the NFA cleaned out many crooked firms. They then had nothing to do. Firing themselves was not an option. They also had what would be called a conflict of interest in any other industry. Members of JP Morgan, Morgan Stanley, and Goldman Sachs sat on their board. These firms wanted more commodity business. Putting all the mom and pop shops out of business would eliminate the competition.

I was the Vice President of Compliance at one of the largest such shops in America. At the peak of our business I was monitoring ninety brokers in six offices. I made sure that every broker who picked up a telephone to solicit business gave a balanced presentation. Clients had to know the risks as well as the benefits. I gave extensive ethics and anti-money laundering training. I was proud to be part of an honest business.

The NFA unfortunately decided to destroy my firm. I am well aware that there are plenty of prisoners in jail claiming their innocence. I have seen with my own eyes good, honest professionals get harassed by crooked regulators.

Regulators feel pressure like everybody else. After a series of high profile blunders from the Bernie Madoff imbroglio to other failed detections, regulators desperately needed to look like they were doing something. They needed some high profile scalps to save their own jobs. They came after my firm.

I wracked my brains trying to figure out the answer to a simple question. Why did they hate us? Why us?

One explanation was that they were coming after everybody without enough money and power to fight all the way to congress. Yet organizations are made of people. The person who hated my firm is one of the top people at the NFA. His name is Dan Driscoll.

I attended a meeting that the NFA put on called their "Issues and Answers" meeting. These junkets allow the NFA top brass to hold meetings in lavish, expensive hotels on the public dime where those top executives talk to each other. Members of my firm decided to attend one of these meetings since all firms are invited. We figured it would be seen as a positive sign that we were friendly with the regulators, and not hiding. When Mr. Driscoll began speaking, I was concerned right off the bat that the main man in charge of enforcing the industry did not know his @nus from his elbow.

One thing he mentioned was that brokers cannot be permitted to state anything on the telephone that cannot be verified by legitimate sources. This makes perfect sense. He then stated that all brokers should be required to state on the telephone that 90 percent of people who trade commodities lose.

I asked him where the 90 percent figure came from. I wanted to be able to direct clients online where they can read about this statistic. Mr. Driscoll responded in front of a room full of people that there is no verifiable source. It is "common knowledge."

Are you kidding me? The man talks about verification, and then asks us to state something he cannot verify himself. He then referenced a study done in the 1960s saying that close to 70 percent of people lost, but that the figure was higher now. This guy is clueless enough to be a climatologist.

His next comment was even more idiotic. He stated that brokers had to mention on the telephone that well-known news events were already factored into prices. I asked him another question for clarification. "Mr. Chairman, is it okay to tell the brokers that such events *may* be factored into the price? If they are definitely factored in, then there is no need for brokers, clients, or markets. I train my brokers to say that events might be factored in. Is that acceptable?"

Mr. Driscoll responded that since markets were efficient, prices rapidly adjusted, and there was no room for trading profits based on news. Everything is factored in.

What planet is this imbecile living on? Markets are not always efficient. There are plenty of people who make a living as traders. I was one of them. My firm had tons of trading profits and tons of winning trades. We also had many losses, but in Mr. Driscoll's world we would lose 100 percent of the time.

When auditors came and saw what we were doing, they recommended certain changes. We cooperated fully with every single change. We requested a meeting with the NFA top brass so that we could sit down with them, find out exactly what concerns they had, and do whatever made them comfortable. They sent us an angry letter filled with insults such as calling us "ignorant." They refused to meet with us, and arbitrarily decided that they wanted us out of business. We had seen them do this to other firms.

In 2009 we pointed out that we had a long history of being cooperative. They decided that we were guilty of violating obscure "rules" in 2005 and 2006. We pointed out that they already spoke to us in 2007 about those rules. We had already made the changes as requested.

They decided that we did not go back and make the changes *before* they spoke to us. Even though we did everything they asked, they decided to punish us retroactively.

If the speed limit today is 65 mph, and I am driving 60 mph, I should be fine. If one month later they lower the speed limit to 55 mph, and I comply, they cannot punish me for driving 60 mph one month ago when 60 mph was legal. The NFA does not operate in the real world. We "should have known" that at some point the speed limit would have been lowered.

The prosecutors were a pair of old men that will most likely be dead soon of natural causes. Phil Raleigh is one steak away from obesity-induced cardiac arrest. Ron Hirst fell asleep several times in the courtroom. This prevented him from being concerned with facts already addressed when he asked about them again.

Mr. Hirst tried to ingratiate himself with me by pointing out that he agreed with my political views despite our being on opposite sides in this situation. I pointed out that he reminded me of my grandfather, who also resembled a walrus. I guess he does not like compliments about his mustache. Mr. Raleigh had a different approach. He hurled an epithet at me. If I had a job where I was never held accountable to anybody I might turn from Sir Philip Walter Raleigh into Lord Acton myself. Absolutely power does corrupt absolutely[39], even in lily-white snowy innocent cities like Chicago.

The hearing panel was a kangaroo court. The chairman of the panel was Bill Maitland. He reminded me of Al Gore. He was pompous, spoke like he knew everything, and was passing judgment on me while his own son was facing legal issues eerily similar to that of Al Gore Jr.[40]

One plaintiff refused to testify. Our motion for that part of the case to be dismissed was denied. No witness, no problem. Let's go forward anyway.

The prosecution was allowed to have their witnesses testify by telephone rather than fly to Chicago.

(A corrupt organization based out of Chicago? Feign surprise.)

We made the same request for our personnel. In most cases, denied.

One prosecution witness with a history of lying claimed that he could not testify because he had to go to the hospital. We requested that the witness provide proof of hospitalization. They lied, we were denied.

Chairman Maitland then approved a prosecution request that their witness be allowed to testify long after both sides had wrapped up their cases and done closing arguments. This would be struck down in a real court of law where facts and evidence matter. Courts are not philosophy based organizations.

Statutes of limitations were ignored. Missed deadlines did not matter.

On several occasions Ron Walrus Hirst told me I should have done certain things differently. I pointed out those were his opinions, which did not alter the fact that how I handled things was legal. He mumbled something about other considerations.

Other considerations? This is why people have no confidence in the legal system. State what the d@mn rules are and be done with it.

Dan Driscoll runs what many honest brokers consider to be a corrupt enterprise. Raleigh and Hirst took orders from him. A twenty-five-year-old kid named Melissa Glassbrenner gathered the "evidence." Some of it was manufactured, with mitigating evidence mysteriously disappearing under a litany of "honest mistakes." After all, regulators would never deliberately suppress evidence to win a case. The panel chairman would never be a shill for the prosecution.

Ms. Glassbrenner's main job was to have her team call up thousands of our clients and beg and plead with them to file complaints. Filing complains costs fees, and naturally the regulators kept these fees. Despite thousands of phone calls and clients, Ms. Glassbrenner found four...yes four...people willing to comply. They were broke, so the NFA gave them expenses paid trips to Chicago in exchange for their testimony.

(Ms. Glassbrenner also was not monitored in terms of proving that her underlings obeyed the law. The NFA ironically wanted me to listen in on private conversations of my own employees, yet refused to do that with their own. The NFA reminds me of leftists in America that worship Hugo Chavez or Fidel Castro from afar but would never actually want to live under such rule.)

The regulators thought they were smarter than the guys working at my firm. They thought wrong.

The firm decided to voluntarily shut down. My boss and many of the brokers simply set up another firm. This new firm does not sell commodities. It only sells physical gold and silver bullion. Physical bullion is not regulated by the NFA. Business as usual quickly resumed.

As for me, I am now on the lecture circuit doing better than ever. I set my own hours, am my own boss, and get to tell my story to everybody. I also do independent consulting, warning every commodity brokerage in America how to handle crooked regulators.

Dan Driscoll can brag on Capitol Hill how he has put virtually every firm out of business. The truth is those brokers are back in business the next day. They are selling stocks, life insurance, vacuum cleaners, dictionaries, or some other product that he has no jurisdiction over.

Ron Hirst and Phil Raleigh are spending their golden years taking orders from a man younger than them. They make more than a living wage, but much less than top salespeople. They look in the mirror and realize that what they are is all they will ever be.

My advice to every person in this world is to get rich. Do what you have to do to get wealth and power. Living an honest life is not enough. Corruptocrats do not back down just because their target is innocent. They back down when met with superior force, wealth, and power.

Crusaders will always exist, be they radical leftists, jihadists, or pseudo-government bureaucrats.

America is the land of entrepreneurship. There is always room for enterprising individuals with actual real talents. For those flunking out of organ grinder school, there is always room for trained chimpanzees at the NFA.

Dan Driscoll and his cronies will be spending their remaining days mired in their own paperwork in freezing Chicago where February equals death.

I will be in my Los Angeles luxury condo building in the Jacuzzi sandwiched between a pair of Republican Jewish brunettes wearing brassieres made out of edible silver bullion.

Nice work Dan Driscoll, you useless, talentless dumb f*ck.

eric

Chapter 7:
Sexual Violence

This is not about anything kinky or perverted. Get back here. I love when a lack of filth is seen as boring and conventional. Liberal women love to scream at the top of their shrieking feminist lungs about how they want to be treated exactly like men. Then the minute things get tough, they pull the girly-girl routine. If women want to be treated like men in an office, they should get used to a boss getting angry and using bad words, even if the boss is a man. Conservative women like Margaret Thatcher act like men by being effective and tough. Too many liberal women despise men. Luckily for men, they despise other women more. That is when men should put their feet on the coffee table, get a beverage, and enjoy the show.

Ideological Bigotry Part XXIV—Maureen Dowd's Sexual Temper Tantrum

Water is wet. The sun rises in the East. Liberals on the Upper West Side of Manhattan delight in the scent of their own bottoms. The *Jayson Blair Times* engages in ideological bigotry.

Whether it is Jewish self-loathing from Richard Cohen, a Bob Herbert racial temper tantrum, or Pinch Sulzberger giving away secret American troop movements, the *JBT* is truly becoming a collection of raving lunatics in the town square. Their intellectual train has long since left the Union Station.

In the name of gender equality, Maureen Dowd fills the victimhood quota required by this long since scratched and broken record excuse of a media instrument.

This woman is so grating that when she tried to interview Khalid Sheik Mohammed, the ACLU stepped in on behalf of the poor sheik and reminded us all that the Eighth Amendment against cruel and unusual punishment protects him from torture. This is a shame because he was ready to say everything under the condition that she say nothing.

This woman is so vicious that she makes Cruella DeVille look like a Dalmatian lover volunteering at the Best Friends Animal Sanctuary.

I don't know what species her parents belonged to, but no wonder she loves the Prius. She is definitely a hybrid of something herself.

(If a liberal were writing this, it would be considered satire and awarded a Pulitzer. I could go on all day. Bring it on Maureen.)

Her latest sexual (perhaps in her case asexual) temper tantrum was a diatribe against Sarah Palin.

I avoided linking to the article to prevent my innocent readers from contracting swine flu from Miss Piggy's more repulsive twin.

Her column entitled, "Visceral has its value," was meant to be a slap at Sarah Palin. Maureen Dud calling somebody else visceral? Talk about the black widow pot calling the kettle black-hearted.

Here is some of the filth she wallows in.

"It's easy to dismiss Sarah Palin. She's back on the trail, with the tumbling hair and tumbling thoughts. The queen of the scenic strip mall known as Wasilla now reigns over thrilled subjects thronging to a politically strategic swath of American strip malls."

Wow. She took a cheap shot at a hot woman with gorgeous hair. That is what the feminist movement has become. Elizabeth Cady Stanton and Lucretia Mott are trying to come back to life so they can put either a muzzle or a feedbag on this creature. Betty Friedan is muttering to her friends that this witch needs to put a sock in it.

An entire town is nothing but a "scenic strip mall." That is beautiful. Denigrate an entire town just to make sure one woman gets hit.

The town is not enough. Everybody who goes to malls is now in her snarling cross (nasal) hairs. Had Black Friday shoppers in 1969 bought her lumps of coal, she could have used them to stuff her bra, snare a boyfriend, and have a family.

(Doing her job is quite easy.)

Hell hath no fury like a she-beast scorned[41], as Stuart Schwartz ably pointed out.

Why does Maureen Dowd hate Sarah Palin with a passion and ferocity so blinding that it makes over-the-hill and kidding herself exotic dancer Katie Couric seem fair and reasonable?

Her contrast of Barack Obama and Sarah Palin reveals everything.

"He struggles to transcend identity politics while she wallows in them. As he builds an emotional moat around himself, she exuberantly pushes whatever she has, warts and all — the good looks, the tabloid-perfect family, the Alaska quirkiness, the kids with the weird names."[42]

He actually is identity politics, but that is for Bob Herbert's next meltdown. Maureen Dowd hates Sarah Palin because Sarah Palin has virtually everything and Maureen Dowd has and is virtually nothing.

Sarah Palin is gorgeous. She is a former beauty queen. She was a successful jock and cheerleader. Boys want to date her. She needs administrative staff to send the declination letters on the deluge of marriage proposals. Sarah Palin and her husband are still in love with each other. They are happy.

Can anyone picture Maureen Dowd as a cheerleader?

"D-O-W-D-I-E, that's the way we spell Dowdy, Dowdy, Dowdy, I'm Maureen and I'm Dowdy."

The "tabloid perfect family" is a grudging admittance that the Palins are good parents. Those that dare go after Bristol Palin had better be prepared for a fusillade against Al Gore's son.

Sarah Palin lives in a world of sock hops, campfires, and sing-a-longs. Maureen Dowd spent decades rotting away in a city that was rotting itself under drugs, crime, and sewage.

Sarah Palin is a successful conservative. Maureen Dowd is a failed liberal. Sarah Palin is authentic. Maureen Dowd is a fraud, although by *JBT* standards, plagiarism is not fraud when done by a liberal.

All her protesting about men being unnecessary will not change the fact that she knows she could never get a catch like Todd Palin. She would never even put the worm on the hook, for fear of chipping one of her typing nails. As for the kids with the "weird names," Miss Dowd apparently has never met a Hollywood celebrity.

Some will correctly point out that Maureen Dowd is a failed human being living a menial life at a long since disgraced and discredited publication. Yet in the same way she advises that Sarah Palin cannot be ignored (She is starting to pursue Palin in a *Fatal Attraction* Glenn Close menacing kind of manner), Dowd must not go unchallenged. Idiocy is still dangerous when the platform is large.

(Perhaps the movie *American Beauty* offers a better theory. Maybe Dowd hit on Sarah Palin. Sarah rejected her, and Maureen went ballistic, targeting her as if she were Kevin Spacey.)

Dowd applies the platform logic to Palin.

Angry feminist pot, meet exploding hysterical kettle.

Maybe if NASA would land a man on Maureen Dowd, she would mellow out. We can even make the Hall and Oates classic *Maneater* her wedding march.

Never mind. KSM won't date her. That pesky Eighth Amendment saves him again.

eric

Ideological Bigotry Part XIV–More Jewish Female Rage

Another Jewish woman railed about where all the good men are, while rejecting huge swaths of them. One train wreck came in the form of Amy Klein at the *Jewish Journal.*

I have never met or spoken to Amy Klein. To the best of my knowledge, nobody I have slept with or dated is friends with or even knows her. If they do, I was never told. This disclosure is a non-disclosure. My only impression of her is based on her own words.

Rocker Cher once said that "Words are like weapons. They wound sometimes."[43] I recommend that Amy Klein buy *Heart of Stone* and listen to the song "If I could turn back time." Perhaps she would retract her most awful comments that she may claim were in jest, as if that makes them acceptable.

The entire purpose of Amy Klein's column was to help her get her M.R.S. degree. She desperately wants to get married, and has desired this for some time. I find zero fault with this. I desired to find my life partner for what seemed like forever.

While one should not compromise their core beliefs, they should examine them to see potential necessary improvements.

I eschewed linking to the column itself to avoid spreading the disease of irrelevance. The first few lines were what offended me. Had Ms. Klein left them out, the column would have remained unchanged. It would have been the same message without the venom.

Here are the offending words of Amy Klein.

"I hate that there's another group of guys who are unavailable to me. Married people, actors, Republicans, and other men who don't like women: Gay men. In this town it's not like you run into that many—I'm talking about Republicans and married men."[44]

I could "lighten up." What are some harmless words directed at a small group of people? Why not tell jokes that are anti-black, anti-gay, or Allah forbid, anti-Islamofascist?

I supposedly belong to a group of oppressors. Apparently I am fair game. Democracy allows me to reply, Ms. Klein.

"Ms. Klein,

Your column on gay marriage was deeply offensive. If you want to announce to the world that you will not date Republicans due to your own prejudices, that is fine. To say that Republican men are unavailable, and hate women, is flat out ideological bigotry.

Ideological bigotry is just as harmful to society as racial or any other ethnic bigotry.

I want lower taxes and dead terrorists. That does not stop me from finding time to tell my girlfriend every day how much I love her. She is a liberal Obama supporter, and I am a staunch Republican and McCain backer. Several of my male friends have married women of different political persuasions, and they are as happy as James Carville and Mary Matalin.

There are significantly more young Jewish Republicans in Los Angeles than you would think. Most of us keep quiet for fear of being attacked. In that sense, Jewish Republicans are the new gays.

I have a ton of single friends, and I have contributed to four marriages. I know plenty of young single Jews. Confirming a potential love interest is like confirming a Supreme Court Justice. It should be based on quality, not ideological litmus tests.

Good luck in your search. I wish no personal animus toward you. I also wish you give up the ideological bigotry and see Republicans as human beings who are capable of human emotions, such as love.

I suggest you use Yom Kippur to reflect on my sincere words. It is not about politics. It is about prejudice. It stings deeply, and you should not use your column to promote it.

Respectfully,

eric aka the Tygrrrr Express"

People like Amy Klein lead to me struggle with my darkest feelings. Part of me wants Amy Klein to remain single and childless, crying herself to sleep every night with the rest of the spinsters. If she were to reproduce, she would just bring more Jewish liberal bigots into the world anyway.

I rescue myself from the precipice to remind myself that I need to be better than her. I should not wish infertility on any woman, much less a Jewish one. There are so few Jews in the world. We have a 52 percent intermarriage rate. More Jews being brought into the world, even if they grow up to be liberals, are a vital necessity. People can change and grow politically. They cannot do so if they cease to exist and the population itself collapses.

Amy Klein is only one woman, but she is symptomatic of a disease that is destroying Judaism.

Hatred is poison. It benefits nobody. I know another Jewish woman who is miserable because she does not have a boyfriend. She rails against other happy couples. She is another feminist with contempt for women who choose to be housewives.

Equality for women gives them the right to enter the corporate world. It does not force them to do so any more than it forces them to stay home. Some women want to be homemakers. It is a tough, honorable job. It does not involve staying home all day watching soap operas. It is hard work.

This left-wing feminist has hostility toward oppressive Republican men. She simultaneously wants to find a good provider with his act together. Enraged females like her cry for a companion while sabotaging themselves from being in a position to lovingly accept one that does not fit every item on their left-wing checklist.

Men with their act together who make a decent amount of money, enabling them to be better providers, often vote Republican. This is not about oppressing women. It is about wanting lower taxes. This allows them to keep more of what they earn so that they can spend it on many things, including their loving wife.

Theresa Strasser occasionally wrote about how screwed up her love life was (I think she finally got lucky). She did a comedy routine where she said, "For this, press one, for that, press two, for this, press three (I forgot one through three), if you are a Republican, press six-six-six for the devil."[45]

Many in the crowd laughed. I was not amused.

I am far from perfect, but I treat people with human decency. Almost every girlfriend I have ever had has been politically liberal. In the Jewish community, especially in Los Angeles, this is normal. Tolerance trumped ideology. The relationships ended because we were not right for each other. Politics was not the deal breaker.

I have plenty of single male friends. I genuinely want people to be happy. I constantly offer to set people up with each other, under the condition that I be spared any wrath if the situation ends badly.

What I will not do is offer to help anybody that suffers from bigotry of any kind, including ideological bigotry.

I admit these women never sought my help. Maybe they should. Many of them are doing terribly on their own. A column with a large circulation (since discontinued, leaving her empty) is no substitute for a lovely warm body to fall asleep and wake up beside.

I pray to God that things work out between the current romantic administration and me. We have to do our part. Caring for each other's politics should be overridden by caring about each other.

Hineni. Here I am. I am Jewish, Republican, proud, and warm-hearted.

eric

Ideological Bigotry Part XXI–Playboy Screws Itself

Playboy is crashing so fast that people may mistake it for the *JBT.*

In an act of tastelessness, hatred, and ideological bigotry, *Playboy* magazine decided to try and destroy innocent people.

Since the beginning of time, men and women have had "hot lists" where they rated the opposite sex. I myself put out an article entitled "The Top 120 Political Yummy Bouncies."

Thirty women were rated based on their bodies, or to be more specific, my perceptions of their bodies without ever seeing most of them in real life.

That may be sexist and sophomoric, but there was no malice behind it.

Playboy published a list of women worthy of a "hate-f*ck."[46]

The idea was that these women were pretty, but evil. The author hated their guts. The hate-f*ck was his having his way and then hurting them. We do not treat people we hate with kindness.

Another word in the real world for hate-f*ck is rape. There is nothing sexual about rape. Rape is a crime of violence. I believe it should be added to the list of capital crimes. It is a form of killing. Rape destroys men and women.

It is one thing to fantasize and discuss people in a sexual manner. To sleep with somebody while hating their guts is destructive for the aggressor and victim.

What made this so awful was that the author decided that he hated these women without having met them. I have met some of them. Amanda Carpenter and Mary Katharine Ham are lovely human beings. Mary Katharine Ham is very funny and easygoing. Amanda Carpenter is an overwhelmingly nice person. They are both dignified people that conduct themselves on television with class.

Michelle Malkin, who I have not met, is on the list. The woman is a devoted wife and mother to two children. She had to move her house because of death threats. She is a minority and a conservative, which triggers rage among the angry left.

All of these women were referenced in my Top 120 Political Yummy Bouncies column. Calling a woman "hot," is not the same as defiling them.

Some on the left will try to claim that I spared them because I agree with them, and that I skewered women on the left. This is also false.

I think Naomi Wolf, Norah O'Donnell, and other liberal women are hot. I would have sex with them if I was single and they were single. I do not hate them.

I became a blogger to combat ideological bigotry. The idea of wanting to sexually humiliate a woman out of misogyny is a sickeningly foreign concept to me.

This is a big deal to me because I do not want to get lumped in with the haters.

I know some women are offended by my discussing respected professional women in a sexual manner. I also know I will most likely keep doing it from time to time. If I ever hurt anybody's feelings, I would be genuinely troubled by it.

There is a middle ground between raging feminism as practiced by the National Organization for Women and the raging anti- female hatred practiced by the disgusting writer behind the *Playboy* article.

Ironically, it was a woman destroying *Playboy*.

Hugh Hefner was about creating beauty and making money. His daughter Christie Hefner is a left-wing ideologue that has donated money to left-wing fringe causes. She also moved *Playboy* into the hard-core pornography that Hugh Hefner did not want to associate with. In his mind, *Playboy* was high-class while Hustler was low-brow. Christie Hefner made them indistinguishable.

(She has since been ousted, which has been a godsend to the brand and the company.)

I would condemn anybody that glorified violating Michelle Obama or Hillary Clinton. Jokes about raping Laura Bush, Sarah Palin, and Condoleezza Rice go unpunished.

I am angry that sweet human beings like Mary Katharine Ham and Amanda Carpenter are spoken about in this manner.

To the author of the *Playboy* article who I will not dignify by name, I have just one thing to say.

Go (hate) f*ck yourself.

eric

Chapter 8:
Sports Violence

Professional sports is one of the last remaining meritocracies. Every life lesson can be learned from sports. Those who have never played sports can always go into jobs that require no skill or talent, such as journalism. Like media critics and political pundits, too many sports columnists get paid to carve up others due to their inability to play the games themselves. They cry about deadlines. Until a three hundred pound linebacker slams them to the ground for having their column come in late, they do not know anything about real pressure.

Oklahoma State—Thank You Coach Gundy

A member of the media took cheap shots at a college athlete. Like a father protecting a son that he may privately scold, Oklahoma State football coach Mike Gundy fiercely defended his benched quarterback Bobby Reid.

Oklahoma sports reporter Jenni Carlson may think twice before she writes her column. This is not chilling for free speech. It is a victory for responsible journalism. The media is despised because it gets stories wrong, hits below the belt, engages in character assassination, fails to verify sources, and refuses to issue mea culpas in a manner that leads to being respected.

It may seem harmless, but why attack a young man because his mother is feeding him chicken in the parking lot? Does this make him a momma's boy? Is he less of a man? Pro Bowl Eagles quarterback Donovan McNabb appeared in *Chunky Soup* commercials with his mom feeding him soup. Should we berate him?

Coach Gundy benched his quarterback. The only issue about this story should have been whether Bobby Reid needed to play better. Questioning a young man's heart after it has just been broken is beyond cruel. As Coach Gundy pointed out, these are not professional athletes earning millions of dollars. They are kids, many of whom will never be paid to perform. They play the game because they love it.

Coach Gundy's YouTube press conference spoke for itself. He looked right at Jenni Carlson when speaking. He thundered into the microphone while holding up the offending newspaper article.

"Three-fourths of this is inaccurate. It's fiction. That article had to have been written by someone that doesn't have a child, and has never had a child that's had their heart broken and come home upset. Here's all that kid did. He goes to class. He's respectful to the media. He's respectful to the public, and he's a good kid. He doesn't deserve to be kicked when he's down. If you have a child some day, you'll understand.

If you want to go after an athlete, one of my athletes, you go after one that doesn't do the right things. You don't downgrade him because he does everything right, and may not play as well on Saturday.

That's why I don't read the newspaper. Because it's garbage! The editor who let it come out is garbage!

Where are we at in society today? Come after me! I'm a man! I'm forty! I'm not a kid!

Don't write about a kid that does everything right and has his heart broken, and then say that the coaches said he was scared. That ain't true! So get your facts straight. Who is the kid here? Are you kidding me?"[47]

Finally somebody said enough is enough. There are young athletes committing robberies, rapes, drug crimes, and murders. Why castigate a guy for loving his mother? Shall we ban crying after winning championships?

I have never been to or watched an Oklahoma State game. I had never heard of any of the people in this story until I saw it on television. If I were a player in Coach Gundy's locker room, I would go through a brick wall for him.

This was not an attempt to distract from other issues. The Cowboys won the game 49-45. The backup quarterback who was promoted seemed to justify making the switch. Why bother canceling a victory celebration of a press conference and get angry because a player that the coach himself benched got attacked in the press?

The player is a human being. Football is a team sport. Every member of the team counts. Many football players at the very end of their careers were sent into the game for one final series, even one final play. Some players sign one-day contracts so they can retire with the team they love. They put on the uniform, go on the field, salute the crowd one final time, and walk off with dignity.

Dignity is what this is about. Winning and losing matters, but for once a coach put human dignity over the final score. The benched player mattered just as much as the players on the field.

Dignity means respecting waiters and waitresses, shoe shine people, and building maintenance people. They matter. A million dollar salesperson might not close a sale if the potential customer sees scuffed shoes. The $4 shoe shine service helps the salesperson earn those millions.

Coach Gundy closed ranks. People do that. Families do this. I can say my cousins are imbeciles, but you will not mock them. Religions do it. Jews, Christians and Muslims argue fiercely within themselves, but tread lightly when criticizing other religions. Politicians have vicious primaries, but (should) back the nominees in the general election. Nations do it. Many Americans mock their leaders, but (should) condemn that mocking from Europe or anywhere else.

I had employers take me in their office and ask me how I could have been so (insert bad word here). When somebody else would try to pile on, that same boss would defend me to the hilt and let the criticizer know what a (worse word here) they were.

Dignity matters. So does loyalty. Coach Gundy gave it. He will get it back in spades.

Bobby Reid was demoted for failing to do his job well enough. Failing does not make one a failure. Bobby Reid is not a failure. Failing makes people human. Coach Gundy has a responsibility to help mold this man. Coaches, teachers and fathers matter. The boss was not happy. He took steps that hurt. Bobby Reid knows inside how the coach feels about him.

Some say this is not a life and death matter, but people commit suicide. They feel like failures, sink into despair, and give up on life. I am not saying Bobby Reid was at that stage, but Jenni Carlson kicked a man who was down. Mike Gundy lifted him back up. Saving a life does not just mean stopping someone from jumping off a bridge. That is extreme. Saving a life can be as simple as finding somebody who let you and themselves down, and patting them on the shoulder. Sometimes my favorite words in the English language come when somebody I respect says, "atta boy!" Atta boys matter.

I have no idea what Oklahoma State's record is on the football field. What I do know is that Bobby Reid being benched does not make him a loser. Mike Gundy pointing that out makes him a winner.

Thank you Coach Gundy. If I am ever in Oklahoma, I might be talented enough to be the team's water boy for a day. It would be an honor.

eric

Rush Limbaugh Fights Back

Rush Limbaugh is a conservative. He exists and breathes air. For those reasons, people on the left hate his guts. It is called Ideological Bigotry.

Luckily for decent society, Rush has a platform to fight back.

Some will say that Limbaugh is an unsympathetic figure. This is code for politically incorrect. Unsympathetic figures are the very people we absolutely must stick up for if freedom of speech means anything.

Carrie Prejean had a crown stolen from her.

Dr. Laura Schlessinger was bullied off the air.

Twenty-year-old Hannah Giles was being sued by a liberal criminal enterprise named ACORN simply because she proved they were a liberal criminal enterprise.

Andrew Breitbart was being sued for supporting Hannah Giles.

Rush Limbaugh was then blackballed from participating in a sports league, despite the fact that Mark Cuban owns a team and Keith Olbermann spends much of his non-sports time engaging in left-wing bile.

By every professional standard, Limbaugh was qualified to own a team. With the left, qualifications are irrelevant. All that matters are feelings.

Leftists see conservatives as sub-human, and therefore lacking feelings.

This is not about mere politics. It is about smearing people with incendiary charges. Dr. Laura is against gay marriage, so she was labeled a homophobe. Carrie Prejean was ambushed, and treated as if she were an anti-gay bigot.

Rush Limbaugh worships at the altar of the National Football League just like I do. Rush was labeled a racist for calling a black player overrated and stating that the NFL promotes social engineering. That is an opinion, and hardly anywhere near as inflammatory as the stuff the left says about the right on a daily basis.

Jesse Jackson and Al Sharpton stepped in because they refuse to get real jobs and benefit society in any way, shape, or form. These two race hustlers are well dressed anti-Semites and nothing more. Limbaugh made his money honestly. Jackson and Sharpton are the ones who spent their lives peddling bigotry for personal financial gain.

This is not about agreeing or disagreeing with Limbaugh. This is about disagreeing honestly, without poisonous and baseless attacks of bigotry.

Nobody is entitled to own a football team. If they were, I would have gotten way ahead of Rush and everyone else. Everybody is entitled to a fair hearing.

Rush Limbaugh needs to take his bigoted left-wing critics and go after them with all the fury that the power of his position brings him. Those who engaged in libel and slander of him must be sued until they are bankrupt. Nobody is allowed to make false charges. If his critics have evidence of racism, they had better put up or shut up right now. Since they can't put up, they should just shut up. If not, Rush must shut them up.

The left-wing bullying has got to stop.

Make 'em bleed Rush. They deserve it.

Once he crushes the leftist haters that made the false charges, those people will not be around to attack other innocent conservatives who have been subjected to slurs and accusations just for being alive and expressing opinions.

Yes, I mean me.

The gloves are off.

eric

Chapter 9:
Hysterical Violence

Some say that liberals lack a sense of humor. That is an overstatement. They just lack sense, period. Many on the left are politically correct McCartheyites with their noses out of joint. My role is to perform verbal rhinoplasty on them. My lacerating tongue is the scalpel. I would ask you to enjoy my finished product, but I am not a miracle worker. After all, when I am done skewering them, they are still liberals.

The Nazi Hunter of Chatrooms

Simon Wiesenthal, you've got competition.

Okay, that's not true at all. He tries to avenge murders. I entertain myself on the Internet. Nevertheless, even frivolity can occasionally rise up to accidentally make the world a better place.

Unlike Al Gore, I did not actually discover the Internet for everybody else. I did discover it for myself in 1997. I saw a friend of mine playing what I thought was a video game on his computer. He was appearing in what appeared to be a conversation. In fact, several people were having conversations.

I had never seen a chatroom before. I was fascinated that people from all over the world could interact with each other.

He asked if I wanted to try it, so I did. I did not know how to set up my own name, so I logged in under his. I just told everybody I was Greg's friend, and my name was Eric. The people were friendly. One girl named Kyrie9 mentioned something about tennis. That caught my attention, so we started talking about tennis. We found out that we both liked 1980s music. At some point we even talked on the telephone. She was a pleasant person. We eventually lost touch, but it was an interesting experience.

This setup, known as WBS, was under the auspices of Disney subsidiary Infoseek. Anything owned by Disney had to be wholesome. This was before one of Infoseek's top executives, Patrick Naughton, was arrested for trying to meet a thirteen-year-old girl at the Santa Monica Pier.[48] They met in the "Daddies and Daughters" chatroom. I realized the Internet had a downside.

I went into a political chatroom, and was bored after five minutes. Most of the people were just hurling insults. I talk politics with my real life friends. Discussing it with strangers seemed pointless. I went into a football chatroom and was equally bored. In real life I care if my team is better than your team. Online, it seemed bizarre. I was never going to meet these people.

I was about to declare the Internet a failure when I found a room called the "Hot Tub." Despite the provocative name, it was a mild flirtation room. The people were funny. What caught my eye was that two people seemed to be more than friendly with each other. It turned out they had met online, then met in real life, and were engaged to be married.

The light bulb went off. This is what the Internet was for. People can use it to actually meet real life people and find happiness. Some of the guys pointed out to me that even if they did not meet the love of their life, there was always the option of simply having sex. Whatever objections I had to the Internet disappeared at that moment.

The Internet was now useful, but one night the Hot Tub got flooded. "Flooding" is when somebody repeatedly types messages over and over. It is a form of spamming. Nobody else could type anything. In an attempt to wait out the flooder, I ducked into the politics chatroom for a few minutes. I was stunned to find a couple people spewing anti-Semitic venom. There were thirty people in the chatroom. Twenty-eight of them were pleasant. The other two were Nazis. I now realize they were probably just teenagers being provocative. At the time it seemed strange for people to go online just to harass other innocent people.

I made a decision to take these guys down and remove the pollution from that chatroom. Rather than engage the Nazis directly, I decided to use them as a foil. I talked through them to the rest of the room. Bizarre entertainment was my weapon of choice. I used the Socratic method. I have no idea why these questions and answers came in my head. Like Robin Williams, warped things happen when the Tygrrrr is out of the cage.

I wanted to know why they had such an unpleasant disposition.

"Why are Nazis always so grouchy? I mean you guys are always ticked-off about something. Why can't you guys just get a burger and a soda, watch a ballgame, get a call girl, and just chill out? What is the point of killing off everybody if you can't even take time to enjoy it?"

Several people found my question amusing, and wondered where I was going with this. I had no idea myself. I then asked the question that allowed me to go off the rails.

"Do any of you Nazis drink Coca-Cola? Be honest. Do you drink Coke?"

Both Nazis replied in the affirmative.

"Congratulations! Coke is kosher! It's certified by a rabbi and everything! It's in your bloodstream! You're Jewish!"

The Nazis sought to refute my claim in an angry manner. The rest of the room continued to encourage me, which may or may not have been bad for society at large.

When the Nazis tried to bring up the Fuhrer, I cut them off.

"I know all about Will Furrer. He plays for the Houston Oilers. He played terrible today."

I then did my best impression of ESPN's Chris Berman, as he did his German imitation. "Ze Fuhrer is down. Ze Fuhrer has thrown another interception. Ze Fuhrer has fumbled again. Ze Fuhrer cannot get it together."[49]

When the Nazis tried to explain that they meant the Reich, I came back again.

"Frank Reich plays for the Buffalo Bills. Fine, he beat the Oilers in 1992, but didn't get it done in the Super Bowl. Ze Reich keeps turning ze ball over. Another German dynasty defeated by American Cowboys!"

I started receiving pms (private messages), which was useful. I now knew I could contact girls in the Hot Tub without other people seeing them. Unfortunately, I often forgot to hit the private button, and became "the king of blown pms." As for these pms, they were telling me I was hilarious, and to keep it up. My ego had been effectively fed.

"In sports news today, Jews six thousand, Nazis twelve. Man, you guys got your @sses kicked!"

The Nazis started typing in capital letters. This told me that either they were angry, or they had trouble with the caps lock key. As ill-mannered as typing in all caps is, I did it for my next comment.

"YOU GUYS COULDN'T EVEN FINISH OFF THE FRENCH IN WORLD WAR II. NOBODY LOSES TO THE FRENCH. YOU GUYS ARE AN EMBARRASSMENT TO KILLERS EVERYWHERE!"

Even Nazis have a line that should not be crossed. Questioning their manhood by bringing up the French set them off. They went ballistic, talking about the Jewish conspiracy. I then let them know in a calmer lower caps voice what they were in for.

"Do you want to know what the real Jewish conspiracy is? It's when my Jewish friends and I go to Germany and get all your women knocked up so you won't want to touch them because they'll be tainted with Jewish blood. Let's see you try and kill off a civilization when you're walking around frustrated because you haven't gotten any in eighteen years until the kids leave for college. Come on. Admit it. Even Nazis need a little Nazi nookie from their favorite German cookie!"

At this point they were stammering. They wanted to spew venom, but seemed taken aback by the approach. The others in the room were highly entertained. I then decided to take a bold step.

"You know what? You guys are not hateful enough. I don't think you have what it takes to truly get the job done. I am banning you from the Nazi movement. You will have to find another hate group to join."

They respond in a confused manner that I could not ban them from their own movement. I let them know how wrong they were.

126

"The hell I can't. I'm an all-powerful Jew. As of this minute, you're banned! You're no longer Nazis! Now find a group of grouchy people and commiserate with them but you're done from this movement. If I find out you tried to rejoin the movement I will call my buddy Alan Greenspan to finish off your economy. By the time he is done wrecking your country German cars will be as popular as American VCRs."

(Sadly I was wrong. Ben Bernanke let the VCR go the way of the dollar. Mercedes refused to act like a Detroit company and immolate itself.)

As these mysteries behind keyboards tried to come up with a retort, I added my final thoughts, an attempt at reconciliation.

"You know something Nazis? You need a hug. There, there, that's a good little Gunther. Give us a big one. Let it all out."

They fled the room and did not return.

I pumped my fist in the air and announced, "Yes! I am the Nazi hunter of WBS chatrooms! I shall now call Simon Wiesenthal and help win the battle for good!"

I was prepared to make a difference in this world. I would save mankind. I would win a Nobel Peace Prize, or instead something useful like gift certificates.

As I prepared to benefit the world, my heroics were interrupted. A friend called to tell me about a Jewish dating Web site called JDate. It was in its infancy. I took a look and noticed that it was wall-to-wall female Hebrew @ss.

I could have spent time on frivolity, but luckily I understood what was important in life. I had a job to do.

Others would fight the Internet wars. I had Hebrew Tang to drink.

eric

Laughing at Liberals

Over the course of existence, liberals have accused conservatives of being uptight and humorless. They even call the GOP the Grumpy Old Party. In the spirit of bipartisanship, it is time to take the lighthearted equivalent of verbal brickbats to their skulls. They have no idea what humor is given that they live in a politically correct bubble where every "edgy" joke is followed by an apology.

There are a million things we can say about these political misfits. I enjoy delivering red meat to GOP audiences. Let's get to it.

"I can't tell you how great it is to be among so many of my fellow gun-toting, bible-thumping fascists."

"I also can't tell you how great it is to be in a room where Helen Thomas does not get to ask a question."

"For those of you expecting a call from Rudy Giuliani's wife, please leave your cell phones on. Otherwise, show the speaker some love."

"I notice that one your Republican Women's Federated chapters has a vacancy for First Vice President. I would like to apply for the job. I know what you are thinking. I don't live in the area and I am not a woman. I am totally unqualified. So what? That never stopped Barack Obama."

"The Pelosiraptor had the nerve to refer to the people attending tea parties as Astroturf.[50] She said we were not grass roots. We were Astroturf. When I heard Nancy Pelosi talk about Astroturf, I thought, 'Oh great. Another woman just admitted to being in Bill Clinton's pickup truck.'"[51]

"Republicans are the party of Rudy Giuliani, John McCain, Fred Thompson, and Michael Steele at the RNC. Democrats offered Barack Obama, Christopher Dodd, and John Edwards. It's obvious why we lost the 2008 election. Americans are bigoted against the follically challenged."

I hope Americans are still bigoted against the follically challenged in 2010, especially in Los Angeles. That way we can get rid of Henry Waxboy and Brad Sherboy.

My plan for them is a government program similar to 'Cash for Clunkers,' because boy are they a couple of clunkers. We are going to pick them up in a truck, and drive them across the country into somebody else's district. Don't worry, it won't be yours. This program is called 'U-Hauls for cue balls.'"

"I did the research as to why the left hates the right. It is because we exist and breathe air."

"Take the word Jewish and replace it with Republican. Now take the words Hamas and Hezbollah and replace them with liberal democrat. The left are verbal suicide bombers, except less warm and fuzzy."

"If you are a minority and a conservative they will try and destroy you. They will try to rip you to shreds if you believe in radical Christian notions such as…I don't know, something sinister like…love thy neighbor."

"I keep being told that radical Christianity is just as dangerous as radical Islam. Late at night I am more worried about Osama Bin Laden wielding a bomb than Pat Robertson wielding a book."

"He can't make me read his book. He can't make me buy his book. The only downside is I can't make him read or buy mine. He doesn't return my phone calls. He told me to stop proselytizing, something about a different faith."

"There is actually one thing scarier than a radical Islamist wielding a bomb. Beware an angry housewife wielding a golf club."

"I recently saw the Batman movie. Batman saves the entire world, and the spoiled ungrateful brats don't appreciate it. He leaves silently and lets everybody figure it out for themselves. The minute he is gone they realize how great he was. Oh no wait, did I say Batman? I meant George W. Bush."

"I guess that would make Obama the Joker."

"I don't want to say that Barack Obama is a snob, but I look at him and think, 'Picture what would happen if Jacques Chirac and John Kerry had a baby."

"I don't want the second coming of Jacques Chirac and John Kerry. I would rather the second coming of Ronald Reagan and Margaret Thatcher, that being Sarah Palin."

"Now I don't agree with Sarah Palin on every issue. For one thing, I can't stand her position on traditional marriage. What I mean by that is I can't stand the fact that she is married to somebody who is not me."

"I know what you are thinking. Sarah Palin is a terrible mother. How dare her daughter Bristol get drunk, and stoned, and drive a car into a tree and… oh, no. Wait a minute. Never mind. That was Al Gore's son."

"It's okay though. At least it was a hybrid."

"I have had it with the Palin critics. David Letterman keeps going after the Palin family. Talk about the pot calling the kettle African-American."

"What can you say about Superwoman? Sarah Palin ran an entire state… had what kids will one day read about called a budget surplus…actually they probably won't read by then, but if they did…

129

Sarah Palin also has five lovely children that she picks up and takes to school. Barack Obama only has two children, and he has Joe Biden picking them up from school."

"For those of you wondering who does less real work and still gets a paycheck than Hillary Clinton, it's Joe Biden."

"Democrats should love Sarah Palin. She has a beautiful special needs child. For this reason alone Democrats should worship Sarah Palin. They are an entire political party of special needs children."

"All these people say is gimme, gimme, I need, I want, I deserve, I'm entitled. No, you're not. When you're two years old it is mildly adorable. When you are sixty-two like Boxer, Hillary, or the Pelosiraptor, it's intolerable."

"By the way, you may call me by my first name or by my last name. Whatever you do, don't call me ma'am. I worked so hard to earn the title of Mister."

"How does somebody earn the title of Mister? They do what Barbara Boxer never did. They grow up and become an adult."

"The left tries to demonize us by going after our military while our soldiers are fighting and dying. *The New York Times* ran forty-seven front-page stories about Abu Gharaib. The good news is that nobody reads the *Jayson Blair Times*."

"Here is even better news. Abu Gharaib was nothing. My friends and I went through something very similar to Abu Gharaib when we were growing up. It was called summer camp."

"They gave us purple nurples and wedgies. They twisted stuff. It was worse than waterboarding. I am actually against waterboarding. Like Colonel Bill Cowan, I prefer electricity."[52]

"In Los Angeles they think waterboarding is like boogie boarding. If we just give Osama a surfboard and let him hang ten everything will be fine."

"Abu Gharaib was nothing. Some liberals complain that we put the prisoners into human pyramids. So what? That is going on at adult parties all across America. The game is called 'Twister.' You spin the thing. It lands on red or green. Whether you have glaucoma, arthritis, or are completely healthy, the whole thing comes tumbling down. Nobody dies."

"Some liberals complain that at Abu Gharaib, we put bras and panties on the prisoners' heads. I ask these liberals a simple question. Have you ever been on a college campus?"

"It's called Rush Week. Rush Week has nothing to do with Mr. Limbaugh. If it did, kids would actually be learning at these Poison Ivy League Universities."

"Only at a Poison Ivy League university could we have gone from Jimmy Stewart to Jon Stewart, from Winston Churchill to Ward Churchill, and from *'Tea With Mussolini'* to Columbian Coffee with Armageddonijad."

"How dare these liberals criticize our soldiers? They called Bush and Cheney liars. They called General David Petraeus a liar. I am sad to admit they were right. President Bush and Vice President Cheney did lie. General Petraeus repeated the same lies. General Petraeus first lied in his testimony to congress when he told them that he was pleased to meet them."

"Then General Petraeus told an even bigger lie when he said that he respected their opinions. Nobody that matters respects Barbara Boxer's opinion on anything."

"I love George W. Bush, but he made one mistake. General Petraeus needs to stop making the same mistake. General Petraeus...stop being so polite. You need to turn into the second coming of Jack Nicholson's Colonel Nathan R. Jessup."

"Miss Boxer...I have neither the time nor the inclination to explain myself to you. You can't handle the truth!"[53]

"Another thing Miss Boxer. You and your liberal friends are not fit to shine my shoes. You know what? Let's put that to the test (slams his shoes on the table). Here they are. Have them spit-shined by o-six hundred hours because that's the only thing your liberal prattling mouth is good for!"

"My parents dislike smugness, but yeah, I am pretty pleased with myself for that remark as well. For those of you vegetarians in the audience, don't worry. You're getting some red meat."

"I have been celebrating my holiday of Hanukkah. Hanukkah is a Neocon holiday. We did not sip tea with our enemies. We beat the daylights out of them. Hanukkah is the Jewish July 4th."

"For those who wonder if Jews believe in the second coming, Jews have our own second coming. Judah Maccabee has been reborn, and his name is Paul Wolfowitz."

"The word Maccabee means 'hammer.' Maybe the second coming is Sir Charles of Krauthammer."

"It is always better to have people ask 'Why you are done speaking?' than 'When you are done speaking?'"

"I will take questions momentarily. I know you have them because my parents have so many. Feel free to exercise your Second Amendment rights and fire at will."

"I will leave you with a Hebrew word. The word is *Hineni*. It means 'Here I am.' Never give up. Never give in. Always fight for what you believe in. Never back down from a fight. Don't bring a knife to a gunfight. Bring a bazooka. We are right. They are wrong. We will win. They will lose. *Hineni*. Here I am. Republican and proud of it always."

Many liberals do not find anything I say funny. This is not for them. I am laughing at them, not with them.

You should too, solely because they are themselves.

eric

Chapter 10:
Historical Global Violence

All around the world there are threats. Third-world genocidal lunatics want to end America, the Great Satan. Volumes have been written about leftists that fail to grasp this. Millions of innocent people have been slaughtered due to Kumbaya-loving leftist appeasement. The good news is that many world leaders truly get it. They are conservatives, but they are leaders first. We need them now more than ever.

My Interview With Colonel Orson Swindle

At the 2008 Republican Convention in Minnesota, I had the deeply humbling honor of meeting and interviewing Lieutenant Colonel Orson Swindle.

Colonel Swindle has had a distinguished career in the military and in government. He is remembered most as the Vietnam prisoner of war who once shared a prison cell at the Hanoi Hilton with Senator John McCain.

One of the reasons Senator McCain is so respected is because he has that difficult to define quality known as "gravitas." Colonel Swindle has gravitas. Anybody can give a political speech. Colonel Swindle is a testament to a truly great human spirit. I cannot begin to fathom his strength of character and courage.

Colonel Swindle was escorting fellow POW Colonel Bud Day to an interview when I approached them. Colonel Day is eighty-five. While Colonel Swindle is not a young man, he and his wife kept a wall around Colonel Day to keep him from getting jostled by the crowd.

In Vietnam, Colonel Day was brutally beaten and tortured, as were Colonel Swindle and Senator McCain. Colonel Day pleaded with John McCain to rebreak his arms and set them properly. McCain did not want to do this, but Colonel Day insisted. McCain broke his arms, and reset them using bamboo. Today Colonel Day has the use of his arms.

Regardless of political affiliation, true greatness is found in men like Colonel Swindle, Colonel Day, and Senator McCain. We are free because of them.

Here is my interview with Colonel Orson Swindle.

1) What are the most important issues of 2008?

OS: *This is about the Presidency. It is not American Idol. This is real, not imaginary.*

Major issues in this campaign are education, the economy, and Social Security.

We need a leader to bring people together and get things done. John McCain is a leader.

John McCain has dozens of character representatives. I am one of them. People will put it all on the line and tell you what kind of man John McCain is. Name five people that are willing to do the same for Barack Obama.

John McCain is proven. He's been tested. He has integrity. He is an intellectual. He offers loyalty. He has courage.

2) Who are your three favorite political heroes?

OS: *Ronald Reagan. Ronald Reagan. Ronald Reagan.*

3) You spent seven years as a prisoner of war. How did you get through it? How did you survive?

OS: *During the tough times...it was mostly tough times...you just hang on. That's all you can do. You hang on. You don't give up. You can't give up. You are driven not to give up. It's your sense of honor.*

That, and you pray to God.

4) How would you like to be remembered one hundred years from now? What would you want people to say about Orson Swindle the person?

He made a difference.

Ronald Reagan once said, "Most people spend their lives wondering if they made a difference. Marines don't have to wonder." [54]

I'm a marine.

I was too choked up to ask any more questions. I am in awe of the man.

I thanked him for his time and his service, but it was not enough.

Thank you again Colonel Swindle. God bless you sir. I'll tell you what I told John McCain when I met him, and what I tell every veteran I ever meet.

Thank you, and welcome home.

Welcome home sir.

eric

Welcome Back Mr. Berlusconi

A victory for conservatives and capitalists reverberated around the globe.

Another fabulous leader reclaimed his mantle. Silvio Berlusconi won a landslide election to become Prime Minister of Italy for the third time.

Mr. Berlusconi is a staunch ally of America, a friend of President George W. Bush, and an absolute friend of Israel and Jews everywhere. Of equal importance, Mr. Berlusconi is a staunch conservative.

Not since the 1980s when Ronald Reagan, Margaret Thatcher and Brian Mulroney led the Anglosphere has conservatism been so powerful.

The "Old Europe"[55] that Donald Rumsfeld poked fun at is dead. The easiest way to defeat American liberals when they run for president is to refer to them as "French." Yet the France that San Francisco and Manhattan admires does not exist anymore.

Liberals worldwide are scurrying for cover like little cheese-eating rats. They can scream to the heavens that they are correct, but the world is not listening. They protest that they are smarter than everybody else, but the world scoffs. They claim to want to change the world, and then find out they cannot govern.

Liberals will claim many things. What they are not claiming is election victories.

In America, Republicans dominated presidential elections for the last forty years entering 2008. Every once in awhile a southern Democrat will run a football play that Haley Barbour refers to as "fake right, run left."[56] A true liberal had not been president since LBJ stepped down. The two Democrats that did win fought with their own party, and failed to move America to the left. Even Barack Obama won as a stealth candidate that is now making rightward concessions to get a shred of his agenda passed. Despite protests that America is despised in the world, the world seems to want clones of George W. Bush running their own nations.

In Canada, Cretin (Chretien, whatever) is a distant liberal memory. Stephen Harper is in power, and relations between our nations are strong.

In Germany, the failure that was Gerhardt Schroeder has been replaced with Angela Merkel. She is cutting through bureaucracy and statism to modernize the German economy. Make no mistake about it. Modernize in this case means Americanize.

In France, Nicolas Sarkozy is loving every minute of his role as Sarko the American. This man is George W. Bush relocated, which makes sense since

Paris is a city in Texas. He cavorts on the beach with his blazing hot model wife. His enemies criticize him. He doesn't care. He has the hot wife. Others can criticize, but he will do as he d@mn well pleases until voters tell him he cannot. He is comfortable in his own skin, and in minutes repaired a relationship that was near fratricide.

In Italy, a billionaire entertainment magnate retook the reins. Silvio Berlusconi is still popular. Despite his prior razor thin loss, two years of leftist governing was enough to have people embrace his return.

The dominoes continued to fall. Israel was next. Ehud Ohlmert had single digit approval ratings, and Benjamin "Bibi" Netanyahu waited in the wings to make his comeback. His critics on the right correctly point out that he moved left when he became prime minister. He has vowed not to make the same mistake twice. His term as finance minister was a rousing success, and his hard-line stance on terrorism is a welcome departure from the Labor strategy of grovel and surrender.

England and Australia are the exceptions, but make no mistake about it. Tony Blair was left of center, but he was no leftist. He showed economic conservatism by making the Central Bank of England independent. Yes, a world leader gave up some of his own power for the good of his nation and the world. He then maintained a stance on the War on Terror that was every bit as conservative as Lady Thatcher and Mr. John Major. Prime Minister Gordon Brown is on the left, but drowning. He tried to fight the American rightward drift, yet was really fighting European trends as well. As for John Howard, it is easy for voters to become complacent and take for granted a man who simply did virtually everything right. His successor has gigantic shoes to fill. Time will tell.

Leftist governments are failing worldwide. Hugo Chavez in Venezuela is a dictator and a thug. He seeks comfort in friends such as Iran because his reforms have failed with the civilized world and enraged his people.

Communist governments in Cuba and China are on the verge of doing their impersonation of J.R. Ewing from *Dallas*. The Chinese are already enjoying rampant capitalism, running happy and wild the way America did in the 1980s. Cuba is allowing ordinary citizens to have privileges that were unthinkable a couple of years ago.

This is not to imply that liberalism is dead, or that conservatism has won for good. What it does mean is that capitalism is triumphing, and socialism is reeling. Corporations, privatization, and free markets are accomplishing what bloated government bureaucracies cannot get done. Most importantly, nations led by conservatives are willing to confront Islamofascism, since allowing the left to handle the problem would be akin to joining the Caliphate. Anybody who thinks that George W. Bush is a cowboy has not heard Mr. Sarkozy speak on the issue.

Even without the retired Mr. Bush, his conservative friends Mr. Sarkozy, Ms. Merkel, Mr. Harper and Mr. Netanyahu have a window.

I would say that liberals look and act French, but that cliché is a French word known as passé. Instead they look like John Kerry, another liberal that confused San Francisco with the rest of a beautiful country that really is the heart and soul of America.

Leftist intellectuals may keep their noses in the air, but those on the right are too busy rolling up their sleeves and governing to notice. The job of world leader is a tenuous one, especially in Italy. For the first time since 2006, there is cause for much optimism.

Welcome back Mr. Berlusconi. Your friends in America are glad to see you again.

eric

Time to Make French and World History Mr. Sarkozy

Dear Mr. Sarkozy,

As one member of the blogosphere, allow me to be as pretentious as everyone else by giving you unsolicited advice.

Congratulations on your victory. I am a proud American, so I hope that does not taint my praise of you. Now that you have been elected, various entities who pretended to merely disagree with you will now tell you they hate you. The only judgment that matters is the judgment of history. You have the opportunity to help write it, ensuring a favorable review. Here are some pointers from an armchair quarterback.

First of all, you might be told to "govern from the center, given the closeness of the election." This is nonsense. You ran as a conservative. You won as a conservative. You must govern as a conservative. If this means leftists will take to the streets, then get your police force ready with tear gas and rubber bullets. Leftists have only one skill, and that is protesting. They could lose 90 percent of the vote and still claim a mandate. Ronald Reagan once stated that "Compromising with liberals is like feeding your friend to the crocodile in the hopes that he eats you last."[57] Keep your supporters happy. You cannot win everybody, but you can lose everybody. You promised conservatism. Keep this promise.

Secondly, you will be told to be less confrontational. This is rubbish. Politics is a tough business. Governing is even tougher. You will make an effort to be amiable, as did George W. Bush. This will be seen as weakness. There is nothing...and I mean nothing...that you can do to make the left like you. Once you accept that they hate your guts, you can be liberated from having to please them. You can be cordial, but make no mistake about it. You set the agenda. At the risk of bringing up King Louis, you are the state. Be confrontational when necessary. If you have to, ram your agenda down their leftist throats. The goal is not to humiliate them. The goal is to get things done. Depressing the left is merely a bonus. Ronald Reagan changed America and the world. He did so with Democrats in congress for much of his tenure. George W. Bush's greatest victories were by single vote margins. Margaret Thatcher dragged her opponents kicking and screaming into a better England. One person can move the mountain. The political streets are littered with politicians who tried to be nice for the sake of "getting along (George Bush Senior, for one)." When you are wrong, you can figure out a way to own up to it. When you are right, do not give an inch.

Thirdly, do not be afraid to be pro-American. One of the reasons I have had such hostility toward France is because I see France as a spoiled little brat that blames America for all her self-inflicted ills. I hated the French for no other reason than they hated me. Someone once asked me what I would do if the French ever liked Americans. I responded that I did not deal in fiction or fantasy. French support of America belonged in the same automobile where I kept Santa Claus, the Easter Bunny, and my pet unicorn. I may have been wrong. As a gesture of support for your presidency, if you keep your word about being pro-American, I will end my boycott of your nation. I am not going to buy my ticket to France just yet. I need to see if you cave in to pressure and begin distancing yourself from America the way Mr. Chirac did. You truly believe that better relations with America will benefit both of our nations. You are right, and I enthusiastically look forward to seeing this relationship flourish.

Lastly, remember again that in the long run, the only thing that matters is the judgment of history. Ronald Reagan was ridiculed. He is now considered one of the greatest leaders of any nation anywhere. George W. Bush was excoriated by the world's unwashed leftist savages. He continued on down the same path because he knew that his critics were not fit to lick his boots. He was respected and feared where it counted. I would tell you to ask Saddam Hussein, but thankfully that is a testimonial no longer available.

There are very few universal truths, but empirical evidence offers some elements of governing that are as close as possible to such truths. Supply-side economics works. Tax cuts stimulate economic growth. Raising taxes stifles growth. Free trade works. Protectionism is a failure. Constitutional law works. Sharia does not. Sharia must not be allowed in France. Law abiding citizens are the good guys. Protesters who block traffic and commit crimes are the bad guys. You rightfully called them "scum." Israel is a democracy, and a friend to democracies everywhere. Syria and Iran are nations led by terrorists, and enemies to world peace and stability everywhere. Business does not oppress the masses. Business produces jobs, allowing the masses to live better lives.

Good luck Mr. Sarkozy. You have an opportunity to make French...and world...history. If your deeds match your words, you will reach your potential for greatness. Your critics try to link you to Ronald Reagan, George W. Bush and Margaret Thatcher. Wear those criticisms like the badges of honor they are. True leaders are often reviled by a plurality. When the history books reflect how these leaders changed the world for the better, very little carping from the sidelines holds any consequence.

Godspeed Mr. Sarkozy. Lead well.

eric

Godspeed Mr. John Howard

Nothing lasts forever. No one is indispensable. Great men rise and fall. In Australia, a true giant fell.

Not since Lady Margaret Thatcher was brought down by a revolt in her own party in 1990 has conservatism…and the world…suffered such a blow. It is the very freedom and democracy that civilized people everywhere cherish that forces us to accept decisions, no matter how horrible they may be. The people of Australia spoke. After four terms, Prime Minister John Howard and his conservative ruling coalition was defeated by his opponents in Labour.

This short, bald, undistinguished looking man who led Australia was a giant. On economics, Australia's budget was balanced. Australia had no deficit when he left. The whole nation had a surplus.

On immigration, John Howard was a hardliner. Immigrants who came were expected to assimilate and conform to Australian values. Those who refused were to leave, with help from the Australian government.

On the defining issue of our time, the War on Terror, John Howard was a staunch ally of America. He articulated the Bush Doctrine better than President Bush did. He, President Bush, and Tony Blair continued what is known as "The Anglosphere." With help from former Prime Ministers Aznar of Spain and Berlusconi of Italy, Australia was on the front lines as being an absolute and unwavering defender of American values.

Australian political analysts, who if they were any less qualified to do anything would be American pundits, kept predicting electoral defeat for Mr. Howard. He kept confounding them. What the pundits failed to understand is that like Ronald Reagan, Mr. Howard talked right past the media that looked down on him. He spoke plainly to the people. The more he was attacked for being a regular guy, the more regular guys liked him.

John Howard won elections because he got the job done. He managed Australia deftly through the Asian financial crisis a decade ago. He went after bureaucracy as vigorously as he went after al-Qaeda. He condemned the nightclub bombings in Bali. He kept pointing out that those bombings occurred well before the war with Iraq. He did not offer excuses. He condemned barbarism in the strongest possible terms, whether it be 9/11, the Bali bombings, or the attacks on Israel that Mr. Howard understood were pure evil. He knew right from wrong, and expressed this with a bullhorn.

Mr. Howard lost his last race because he was a victim of his own success. When there are no more perceived external threats to conquer, be they Islamofascists or inflation, people gaze inward. This is why the Roman Empire fell, and why Lady Thatcher was brought down. When people are happy, they become complacent. Laziness leads to a yearning for more. Governing is not sexy. Mr. Howard was not sexy. He did the job in an unflashy way. For many people, peace and tranquility is equated with stagnation and boredom.

In America, presidents only get up to two terms. Despite leftists howling over a loss of civil liberties, George W. Bush did not try to extend his stay into a dictator-for-life reign of terror. Hugo Chavez of Venezuela did. While Mr. Chavez started out autocratic, many leaders start out good and then stay in power too long. They cling to power or try and rig elections, like Pinochet in Chile. In a true democracy, they are simply fired. Winston Churchill was fired, proving that even the very best of the best are replaceable.

John Howard's last day in office was a day of joy and mourning for people all over the world. The joy comes in the form of a free and fair election. After ruling for so long, a prime minister relinquished his seat without bloodshed or lawyers contesting the results and crying about fake fraud. A peaceful transition of power occurred. Australia continued to go about daily life. Some say things are so peaceful that the difference in power was negligible.

The mourning comes in the form of seeing one of the greatest world leaders in the history of government go down to defeat. John Howard was one of the very best. His electoral loss is a loss for the world.

From one American citizen, I say thank you Mr. Howard. Thank you and God bless you for your fine principled leadership. The twenty-first century has gotten off to a brutal beginning. Very few people could have navigated through such torrentially monstrous waters. Thank you for being one of them. You will be missed.

Godspeed, Mr. Howard.

eric

India Burns, Liberals Plan Tea Parties

Let me say this real slowly so that liberals can follow along.

The…world…is…on…fire.

While this is happening, liberals plan to get to the "root causes" of terrorism.

A movie about a comic book character summed up the complexities of terrorism perfectly. I recommend that every person on Earth watch the 2008 *Batman* movie.

When others are trying to understand terrorism, Michael Caine as Alfred the butler offers quiet wisdom. He understands why terrorists do what they do.

"Some people just like to watch the world burn."[58]

That is it. Every PhD in sociology can now go find something else to do.

There are no "reasons" why some people do bad things. Some people, to quote rocker George Thorogood, are just "bad to the bone."[59] Continuing with the Thorogood train, some people are just "born to be bad."[60]

Willie Sutton robbed banks because that is where the money is.[61] The guy climbed the mountain because it was there.

Terrorists blow stuff up because they feel like it. They enjoy it. It is a hobby for them. It is the same reason some children burn ants with magnifying glasses or put birds in microwaves.

Water is wet. Sadists are sadistic.

Before going any further, many in the media have already decided that a girl on spring break in Aruba or a teenage celebrity drinking and driving are more important than terrorists engulfing innocent world citizens in balls of flames. Rather than look to Deepak Chopra or Deepak Kalpoe for anything about anything, I prefer listening to people that actually know things.

Between Ralph Peters, Sir Charles of Krauthammer, and the geniuses at the *Wall Street Journal*, there is hope. These glimmers of sanity unfortunately get drowned out in an ocean of idiocy.

Deepak Chopra is the ShamWow! Guy with an accent. Instead of selling home products, he sells new age gobbledygook. Only Larry King could consider his opinion on terrorism to be one of expertise.

I was raised in New York. I watch football. I should therefore be the head coach of the New York Giants. Who needs Tom Coughlin? He won the Super Bowl with them, but I have thirty years of armchair quarterbacking experience.

We have a media that thinks a big story is some woman who married a successful politician but failed on her own. She was given a job that contributed nothing, which is somehow news. She had thirty-five years of experience, which meant that she graduated law school at age twenty-five and eventually turned sixty.

I am delighted that Hill-Dawg is secretary of state. The feminists can now cheer that the man became the CEO and the woman became his secretary. How traditional. What matters is what does not matter. What does not matter is the secretary of state. Hillary is out of the senate. New York no longer has to fear becoming a banana republic with her as governor.

The secretary of defense has to save lives. Secretaries of state engage in "diplomacy," which is code for having tea parties and accomplishing nothing. Worthless phrases such as "tough diplomacy," "aggressive diplomacy," and "smart power," are code words for fancy dinner parties at five star restaurants to decry world hunger and poverty. John Kerry or Al Gore could have bored the enemy to death. Instead Hillary could just nag them to death. Men will do whatever it takes to stop a woman from shrieking.

Oh no, wait a sec. That is in America, where we have free speech. In Arab Muslim countries, the women who nag just get shot to death. Other offenses that get women shot to death include speaking and breathing.

Hillary failed before being sworn in. She spoke about how we needed to move beyond force. Apparently the terrorists seem to be doing quite well with the force approach. We might wish to fight fire with superior fire.

Hillary could emulate Nancy Pelosi, put on a burka, and sip tea with Bashar Assad. That worked out real well. He renounced violence and promised to be more understanding.

Oh no, wait again. That would be congressional demotards. They can't support a single worthwhile military mission, but they can issue resolutions on whether or not their visit with Armageddonijad should be centered around Mint Medley or Earl Gray. Liberals will understand the use of military force the day Islamofascist terrorists have their children Bar Mitzvahed.

It is not about poverty. Osama Bin Laden inherited $300 million.

It is not about the United States. We are not located anywhere near India, Madrid, or Bali.

It is not about Israel. There are only one thousand Jews in Mumbai, and ten thousand Jews in all of India.

It is not about the Israeli-Palesimian conflict.

It is about a radical Islamic culture of violence that has existed for fourteen hundred years.

America is told by pious liberals that we should consider another approach besides force. How about the terrorists try another approach besides murder? Why is nothing demanded of them?

America gets criticized for subjecting Muslim prisoners to hijinks one would see in the fraternity movie *Animal House*. ACLU liberals wring their hands over the equivalent of a college fraternity hazing while Jews, Christians, and moderate Muslims get blown to bits trying to enter a pizza shack or a nightclub.

The only solution is to let the liberals get their wishes against their will. We should give them what they want until they realize they no longer want it.

Liberals love multilateralism. They think we need to be more humble. They are also against Americans using coercive interrogation techniques, preferring to ask nicely.

We should therefore turn the genocidal lunatics over to foreign governments and pretend not to know that the tar will be beaten out of them. To try and convince India, Pakistan, or other nations not to waterboard somebody would be America bullying another nation.

Rather than argue about Guantanamo Bay, we can deport the terrorists to the most brutal regimes that support us, and wash our hands. When the brutality "leaks," conservatives can express shock and outrage while privately high-fiving.

We could also just be honest and loudly state that we are not here to have tea parties.

The only successful diplomatic missions that liberals have ever engaged in have been the ones that accomplished nothing. Even conservatives benefit when diplomatic movements lead to wonderful photos, good food, and status quo. Annapolis is a perfect example of a useless meeting that succeeded wildly by leading to nothing.[62]

The stock market crashed almost eight hundred points in one day. Liberals cried that we must "do something." No we must not. The same applies for foreign policy. Don't do anything unless it is going to be done right.

Those who keep insisting that only political solutions will work do not understand the military or politics.

Until we trust Ralph Peters over Deepak Chopra, the problems will continue.

We do not need to sit down with animals. We need to kill them and use them to feed the more likable animals at the San Diego Zoo.

Good people are burning. The world is failing to protect them. Good people need to support military actions by democracies. Those democracies must have the courage to use it. When we see militants gathering at a funeral, we have to eliminate them all, rather than let some nonsensical cultural norms allow them to walk away.

The death penalty prevents repeat offenders. When terrorists have their own villages razed, their own families executed, and their own plans forcibly disrupted, things will be better. Will this change their hearts? Who cares? The goal is to defeat them, not get them to behave.

Liberals issued pious speeches about the tragedy in India. They followed up their speeches with more speeches. These are the same people that change the ribbons on their shirts more than they change their underclothing. I believe burnt sienna ribbons show solidarity with "Lesbian Vegans for Libya."

It is time to stop talking and actually do something.

President Bush left office. There are no consequences to anything he does that he will have to deal with. His successor will have to learn to cope.

Dubya quietly worked with India and helped them find the monsters that committed the Mumbai atrocities. Burning their entire villages to the ground is an appropriate start.

Collateral damage is as important to me as Lady Gaga Zsa Zsa Gabor. I will sleep like a baby knowing terrorists are dead.

No more dialogue. No more tea brunches with despots. No more anti-American and anti-Semitic U.N. resolutions.

We talked. They murdered. Liberals dithered.

If liberals want to be liked, they should just talk to each other. They are the only people who listen to them.

Terrorists don't like us. They will not listen. They only understand brute force.

Terrorists want to die. We should happily oblige every last murderous zealot.

Liberals will spend the next century not learning, understanding, or accomplishing.

Given their short attention spans, I will again remind them why terrorists do what they do.

They like watching the world burn.

India does not need platitudes from Dipstick Hopeless. It needs American solidarity.

We must kill terrorists. We must turn over the ones we capture to India provided they promise to use brutality against them. Don't worry if we publicly criticize. Like most American diplomacy, it will not mean a thing.

eric

My Interview With Ambassador John Bolton

Larry King insisted he was not deceased while interviewing Iranian President Armageddonijad, who wanted him deceased. Larry thanked the madman for his graciousness and asked him about his family.[63]

Adult conversations with intelligent questions of people who possess insights actually worth sharing also took place that same night.

Sean Hannity interviewed Ambassador John Bolton. Three weeks earlier, at the 2008 Republican Convention in Minnesota, I did as well.

Ambassador Bolton was the man who successfully overturned the horrible U.N. Resolution that stated "Zionism is Racism."[64]

His appreciation came from the cancerous wing of the Democratic Party. Consisting of many liberal Jews, the leftinistras tried to block him from becoming ambassador. As he communicated to Sean Hannity, Ambassador Bolton remains undaunted.

Out of respect for Mr. Hannity, I will present his interview with Mr. Bolton first. For the cynical among us in society, I am giving myself last licks. Here are some remarks of Ambassador Bolton answering Sean Hannity.

"What has the UN done to stop terrorism? They can't even agree on a resolution on what terrorism is."

"Five years of Europe trying to talk Iran out of acquiring nuclear weapons has left Iran five years closer to achieving that objective."

"He (Ahmadinejad) also said that Zionists control the financial markets."

"Deciding when you negotiate should come from a cost-benefit analysis. With Iran we do not have to calculate. We have had five years."

"As unattractive as the military option is, Iran with nuclear weapons would be even more unattractive."

"Iran is the largest financier of international terrorism in the world today. The notion that they do not possess the same nuclear arsenal as the former Soviet Union does not mean they are not a serious threat."

"Many Americans are at that point (saying enough is enough with the U.N). I have one reform regarding the U.N., and that is that we make our contributions voluntary. We abolish the system of mandatory contributions."[65]

Mr. Hannity sat down with Ambassador Bolton for several minutes. I had a rapid-fire walk-and-talk with him. One thing that is evident from the very first glance is that Ambassador Bolton is a serious man with a serious purpose.

Like many people, he wants to save civilization from blowing up. Unlike most people, he actually understands what civilization should do to rescue itself.

Here is my interview with Ambassador John Bolton.

1) How do you feel about the vice presidential nomination of Sarah Palin?

JB: *It is a good nomination. Sarah Palin will be an asset to John McCain. She was a good choice, and has a history as a reformer who fights corruption. I'm happy with the choice of Sarah Palin.*

2) Who are your three political heroes?

JB: *Edmund Burke, John Locke, and Ronald Reagan.*

3) With regards to the situation between Israel and Iran, is it time for Israel to strike Iran, or is there any diplomatic option that is still feasible?

JB: *I don't see anything other than two options. There is regime change, and the targeted use of force. It is a choice between a bad option and a worse option. Diplomacy has not worked. As awful as having to enact regime change can be, allowing Iran to acquire nuclear weapons is worse.*

4) How would you like to be remembered one hundred years from now? What would you want people to say about John Bolton the person?

JB: *I was somebody who did his best to stand up for human freedom.*

I thanked Ambassador Bolton for his time, and for his staunch support of Israel. I also appreciate his recognition of the United Nations as a worthless entity. Those are my words, not his. For somebody who is not accused of being diplomatic, he is more diplomatic than me.

I wish that sharpshooters outside the CNN studios, after Larry King fell asleep, put a couple bullets into Armageddonijad.

This is why I am not an ambassador. I may not know diplomacy, but I do know that the world would all be better off if John Bolton were allowed to do his job.

It was my honor Mr. Ambassador.

eric

Chapter 11:
Musical Violence

There was a time when the entertainment industry wanted to help make America a better place. Granted this was before I was born, but I have heard such stories. If Hollywood liberals were airlifted and dropped in Nashville to learn from men like Toby Keith and Trace Adkins, maybe America would be a more musically intelligent place. I am not interested in understanding America's enemies. Like sane people everywhere who value western culture over eighth century barbarism, the solution is to go country on these monsters and put a boot in their @ss.

War is For Tough Guys—Bring On the '80s Rock Music

Where are the pro-war movies?

Hollywood did not always make its living aiding and comforting the enemies of the nation that pays their mostly undeserved salaries. There was a time when the entertainment industry loved America. During World War II Hollywood loved America as it was, not the obscure utopian society they wished it to be. The movie industry depicted America and the Allies as the good guys. The Axis were the bad guys, and the twain did not meet. Patriotic movies had rich soundtracks with music designed to pump up emotions and tug at heart strings. It is time to write that movie today.

My knowledge is not movies. I know 1980s hard rock music, which had its zenith from 1986 to 1992. There are many songs that could be used at various scenes in the movie. I have no knowledge of the political views of many of the artists. I don't know if they would approve of their music being used to promote America's justified struggle to win the War on Terror. Nevertheless, let freedom ring and the music blare.

The movie could start out with Osama hiding in a cave, as Firehouse's "Reach for the sky," starts to play. "Well I'm an outlaw/I make my living on the run/ my life is lonely/but I was born to need no one/always on my own." A video camera can then pan away to soldiers training by shooting at bull's-eyes of Bin Laden. "Reach for the sky/I'll shoot you down, in the blink of an eye/ nowhere to run, nowhere to hide/I've got the drop on you, so raise 'em high/ reach for the sky."[66]

As Lynyrd Skynyrd's "The smell of death" booms loudly, the American soldiers refuse to let anything stand in their path. "Whiskey bottles/brand new car/oak tree you're in my way."[67] The troops soldier on, very motivated.

There would be car chases, explosions, heroes saving lives, and testosterone filled rock music. There would be fierce firefights, one of which would take place with a song by "Kiss" star Paul Stanley. As we kicked in doors and hunted terrorists one by one, loudspeakers would blare. "Day by day/kicking on all the way/I'm not caving in/Live to win/till you die/live to win."[68]

One of the bloodiest firefights of the movie would contain Sammy Hagar's "Winner Takes it All" from the Sylvester Stallone movie *Over the Top*. A movie about arm wrestling is a great metaphor for a movie about hand-to-hand combat. "A burst of light/inside your soul/and when the heart/gets pumped up for the gold/there's no defeat/you'd sooner die/it's man to man, as we stand, eye to eye/Winner takes it all/loser takes a fall/fight to the beginning of the end/Winner takes it all/till he breaks or falls/time to make it over the top."[69]

At that moment an American soldier would find Osama, shove him up against the wall, deck him in the face, and force him to submit to American will and steel before he is beaten up some more.

(In this movie Eric Holder does not exist. The good guys do not get prosecuted.)

War is hell. No sane person wants it. America never asked for war. We were attacked and are fighting back. It would help if we could win the public relations war. The soldiers are fabulous. The media undermines them.

Manuel Noriega was brought down not just by military force, but by rock music. He was holed up in a church. The church should have lost its protection under the Geneva Convention since it was used for criminal purposes. We blared rock music so that Noriega could not sleep. He caved.

Caved is the appropriate word. We need to go to every cave, and let every cave dweller know that they will not sleep peacefully until they turn over Osama. Anybody who thinks this would fail has never witnessed an American parent trying to think when their teenage son is listening to rock music. The ACLU would consider this torture. To pacify them we can offer to switch to easy listening or show tunes depending on the level of cooperation.

A clip of Osama and his fellow terrorists plotting strategy and justifying their lunacy could be dubbed over with Santa Esmeralda doing his remake of a classic 1960s song by "The Animals (how appropriate)." "I'm just a soul, whose intentions are good/oh lord, please don't let me be misunderstood."[70]

For those who like 1960s music, upon capturing Osama, we can have a hard rock remake of the classic song made famous by the Bobby Fuller Four. Osama is dragged away in chains (with a couple bullet holes in him leaving him alive but wounded) to the song, "I fought the law, and the law won."[71]

Captured homicide bombers will be forced to listen to Bon Jovi. "Better stand tall when they're calling you out/don't bend, don't break, baby don't back down/It's my life/it's now or never/I ain't gonna live forever/I just want to live while I'm alive."[72]

1980s rock music would be a great choice because it represents the gaudiest of American culture. There was long out-off-control hair, men wearing lipstick, high falsetto voices, and reckless sex. It is every stereotype that causes the lunatics to hate us. The AC/DC song "Moneytalks" could show Americans at our materialistic, imperialistic finest. "Tailored suits/chauffeured cars/fine hotels/and big cigars/up for grabs/up for a price/where the red hot girls keep on dancing through the night/Come on, come on, love me for the money/come on, come on, listen to the moneytalks."[73]

Imagine how humiliating it would be for al-Qaeda murderers if right after we captured Osama, General David Petraeus had his feet on the coffee table lighting up a big, fat stogie. Some may think this is based on the Will Smith movie "Independence Day." It is actually reflected in Alberto Fujimori, the Japanese former President of Peru. After some leftist rebels took hostages, he had his men storm in. They killed all the rebels and saved almost every hostage.[74] He was criticized for his post-victory machismo. He was right.

Fujimori did not negotiate. Neither did Ariel "the Bulldozer" Sharon. Neither did Vladimir Putin when terrorists took over a school. Neither did Margaret Thatcher when dealing with the Falklands. Neither did George W. Bush when 9/11 happened. The time to negotiate is when your enemy is on his knees and his face is bleeding.

If only the media, especially Hollywood, could understand that most Americans love America. We are the good guys. We feed, clothe, protect and defend the world. We bring God's gift of freedom and liberty to places that have never had it.

This is not done through "Kumbaya" or love trains. It is done through blood, sweat and tears. It is not pretty, but it is noble, decent and right.

In the final firefight, Asia's "Heat of the moment,"[75] and Europe's "The Final Countdown,"[76] blare loudly. The troops kick in the door, and ask Bin Laden if he believes his warped, bastardized version of Allah that justifies 9/11. When he says yes, we reply "Good, because you're about to meet him."

Def Leppard's "Rocket,"[77] Guns n Roses's, "Welcome to the Jungle,"[78] and Aerosmith's "The Other Side,"[79] are used to break his will. We then make sure every camera is on Bin Laden's terrified weakening excuse for a soul. Just before two bullets are put in his heart, Golden Earring's "Twilight Zone," plays loudly.

"You will come to know…when the bullet hits the bone."[80]

As the credits roll, Metallica's "Enter Sandman," plays. "Exit light/enter night/ grain of sand/off to never never land."[81] The Rolling Stones would end the credits with either "Sympathy for the Devil,"[82] or "Paint it Black."[83]

9/11 will be avenged against everyone who either commits, supports or harbors terrorists in any way, shape or form. For those who hate America…bring it on. For those who love America…Help make this pro-American movie. Bring on the 1980s rock music.

I applaud those who "get it." For those who do not, "You'll come to know… when the bullet hits the bone."

eric

President George W. Bush, Meet Dee Snider of Twisted Sister

It is one thing for Oliver Stone to make terrible movies that nobody of any human value cares about.

Imagine the possibilities if people with actual talent told the true story.

It is for this reason, that on the silver anniversary of Twisted Sister, I decided to tell the real George W. Bush story.

For those who do not remember Twisted Sister, be older (or younger). Back when MTV actually played music videos, Twisted Sister created a classic. The video begins with a son listening to loud rock music in his room. The father comes upstairs and asks his son loud, angry questions that forever change their relationship.

Dad: "Well, Mister Sister...Who are you? Where do you come from? What do you want to do with your life?"

Son: "I WANNA ROCK!"[84]

Twenty-five years later, as Oliver Stone continues to trash all that is decent and right in this world, I have obtained a copy of a conversation between a father and son that forever changed history. The story took place around 1999 and extended through 2004. Details were released in 2009. That music video is here. The movie will be out in good time.

President George Herbert Walker Bush: "Well, Master Bush. Who are you? Where do you come from? What do you want to do with your life?"

Governor George W. Bush: "I wanna be president."

President George Herbert Walker Bush: "Why do you want to be president?"

Governor George W. Bush: "I wanna finish what you started but didn't finish!

I want Saddam Hussein's head on a platter!

I WANT IRAQ!"

(At this point the elderly realists will be blown out of the room by blaring guitars and flares that take the roof off of the house.)

1) "Tell me don't invade, well all I can say, when you tell me don't invade, I say no! No no, no no, no!

Scowcroft and James (Baker), you tell me what they say, well I'll tell you where they can go! Go go, go go, go!

If you ask Cheney, he and Rummy and Wolfie are ready...

Tell Tommy Franks that it is time to go...

I WANT IRAQ...I WANT IRAQ

2) Some say don't invade, we can dialogue and all sing 'Kumbaya'...Ya ya, ya ya, ya!

Screw the Carter approach, look what happened when we let down the Shah...Shah Shah, Shah Shah, Shah!

Like Noriega, Saddam needs music shooting through him...

along with a couple bullets through the heart...

I WANT IRAQ...I WANT IRAQ

3) Let the leftists cry, that is all, they do anyway...Way way, way way, way!

Saddam had chances, seventeen of them since 1993...Three three, three three, three!

We can let the liberals serenade to sweet surrender...

Or we can win one for the U.S.A...

I WANT IRAQ...I WANT IRAQ

4) War is what they wanted, now we can say that war is what they got...Got got, got got, got!

9/11 came, but it was America that fired the last shot...Shot shot, shot shot, shot!

The liberals carped on every little thing that I was doing...

I was saving their candy @sses, whether they liked it or not!

I WANT IRAQ...I WANT IRAQ!"

Once again, history will show that I was right where it counted.

The 1986-1992 golden age of rock music occurred with the seeds of military greatness still to come in the 2003 Iraq War.

No president rocked harder and got the job done like George W. Bush.

Saddam Hussein is dead. The world is better off.

It became better off as soon as President Bush picked up that bullhorn and let the world know that the people who knocked down the Towers would hear from all of us.[85]

Saddam Hussein did not cause 9/11. He absolutely was a terrorist. Removing him was 100 percent right.

He called our president's bluff. He forgot that the Democrats had left the White House. The men with steel boots and balls were in charge.

The leftists were terrified we would lose (or perhaps win).

"The Dub" was having none of it.

Saddam Hussein was done the day Dubya banged his fist on the table. It was only a matter of time until Saddam would be found in a spider hole and checked for head lice.

It all started with that fist on the table.

"Who are you?"

"I am George W. Bush, President of the United States."

"Where do you come from?"

"The right place."

"What do you wanna do with your life?"

"I wanna save your @ss whether you like it or not.

I WANT IRAQ!"

You got it sir. Saddam is dead. As always, well done.

eric

Trace Adkins For President

After watching *Celebrity Apprentice*, I became a fan of Trace Adkins. I was unfamiliar with his music, but subsequently (legally of course) obtained some and listened to it. As I suspected, I liked it, especially "Honky Tonk Badonkadonk."[86] I did buy his book. Only eight pages in, I became a die hard fan of this guy. I know he is a busy guy, but if I am ever in Tennessee when he is, I will buy him a beverage.

His book is entitled *Trace Adkins...A Personal Stand: Observations and Opinions From a Freethinking Roughneck*. It should be mandatory reading for every American. It is simple common sense, which can often be found in the heartland.

I am already prepared to ask Mr. Adkins to run for President of the United States provided that he is willing to take a 90 percent pay cut and a loss of prestige.

Mr. Adkins is plainspoken, but the bottom line is that he "gets it."

With that I bring wit and wisdom from country music sensation, *Celebrity Apprentice* candidate, and all around good human being, Trace Adkins.

He starts out telling a poignant story about how he explained 9/11 to his then three-year-old daughter. To witness an atrocity like 9/11 as an adult is horrifying enough. Thankfully for him, his daughter was too young to understand what had happened. He wanted to let her know in his own calm, reassuring manner that it was not a normal day.

"My little girl loved to watch the planes come over. I leaned over to Mackenzie and said, 'Let's see how many airplanes we can count.' She was excited. So we waited. And we waited. There were no planes. No planes at all. Now you can't keep a three-year-old's interest for very long.

'There are no planes,' she finally said and jumped up. 'C'mon daddy, let's go do something else.'

I held Mackenzie in my arms for awhile. Then I said to her, 'Look at me sweetheart, and I want you to remember this. There was a day when daddy took you outside to see the planes and there were no planes flying anywhere in the sky. No planes.'

'Why Daddy?'

'Today the president said, 'No one can fly planes today,' so there are none. Today's the only day this will happen. You will never see this again. I want you to remember what daddy showed you on the day there were no planes.'

That was the only way I could impress upon a three-year-old the importance of that sad and terrible time."

I am not a father. I cannot imagine how much bloodlust I would have if one of my children were harmed in any way. If someone comes after me, I can deal with that. I am a pretty tough hombre. Going after people I care about crosses the line. Ask those that have done so.

His reaction to 9/11 was exactly how I felt. It was a combination of immediate rage, but with an understanding that calm must carry the day. Like many people I wanted President Bush to simply blow up every nation that was a suspect, regardless of whether or not they had anything to do with it. Guilty until proven innocent was fine by me. I also understood that the president needed to be a cooler head than me. Thankfully, he was.

Trace Adkins would have immediately held a conference call with every Arab leader. He would have then laid it all on the line.

"Listen. If this is the first salvo, the first shot, and if this is going to continue, then let it be known today that it will not continue for very long. We have the firepower to end this, and we're willing to use it. My children and my grandchildren will not live in fear for the rest of their lives because that's not living. That's just existing.

I'm warning you folks right now, I'm willing to end it all. I will incinerate this rock starting with Afghanistan, and I mean it. If you're not going to get with the terrorist eradication program and get your sh*t (sic) together, and if you permit this stuff to go on in your own countries, by God, I will end this now. We will all go to our maker and we'll let him decide who was right."

Trace Adkins then lets the readers of his book know in parentheses that cooler heads around him would be necessary. He lets us know that after his fiery speech to the Arab leaders, "it would have been at that moment, hopefully, that some sensible person in my administration would have dropped a horse tranquilizer in my coffee."[87]

President Bush waited over three weeks before hammering the Taliban. Some people wanted us to carpet bomb everything in sight within three minutes, but we needed to get it right. We needed a plan in place. We needed cold, decisive leadership, and we got it.

As for Mr. Adkins, he is just another example of why conservative Christians are better for Jews and Israel than liberal Jews will ever be. I have often said that liberal Jews need cranial-glutial extraction surgery. Trace Adkins uses simpler words, but he is not afraid to tell somebody that they have their head up their hide.

One month after 9/11, Trace Adkins was a guest on the Bill Maher program *Politically Incorrect*. Playing the role of typical know-nothing, cranial-glutial-linked liberal Jew peacenik appeaser was Julian Epstein, a former chief Democratic counsel for the House Judiciary Committee.

The show usually featured three liberals and one token conservative who was there as an entertainment foil for the left-wing Maher. Many liberals did not understand that after 9/11, this country did swing to the right. They did not want dialogue. They wanted to take the bad guys and b*tchslap them. After the three liberals spoke their typical nonsense, Trace Adkins offered his common sense.

"This is going to come down to a scrap, and it's going to be big and we're going to have to settle this thing once and for all. We're gonna have to end this thing. We're going to have to fight it out till it's over and until they don't do this anymore. We're going to have to go into Afghanistan and take care of this, and if Pakistan doesn't like it, we thump their @ss (sic) too. That's what we have to do. It's inevitable."

As the liberals stayed shocked, he continued.

"I don't care what it's about. I don't care if it's about religion or politics or economics or what it is. I know that they want to kill us and we have to kill them to stop it from happening. I don't care what the reason is. They want to kill us! That's all they care about. If we don't kill them, we might as well just give up and say, 'Okay, come live over here with us.'"

Liberal Jew (I will continue referring to him in this manner. As the son of a Holocaust survivor, I want to call out those who destroy their own people through naivety) Julian Epstein said to Mr. Adkins, "Man, you are really off the deep end and barbaric about this."

Once again, Mr. Adkins offered common sense to a man who should have known better.

"You're d@mn (sic) right I am! And of all people, you should be too. Your last name is Epstein for God's sake. Those anti-Semitic monsters hate you a lot worse than they do me! They might not give a sh*t (sic) about me, but they wouldn't even waste time talking to you. They'll just kill you. All they have to see is your last name and you're a dead man. And you're going to sit here and try to figure out why they're doing all this stuff? Give me a break, man. Get on board the train, Hoss. We're pulling out, and we're going to kill these (expletive) b@stards (sic)."[88]

Mr. Adkins has a message for America today that is every bit as powerful and relevant as it was after 9/11.

"I stand by those words I uttered one month after the invasion. I still believe the only way to fight Islamic terrorism is to crack skulls. After eight years, al-Qaeda is not going to go away through kindness, education and tolerance. We need to flush them out of their caves and kill them. Then stream that footage live over the Internet."

As I said, I would be happy to vote for Trace Adkins for President of the United States.

Given that he most likely would not want the job despite his being well qualified (any father of five daughters knows how to babysit liberals in congress from a temper tantrum standpoint), the best we can do…and should do…is buy his book (after you buy all of mine) and his music.

God bless this man and his family.

eric

Chapter 12:
Educational Violence

For parents who despise their own children, send them to public school. Between the guns and the drugs, kids are lucky to come home alive. When kids start fights with other kids, the kid who retaliates gets in equal trouble because school principals are like state department employees. Everything is about moral equivalence. The kid who retaliates is told that they should let the system handle it. Does anybody think that a teacher's lounge is where teachers discuss handling anything? It is where they go to escape from future criminals (students) and oppressive bureaucrats (principals). They answer to superintendents, who were put on this Earth to stifle innovation and destroy education. Home school your kids. It is their only chance. Turn the public schools into Fallujah. Blow it up and start again. Better yet, blow it up and don't rebuild.

Creative Destruction and Academic Intoxication

I read an article by a sportswriter that has the potential to reverberate far beyond the world of sports.

The writer stated that in twenty to thirty years, college sports would not exist. It was an interesting hypothesis.[89]

The writer posited that to stop the bleeding red ink that has led to tuition fee hikes, more and more schools would cut back on athletics.

It is a fascinating potential chain of events, but let's take it one step further way beyond college sports.

What if changing technologies and cost structures render universities irrelevant? Is it possible that in half a century universities will cease to be?

Even more importantly, let's dare to ask the charged question. Does this even matter? Is it possible that the end of campuses will result not in a bang, but in a whimper? Is it also possible that this will be an overwhelmingly positive development?

The reasons to dislike universities are numerous. They are hotbeds of liberalism where knowledge takes a back seat to activism and protests. Ideological bigotry has replaced the true purpose of universities, which is to educate.

College professors often have tenure, which breeds complacency. No other industry has this. While a fear of being fired can be chilling, people in every industry somehow cope. Remedies exist for true victims. In professional sports, coaches can stay on the sidelines for decades. When they stop winning, they get their gold watch and rubber chicken banquet. They then become "ambassadors." Professors stay on forever, which does more than lead to laziness. It also stifles creativity by preventing a new breed of professors from engaging students with new ideas.

Even for the apolitical, universities might be going the way of the horse and buggy. This is positive. It is called creative destruction.

Creative destruction is what capitalism is all about. Things die and are replaced. Eli Whitney and Cyrus McCormack invented the cotton gin and reaper, respectively. These devices put many people out of work. Yet life involves adapting and learning new skills.

Wall Street used to have people running around on trading floors yelling. Nowadays much of this is electronic. The Pacific Stock Exchange does not even exist any more.

Satellite television means that we no longer need to hire college students to stand for hours on end holding the antenna at the exact angle to prevent snow.

People adapt or die. Retailers chose to adapt. Rather than try and fight eBay, book and clothing stores chose to use online sites. Brick and mortar stores still exist, but they have online presences. Record companies chose to try and destroy Napster. They won the battle but lost the war. File sharing still exists. Tower Records is out of business.

The question then becomes whether or not there is anything that a university offers that cannot be offered elsewhere. Do universities have a unique product or service that cannot be obtained elsewhere?

No. People are getting online degrees.

While liberal arts colleges may already be obsolete, some will argue that advanced degrees are vital. Do people really want heart surgeons without a medical school degree?

This argument is weak. Rather than go to UCLA Medical School, why not build an education wing at UCLA Medical Center? Hospitals can have schools in them. Medical students have residency periods. Most industries have on-the-job training that is more valuable than college.

Other people will point out that universities are more than just facts and books. There is the "college experience."

The college experience is code for socializing. If I want to hang out, get drunk, and be around people with bras and panties on their heads, I can go...well, the point is there are places to go for that.

I treasure the lifelong friendships I made in college. Had I skipped college, I would have had different experiences and made different friends.

Closing down universities would make life tougher for drug and gun dealers, but that is a painful aspect of change.

There are those who will try to use nostalgia and tradition as an argument. New traditions can begin. The "good old days" were not that good. We have gone from pestilences that wiped out millions of people to cures for once-deadly diseases.

No person, business, or entity of any kind is "too big to fail."

We got it right when we let Lehman Brothers burn. We got it wrong by propping up other firms that should have been treated like Old Yeller. This is cruel, but so is life. I support good CEOs getting millions of dollars in bonuses. I also support bad CEOs being denied bailout money, especially when I have student loans.

The loans bring this all full circle. I spent thousands of dollars for a piece of paper, yet I make most of my money in ways that have nothing to do with that expensive piece of imitation parchment.

Universities claim that they make "well-rounded" individuals. That is more code for social engineering. Some of the least well-rounded people I know are the ones teaching our young people.

The world would go on just fine without Harvard. The late William F. Buckley opined that he would "rather be governed by the first few hundred names in the phone book than the Harvard faculty."[90]

I received my MBA from USC. At USC, we were analyzing Harvard case studies. I can claim a Harvard education. It was the same material.

Nothing about a university should make it exempt from the creative destruction that affects everything else. Nothing in any other entity should make it immune from the constant winds of change.

Only one group would argue against all of this.

College professors dissent. They wax poetic, but are like anybody else engaging in rational self-interest. They do not want to fire themselves. In the same way unions want stronger unions with more benefits even if it cripples the overall business, professors are about self-preservation.

College professors suffer from "academic intoxication." Too many of them simply love the smell of their own scents. They are the entrusted caretakers of our knowledge.

This is a fancy way of saying "elitist gasbags."

Harvard professor Henry Gate barked at Police Sergeant William Crowley "Don't you know who I am?"[91] My response was "Yes. You are an overrated snob with an inflated sense of self-importance harassing a police officer for doing his job."

Does anybody think the world needs Ward Churchill "teaching" our children?

I am not advocating that we shut down all universities, fire professors, and force them to get jobs in the real world (although it would be nice to force them to trade in their ivory towers and tweed jackets for some construction work boots). Some of them are honest professionals that contribute something positive.

I am saying that the marketplace should decide. If universities can revitalize their business model and provide a valuable service at a cost that keeps them in business, so be it. If enough people decide that Harvard should go the way of Tyrannosaurus Rex, we should not keep T-Rex alive for thousands of years for fear of hurting his feelings.

The battle is one of creative destruction vs. academic intoxication. Academic intoxication benefits only the sources of the self-love. Creative destruction, which hurts many people including me in the short run, benefits society as a whole in the long run.

If professors taught this to students early on, we would all benefit even more.

eric

David Horowitz at USC

From soldiers to private citizens, we must all do our part to fight for freedom. One man helping fight for freedom is David Horowitz of the David Horowitz Freedom Center.

I had the privilege of seeing and listening to him when he spoke to the University of Southern California College Republicans in Los Angeles.

The seventy-year-old Mr. Horowitz is a former leftist radical turned conservative. He has devoted this part of his life to combating and defeating radical Islam. His focus is the universities, fighting Islamism on college campuses.

Because of this, Mr. Horowitz has faced death threats, and requires a bodyguard. Leftist radicals on campus take delight in engaging in protests ranging from moderately rude to violent. Some of these future community organizer thugs actually think that "silent protests," such as standing up in the middle of a speech and turning backward, are civilized. "Peaceful" protests mean that no yelling or pie throwing is involved.

Standing backwards involves blocking the view of people. Not all forms of protest are out of bounds. These "silent protests" are disgusting. They do absolutely nothing to further discussion. Also, it seems that conservatives do not behave in this way. Leftists are fine with this behavior because they do not see conservatives as human beings. Acting human toward them is therefore not required.

There were so many aspects of the event itself, rendering it difficult to do the event justice. Before kickoff, there were pregame left-wing warm-ups. This involved an attempt to discredit the event before it began by demonizing the speaker.

I know David Horowitz. I have met the man many times. He is a good human being that has had more pain than any human being should have to suffer through. He is an intelligent person that does not have an ounce of bigotry in him. Let me emphasize this again for the liberals who like to throw around charges of bigotry to demonize conservatives. I know this man personally. There is not an ounce of malice in his heart. He wants to defeat radical Islam. He has nothing against moderate Muslims. Charges that he does must be forcefully, immediately, and repeatedly condemned lest they take hold.

One reason I have such contempt for leftist protesters is their unwillingness to debate on ideas. A phony flyer circulated was meant to look like it came from the USC College Republicans. It stated, "Hate Muslims? So do we."[92] The College Republicans fought back, and pointed out that the flyer was a fake.

Another leftist tactic before the event was to try and criticize the College Republicans for banning many people from the event. RSVPs were required in advance. Perhaps these future community organizers might wish to understand that when people have their lives threatened, they are going to require that extra precautions take place. It is a disgrace that twelve security guards were required to protect a seventy-year-old man simply trying to express opinions. Only those affiliated with a university could object to this while preaching diversity.

Many people banned were members of "Students for Justice in Palestine." That organization spouts incendiary rhetoric where justice is code for "kill the Jews." Members of the "Progressive Alliance" also have a history of agitation. Shockingly enough, they were enraged at their inability to spread more rage.

USC College Republican President Alexandra Ekman saw a Facebook posting by the Students for Justice in Palestine that read in part that they voted "to oppose this speaker in any way possible…"[93]

In any way possible? Who acts like this? Oh yes, leftists and Palesimians. Any measure possible must be taken when it comes to self-defense. It only takes getting it wrong once for a tragedy to occur. People who throw pies at speakers and shoes at a president need to be jailed and beyond until the behavior stops.

The event itself consisted of remarks by Mr. Horowitz followed by questions and answers. I did not stay for all of his remarks. I have heard him speak before, and I agree with him. Here are a few selected remarks.

"The behavior on this campus this past week has been an utter disgrace."

"I have a bodyguard. I have been physically attacked."

"I have to be protected from groups like the Students for Justice in Palestine and the Progressive Alliance. They call us fascist. They are the ones who are fascist thugs. "

"They see Fascist as anything they don't like."

"The only persecuted groups on campuses are conservatives, Christians, and Jews."

"Muslim students are coddled on campuses. They get more money, more privileges, and campuses bend over backwards for them."

"The *Daily Trojan* did not print a response to the 'David Horowitz is a beast' column."

"I marched in the civil rights movement before these leftists were born."

"I don't know if they teach history in schools anymore."

"Leftists scream, rant, and call people names to try and shut them up."

"'Racist' is a useful term to demonize conservatives, run them out of society, and dehumanize them."

"An attempt to conduct a second Holocaust is being done by the war against the Jews on campuses."

"Islamofascism Week initially began to protest the fact that women were being genitally mutilated in Muslim countries."

"If you find that offensive, you are called anti-Muslim. I defend the women, not the Taliban."

"There are good and bad Muslims. Most Muslims want peace and are law abiding."

"The KKK began as a Christian organization, yet most Christians and churches today condemn the KKK. In Islam, I don't see the condemnation of radical Islam."

"In the Koran, Jews are called apes and pigs."[94]

At this point some leftist protesters stood up and engaged in one of their protests that only college campus liberals could find acceptable. They stood up and turned their backs. They were all escorted out as some complained about being oppressed. Others laughed and bragged about their great victory.

At this moment I decided to leave the event because observing the protesters in their natural habitat would make a good study in the argument of evolution vs. creationism. I believe in God, but if anybody came straight from baboons, it would be leftist protesters. In fact, they were confined outside to a specific area resembling a cage. I did not see any of them eating bananas.

Ever so slightly changing "Sumpin' New"[95] by rapper Coolio, they chanted, "Ain't no party like a freedom party 'cause a freedom party don't stop."

They also started chanting "bigots go home." In an act of hypocrisy, they did not leave themselves.

These twenty people were not useless. They make for a very important teaching tool. While observing them, I ran into an eighteen-year-old Muslim freshman girl named Heba (last name redacted).

She was pleasant, polite, and thoughtful. We ended up speaking for close to twenty minutes, maybe longer. She was dressed in her Muslim garb. We both laughed when I asked her what her scarf was called. Apparently it is called a "scarf."

She told me that people had called her a terrorist. I told her this was awful. We actually agreed on more than we disagreed. I told her that I would defend to the death her right to wear her traditional garb, but that I drew the line at somebody wanting their face covered in driver's license photos. Religious law cannot supersede American law. She agreed. She asked me why I had such hostility toward the protesters. It was a totally fair question, and she respected my answers.

The twenty protesters ejected from the meeting accomplished nothing. They were trapped in a protest cage talking to each other. The goal is to persuade people. Their tactics had the reverse effect. She asked me what I thought would be better.

My response was that people who disagree with speakers should come to the event, sit quietly, listen, and then ask very polite but tough questions during the question and answer session. Some events do not allow questions, or require them be submitted in writing. Mr. Horowitz showed more tolerance than many by allowing tough verbal questions.

Heba understood my point, and had another fair question. How can people ask tough questions if they are not allowed in?

My response to her was that the system is not perfect. When members of a group behave badly, a few rotten apples spoil the entire bunch. I knew she was not a terrorist, and felt terrible for her that other Muslims gave her a bad name. I knew what she was going through. I am a Jewish stockbrokerage professional. Bernie Madoff gave Jews, stockbrokers, and me black eyes. I knew that when terrorist acts happen, she prays that there is no connection to Islam. I pray that crooked financial scandals do not involve Jews. Jack Abramoff hurt me. She understood, and questioned where we go from here.

I told her that I loudly condemned Madoff and Abramoff. The main perception in America among Mr. Horowitz and his many supporters is that moderate Muslims are not loudly and forcefully condemning the terrorists. In the Middle East, Muslims stay silent to avoid being murdered. In America we are free. Freedom comes with responsibility. This means standing up for what is right and condemning bad behavior.

She conceded that she personally did not know enough about Mr. Horowitz to label him. I thanked her for being a friendly and reasonable person.

I reentered the room where Mr. Horowitz was speaking. The post-game show featured a fiery question and answer session. Those outside remained ignorant. Those inside who were civilized enough to let him speak were rewarded with a real exchange of ideas that campuses theoretically pride themselves on but rarely ever live up to ideologically.

Mr. Horowitz concluded with a stinging indictment of the pacifist movement.

"Stalin, Mao, and Pol Pot have murdered millions of people. They and their supporters Jane Fonda, Ted Kennedy, and Howard Dean all have blood on their hands. These people do not spread equality or peace. All they spread is leftist misery."

I would like to thank David Horowitz for risking his life in the name of freedom against the Islamists who want to kill us all, and their leftist excuse-making enablers.

As for the College Republicans, they have faced disgusting acts of bigotry. Some of them are also Jewish, subjecting them to unimaginable abuse. They showed tremendous courage in putting on this event, and were ultra-professional in their demeanor all night.

It is sad that such courage is even required. Universities long ago plummeted from bastions of ideas to laboratories of social engineering.

Combating anti-Semitism and Islamofascism on campuses is so important. For a free society to remain free, people must be able to learn in peace. This requires listening, learning, and asking hard questions.

Until David Horowitz can speak in peace, and College Republicans can put on events without being slandered and libeled, none of us in America are free.

This is a fight for the core American value of freedom. Without freedom, there is no America.

When we stand up for freedom on campuses, we stand up for good and decent Americans everywhere.

eric

Terrorism and Blood Libel Reaches UCLA

I have never infiltrated a terrorist sleeper cell, but it seems that the enablers of terrorism congregate at UCLA, specifically in their "Middle East Studies" Department.

I attended a symposium on "Gaza and Human Rights." For conspiracy buffs, combining "sympathize" and "terrorism" gives us "symposium."

UCLA now stands for the University of Crooked Lying Arabists.

This was no human rights symposium. It was a conference on how best to spread anti-Semitism, anti-Zionism, anti-Americanism, and blood libel.

The audience did have some Arab attendees. A healthy plurality of the crowd consisted of fifty-year-old bald white guys and their various leftist causes that have no common links with Gaza issues outside of extremism and wrongheadedness.

The Che Guevara supporters and the Communists were there. Many of the students clapped when they saw others clapping, but spent the bulk of their time text messaging each other and checking their Facebook profiles. This might be the only benefit to their miniscule attention spans. The indoctrination process may not have succeeded, since lengthy diatribes do not fit into a one hundred-forty character Twitter world.

UCLA Near Eastern Studies Director Susan Slyomovics put together the spreaders of bile on this hate-filled occasion. She was listed as the "moderator," an ironic term given that there appears to be nothing moderate about her. She began this session with typical left-wing academic condescension.

"I have done extensive research on Israel and Palestine. After all, this is not Fox TV. This is UCLA."

Perhaps she meant Fox News, unless of course she was comparing her research abilities to Homer Simpson. She is one elitist that needs a research insult assistant.

Snide insults are expected. Even for this group, blood libel was over the top.

UCLA History Department "Professor" Gabriel Piterberg spoke next. His job was to invent history out of thin air. He spoke of an "Israeli onslaught on the Palestinians of Gaza." He accused IDF soldiers of committing war crimes.

He referred to the current conflict in Gaza as one between two peoples with an unequal moral claim. In his eyes the Palesimians are the "Native Indigenous Population." The Israelis are "Settlers from Europe." These labels are as vicious as they are preposterous. Palesimians are as indigenous to Gaza as the French are to Japan. Mr. Piterberg spoke of the "forced removal of the indigenous people in favor of the settler nation-state."

He also offered an incomprehensible parallel between the Arab-Israeli conflict and Karl Marx observing situations in China and India.

He then spread the first poisonous blood libel of the symposium when he accused Israel of using white phosphorous to smoke out and kill Palesimian children. This completely debunked lie was repeated throughout the symposium.

He concluded by comparing the struggle of Palesimians in the Gaza Strip to the Algerian struggle against France.

UC Santa Barbara Law and Society Chair Lisa Hajjar spoke next. She was by far the most dangerous member of the panel due to her crystal clear voice.

She falsely claimed that Israel was violating the Fourth Geneva Convention. The Palesimians are not a nation. Geneva does not apply to them or al-Qaeda.

Throughout the event, Israel was referred to as an "occupier." The Gaza Strip and West Bank were referred to as "occupied territories," rather than the actual term of "disputed territories."

Ms. Hajjar did concede, to the consternation of the leftists in the room, that "War is permissible. Not all war is illegal." She also surprised the crowd by stating that collateral damage by itself is not necessarily a violation of war. She then thundered that "Civilians have a right to immunity. Intentionality is the key."

This preceded the second blood libel of the evening, the fraudulent claim that Israel deliberately targets Palesimian civilians. She repeated the white phosphorous charge. She claimed that Israel should "only target what is necessary." She went further by stating that "Mayor Bloomberg needs a lesson in war."

She claimed that "denying food and water is inhumane. It is a war crime." Perhaps she was stating that Hamas, and the late murderer Yassir Arafat, are war criminals. They starved their own people, diverted funds meant for food, and purchase munitions. Upon further review, the only war criminals she mentioned were Israelis.

She brought up the phony issue of "proportionality," before concluding with the bizarre and irrelevant statement that "Dick Cheney is the enemy of all mankind."

UCSB Global and International Studies Professor Richard Falk began by declaring the situation an ""unequal war." Maybe Hamas should be rewarded for losing with the war equivalent of affirmative action.

He falsely claimed that Hamas tried to initiate a ceasefire in July of 2008 that would have avoided cross-border violence. He actually claimed that this mythical Hamas ceasefire "was a diplomatic initiative that would have ended the conflict."

He completely whitewashed the fact that Hamas fires rockets into Israel on a daily basis. He claimed that Hamas firing rockets was "wrong, imprudent, and immoral, but the rockets did little damage, and were not a significant threat."

Translation from the original Terroristus Enablus vernacular leads one to conclude that perhaps Mr. Falk feels that the Palesimians should be rewarded for being the Inspector Clouseaus of murderers. In the real world, there is no difference between an incompetent murderer and a successful one. First he claims Hamas enacted a ceasefire. Then he claims that attempts to violate the fictional ceasefire at every turn failed to murder Jews. Jews therefore had no right to retaliate. This guy's logic reminds me of congressional liberals enacting tax policies.

He decried "Israeli aggression against a defenseless society," forgetting that only moments earlier he justified their right to defend themselves using rockets. Forget a homeland. These people need a thesaurus. Perhaps they could take a linguistics class with Noam Chomsky, who shockingly enough did not attend this oppression session.

Mr. Falk insisted that the Palesimians were winning the public relations war. Apparently the one hundred people in the room were his sample size. He wrapped up his lunacy litany by stating that "The United States and Israel are the most addicted to a reliance on moral superiority. They practice a genocidal geopolitics."

UCLA English Professor Saree Makdisi spoke last. Apparently he lacks friends in the mathematics or social studies departments. He offered incorrect statistics, inaccurate geography, and deficient logic.

He claimed that the Irish Republican Army murdered more Brits than Palesimian rockets murdered Israelis. He again used a lack of technological craft as an excuse. He also claimed that "dropping ordinances is not ok." He neglected to mention that those leaflet ordinances that the IDF drops are evacuation warnings that save Palesimian lives.

175

He labeled Gaza a prison with seven hundred-fifty-thousand children. His nonsense that "the goal of Israel is to deliberately starve children," added more blood libel to the event. He babbled that "refugees have a moral and legal right to go back home." This is contradicted by the fact that there is not one single Palesimian refugee in existence with Israeli roots. They came from Egypt and Jordan.

The questions asked showed more evidence that many attendees had little interest in Gaza. A "Democracy Now" spokesperson made a speech. Another person stated that "we need more Dennis Kuciniches."

One person from the "Leninists Workers Revolutionary United Party" made the preposterous claim that "Iran needs nuclear weapons to protect itself against the United States and Israel."

Another individual cited Kitty Dukakis, the Jewish wife of failed Massachusetts 1988 presidential candidate Michael Dukakis. That was the second most perplexing moment, behind the elderly Korean peace activist who was hurt by 1950s actions taken by Japan and North Korea.

One individual claimed that "Israel has violated the norms of civilized behavior," and that Palesimian resistance is the non-violent alternative. I failed to see what was non-violent about the "resistance," but time was running short.

There was still enough time for two of the panelists to spread more hatred.

Saree Makdisi thundered that, "If you want to stop the rockets into Israel, Israel must end the occupation."

It took forever, but finally this was the expected admission of celebrating violence that the panel tried to suppress.

I then asked a question in a calm manner.

"You express anger at the killing of Palestinian children. How come you have not addressed the fact that Palestinians are killing their own children? What are your thoughts on Hamas deliberately using their own children as human shields? Do you object to the massacre of one million of your people by Jordan? What about after the 2005 Gaza pullout where Hamas and Fatah killed each other and their children with no Jews in sight? Lastly, what about the fact that Yassir Arafat stole money from your children that was meant to feed them, and instead spent some of it on munitions that got your own kids killed, and diverted the rest of it to Suha Arafat in France?"

The moderator, who let everybody else have free reign provided that they agreed with the panel, demanded that I "condense" my question. I did.

"At what point are any of you going to ask the Palestinians to take personal responsibility for their own corruption and failures, and admit that they are virtually entirely responsible for their own miserable lot in life by choosing suicide bombings and terror over protecting their own children?"

Lisa Hajjar fielded the question. She began by stating that "this was not about the entire history of the conflict. It makes no sense to argue about who started things." That is usually what those who start conflicts say. She also stated that the issue was Gaza and the occupation. Everything else was outside the scope. She added that it was expected for oppressed people to want to fight against their oppressors. I then interrupted her.

"What about suicide bombings?"

Ms. Hajjar then lost her cool, forgetting that the event was being videotaped. She snapped.

"If you think that I am in favor of suicide bombings, then that Zionist hat on your head is screwed on way too tight!"

I did not let her off the hook. I replied forcefully that I was not a Zionist (although I deeply respect Zionism). My hat was actually a fedora, not a Chasidic hat. An "educated" woman such as herself should have known the difference. I then even more forcefully told her that "Your comment was out of line. It was bigoted and racist."

While I doubt she regretted her attitude, she did realize that such comments hurt her cause from a public relations standpoint. This is the same tacit language that is used when describing suicide bombings as "not helpful." She backed down and apologized twice, while making it clear that everything else she said was justified.

The final moment of incredulity came when Saree Makdisi was asked to condemn Iran for funding Hamas with weapons.

Mr. Makdisi replied that, "Hamas is a political group. I have no idea where they get their weapons."

This symposium should be a clear message to the world that Hamas and the "Palesimians" are one and the same. This panel of "academics" made no effort to distinguish them or disavow murderous tactics. Unmentioned were Israel's right to exist, Palesimian blame for any the current conflict, or Palesimians murdering Israeli children.

America may not be willing or able to directly help Israel secure their homeland against an enemy who is defended by professors for being unsuccessful in their genocidal ambitions. The heavy lifting is left to the Israeli Defense Forces.

The least America can do is secure the perimeters of UCLA and root out the threats to our way of life emanating from that campus. After all, those who finance, harbor, or enable terrorists, are terrorists.

This symposium was a terrorist training camp. Luckily enough of the young minds were too busy being indoctrinated by Blackberry video games. Then again, those games involve blowing stuff up.

eric

An Arab Terrorist Professor Surrenders

A small victory in the War on Terror took place.

A vicious university professor and terrorist supporter was brought down.

The blood libel terrorist conference at UCLA led to a deserved Islamist casualty

Not all Arabs are terrorists. Even some Palesimians avoid terrorists (collateral damage).

Now that the politically correct drivel is out of the way, let's get back to the facts.

Most terrorist acts are committed by young Arab Muslim men. Timothy McVeigh was a statistical aberration.

The Bush Doctrine declared that those who support, harbor, or finance terrorists are terrorists themselves.

Lisa Hajjar may not have ever helped somebody put on a suicide belt (unverified). She absolutely has fostered a climate in academia that offers the most mild and tacit criticism of Palesimian terrorism. She was one of the "academics."

When I first came back from that event, I gave myself a good scrubbing. As for Lisa Hajjar, she is no dummy. She is smart and articulate, making her all the more dangerous.

Yet she blundered when she angrily let her anti-Semitic slip show.

This is a woman educating our children. By the grace of Yahweh, she has finally been shut down.

Who knew something positive would come out of the financial crisis?

I would prefer she be shut down for moral reasons, rather than the traditional budget crunch, but anything that shuts her up improves society.

I wonder if she had the chance to visit Judea Pearl, the father of slain Daniel Pearl, while she was spreading her bile at UCLA.

She plays the ethnic card almost as well as the moral equivalence card. She takes criticism of her and turns the tables by claiming that her critics are just Zionist, imperialist (insult typical anti-Semitic epithets here).

"It is unfortunate that students will not have the opportunity to pursue a wonderful curriculum of socio-legal studies, that range from domestic issues and legal and political theories to the study of conflicts and rights-oriented social movements around the world,"[96] Hajjar said.

Don't worry Ms. Hajjar. There are plenty of places where students can go to become ill-informed, know-nothing zealots. After all, not every university has their Middle East Studies Department shut down.

The War on Terror will not be easy. We kill one university program, and another one sprouts up.

I should take personal credit for this situation so that Ms. Hajjar and I can both benefit. She can rail about the Zionist conspiracy. I can build my street cred and impress Republican Jewish brunettes. They do love heroes, and a soldier taking down evil is quite studly. This might even impress the toughest of Jewish mothers.

I would respect Ms. Hajjar more if she would just admit that she did not believe the garbage emanating from her mouth. If she is just taking advantage of dopey college students to further her own career, she would be your typical soulless academic parasite.

I suspect she actually does believe what she says.

I am not a psychologist. All I know is that she is a verbal homicide bomber.

Some will argue that with terrorists and cockroaches, killing one just breeds more.

I disagree. Once her program is completely dismantled, her students will be forced to actually learn something useful and use real majors to become productive members of society.

Her training camp has been busted. The next generation of academic thugs will not learn from her.

Lisa Hajjar has spent her life bashing Israel. My real objection is that she teaches others to do this, and gets paid for it.

As of now, like the War on Terror itself, her plans have been slowed.

I have smoked three cigars in my life, the last one in 2002. I had planned to have the fourth one by age forty. I considered a stogie the day her department died.

Then again, there is no time to rest on laurels. One terrorist sleeper cell has been given the Gaza treatment, with equal justification. Many more still remain.

Like all cockroaches and terrorists, academics talk a good game. When enough pressure is applied, they surrender quicker than they can yell, "jihad, infidel, Zionist donkey aggressor!"

She may be ugly on the inside, but her outside is not horrendous. Perhaps she can get a backup career doing Palesimian porn. "Ketushah Rocket Launch" is always an option.

Perhaps I should not anger her. As a lawyer, she might sue. Worse, she might get angry and explode (near a pizza shack or disco parlor in keeping with tradition).

If she does so literally, I just hope no Jews are in the vicinity.

Either way, the only thing that blew up was her wretched academic department. That is good enough.

Excellent riddance.

eric

Seddio Burns a Brooklyn Building With a Malakoff Cocktail

I rarely ever discuss my family. They usually keep to themselves and mind their own d@mn business. I recommend that everybody does this.

"Family" is not the same as "relatives." Family consists of people you wish you had more time to see. Relatives are the ones that never leave. Family members die too soon. Relatives live longer than Abraham and Helen Thomas combined.

Family matters should be kept quiet. Relatives are fair game, since helping others deal with their own relatives is a noble public service.

Sadly enough for decent society, my mother was preceded by a defective sibling. The woman is too old to be returned to the manufacturer. Apparently the feminist movement failed miserably in their attempt to get abortion legalized after the three-hundredth trimester (Thank you, *South Park*).[97]

I will not reveal her name. I will only say that when one mixes several recessive genes with splashes of incompetence, vindictiveness, rat poison, and nitroglycerin, the result is a toxic blazing concoction known as a Malakoff Cocktail. She storms into rooms like a cross between Jack Nicholson and Janet Reno yelling, "You can't handle the Ruth!" I saw a building burn myself.

The Malakoff Cocktail spawned Adam (a well-intentioned son), Eve (a kind-hearted daughter), and the viper (a daughter who spread her legs for a wealthy man, resulting in a sense of entitlement and avarice that surpasses her parents).

My parents worked hard, played by the rules, and lead honorable lives. In keeping with political conservatism, they want to be left alone to live the most of their own lives.

The Malakoff Cocktail is that lovely combination of politically opinionated liberalism and a lack of knowledge about anything. She was a schoolteacher, which is another reason public schools should be shut down.

Despite having no discernible skills or moral compass, her lack of ethics gave her the ability to lie, cheat, steal, embezzle, and engage in other unsavory activities.

Like many liberals, she responded to being caught by lashing out.

She made a decision that her final years on Earth would be spent harassing my family. To do this, she needed the help of people who are not bound by any code of ethics. She needed people that have "win at all costs" tattooed on their elderly wrinkled (redacted). Her lawyer husband found a couple that would fit the bill.

Combine John Gotti with *Matlock*, and one gets attorney Frank Seddio.

"In recent years, one Brooklyn surrogate, Michael Feinberg, was removed in disgrace for improperly taking excess fees from estates and giving them to a law school buddy. Feinberg's successor, Frank Seddio, resigned after less than a year in office amid allegations he violated campaign finance laws."[98]

"There have been reports speculating that Seddio, a native Canarsien, may have been involved in legal, albeit suspicious, contributions to ensure his judgeship. A recent Daily News editorial charged, 'Frank Seddio opened his checkbook for the Brooklyn Democratic organization three times last summer, contributing a total of $17,500 to a legendary clubhouse, just as the party was deciding whom among the faithful to reward with a powerful judgeship.'"[99]

Many living outside of Brooklyn have never met Mr. and Mrs. Seddio. Ideological violence is more than their hobby. It is their lifeblood. When politically leftist scoundrels go after middle-class Republicans wanting to live their lives, a fair fight does not exist.

Frank Seddio is a New York assemblyman turned corrupt former judge. He had one of his Democratic cronies in New York create a special judgeship just for him. He was removed from office after just over one year. Picture somebody trying to be on the United States Supreme Court and being told that all nine positions were filled. In Frank Seddio's world, a tenth spot would be created. While this could lead to 5-5 decisions that could paralyze America, Mr. Seddio never let the greater good get in the way of the greater ambition. To put this in perspective, his situation was considered too corrupt for New York. While the record technically says he resigned, he has influential friends that bathe each other in (redacted) sanitizer.

While Frank Seddio helps destroy the honor of the judicial system, he is only capable of harming adults. His wife is a much bigger threat. Like many destructive liberals, she understands that the path to dominance comes through the education system.

School principal Joyce Becker-Seddio did not like the fact that schoolteacher Jillian Caruso was active in Republican politics. In a police state, outside behavior can be regulated and banned provided that the one enforcing the rules is liberal and the innocent victim is conservative. There was no evidence that Ms. Caruso engaged in any inappropriate conduct. Liberals cannot make this claim since their entire curriculum is inappropriate.

A George W. Bush picture hung on the wall. Today children sing songs to Barack Obama with a fervor matched only by the musical worship of Chairman Mao. China is a democracy compared to the New York public school system. A picture of a sitting Republican president was too much for leftist thug Joyce Becker-Seddio.

"Jillian Caruso, a teacher on Long Island, was literally forced to resign her teaching position against a threat of termination when her principal, Joyce Becker-Seddio, found a portrait of President Bush hanging in the teacher's classroom. This egregious offense was compounded by the even more horrible fact that Miss Caruso was an active Republican who did volunteer work for the party on her own time. Ms. Becker-Seddio threatened to fire the young woman if she didn't resign, the result of which would have been bad performance evaluations and no future job prospects.

Oh, and by the way, Ms. Becker-Seddio's husband just happens to be a Democratic assemblyman in Brooklyn.

Perhaps Ms. Becker-Seddio also didn't know that hanging a portrait of the sitting president in your classroom (along with other past presidents, as Miss Caruso supposedly did) is not illegal and is, in fact, the right of any teacher under the First Amendment.

One's political activism on one's own time is never anyone else's business. I could understand some concern if Miss Caruso was working to protect the right of NAMBLA members or child molesters, but we're talking about a women who volunteered to work at her party's convention. I wonder if anyone in the Massapequa Union Free School District questioned the political activities of Ms. Becker-Seddio regarding her husband's election to his Democratic assembly seat in Brooklyn? Can she convince us that she didn't assist him in any way whatsoever?"[100]

These are liberal thugs. This is how they behave. Most people have no idea what happens when liberals get their corruption-stained hands on schools, judgeships, and other powerful local positions.

We know about national scandals, such as presidents frolicking with interns in the Oval Office. Below the state level, most people have no idea where power is concentrated. Tip O'Neill used to say that all politics was local.[101] Backyard junkyards still matter. Local politics matter because New York viruses can spread to California and even infect Middle America.

I only learned about the Seddios because the Malakoff Cocktail married a shark who swims with fellow sharks in black ocean swampland.

It is too late to protect my family. I pray that other families have the resources to fight back when ideological bigots aim their guns.

The only solution when dealing with terrorists or leftists is overwhelming brute force.

Conservatives need to stop bringing knives to gunfights and start bringing bazookas.

If the Seddios of the world win, the judicial and educational systems lose. Decent people everywhere burn to death when the Malakoff cocktail crashes through their windows.

eric

Chapter 13:
Community Organizer Violence

Some people are under the naïve mistaken notion that community organizers are noble, selfless creatures that stand in line at soup kitchens and feed people. Community organizers are political agitators. Al Sharpton and Jesse Jackson are community organizers. For liberals who value intentions, community organizers are fabulous. For conservatives who value results, the communities being "helped" are a mess. Businesses leave, and the communities blame Republicans. Maybe if some of these agitators got an MBA (home-schooled preferably), they could build a soup kitchen and actually employ people who can make a difference. The truth is that community organizers want only one thing organized. They care about the dead presidents in their own wallet "earned" by leeching off of the suffering of others dying in their communities. It does not take a village or community organizers to truly help people. It takes conservatism.

President Obama, Your Soul is at Stake

Dear President Obama,

Although I did not vote for you, I wrote you a very warm e-mail congratulating you on your victory. I told my conservative friends that I owed you the benefit of the doubt.

My disagreements with you were political, not personal. I am a conservative Republican, and you are a liberal Democrat. I never disliked you as a human being.

If you do not believe me, feel free to read my blog. Recommend it to your conservative friends. I could use the traffic. If you truly are as bipartisan as you claim, then you have conservative friends.

I am writing this letter because of something your wife said awhile ago. She said that your election would help "fix America's broken soul."

Mr. President, it has become clear that it is your soul that is on the verge of breaking.

You must stop demonizing people simply because they disagree with you. It is not just bad politics. It is bad for humanity.

I don't expect you to change your views on healthcare or other policy issues. Yet you must change your tone.

I told my fellow conservatives that you were a good, decent man, and a good husband and father who loves his country.

If you love America, you have to love what makes America great. American greatness emanates from the American people.

When I wake up in the morning, I think of what I can do to improve America. Sometimes my vision of progress conflicts with yours. This does not make either one of us evil.

You have spent far too much time criticizing your predecessor, despite the fact that he has been overwhelmingly gracious to you and your family. He refuses to publicly criticize you.

You have attacked Rush Limbaugh, who has never flown planes into towers or committed any evil act against America. The last time I checked, all he has done is hosted a political program where he criticizes your policies.

Then you are attacked Fox News with the same passion and ferocity that President George W. Bush used to topple the Taliban and Saddam Hussein.

This verbal carpet-bombing of people just for disagreeing with you must stop. Every minute you engage in the politics of personal destruction, you lose the ability to work with people. You may need such people to help with policies that could feed children, get kids off of drugs, improve schools, strengthen families, and keep America strong.

Afghanistan and Iraq need your attention, and you are distracted...and distracting...with nonsense.

Senator Lamar Alexander of Tennessee gave you a very courteous reminder that you must treat your political opponents with basic human dignity.[102]

President Obama, do you remember President George W. Bush ever attacking MSNBC, the *New York Times*, NPR, and a myriad of other news outlets that hated his guts because he was a conservative who existed and breathed air?

You have been treated with kid gloves while punching your opponents with gloves filled with rocks.

It is time for you and your administration to stop acting like verbal suicide bombers.

I have repeatedly stated that I thought you were a good person with some bad policy ideas. Now I am questioning how good a human being you are.

President George W. Bush is a good human being. He disagreed with people without personally trying to rip them to shreds. Perhaps this is due to his religious faith. Perhaps he has a discipline inside him that I know I do not always possess.

President Obama, American conservatives and Republicans are not the enemy. Bob Dole once said that Bill Clinton was not his enemy, but his opponent. You must get to this point with your political opponents.

The enemies of America are trying to kill us. We are in the midst of a global life and death struggle between civilization and barbarism. Republicans cannot win the War on Terror without you. You are our leader. Yet you can't be a success without them either.

Sir, you need to start acting like an adult. The daily temper tantrums will backfire in the long run. To quote football coach Dennis Green, "Only babies get what they want all the time. Men have to do it the hard way. There's no room for crybabies."[103]

Your election will have been a very hollow victory if you fail to effectively govern. This will happen if you refuse to work with people that have good ideas different from yours.

Your soul is at stake sir. It is on the verge of being irreparably broken.

You told Iran that you would offer an outstretched hand if they unclenched their fist.

You reached out to Iran. Surely you can reach out to your fellow Americans. Some said your words of bipartisanship were phony and insincere. I am still willing to wait and see.

Get beyond the hate. Reach out that bipartisan hand you promised. Let's get down to business.

eric

Hillary—Insincere to the Last Drop

In January of 2003, the Oakland Raiders played the Tampa Bay Buccaneers in the Super Bowl. It was the battle of Bays and pirates.

Late in the game, the Raiders scored three straight touchdowns. The Buccaneers did score a pair of touchdowns at the end, but the Raiders eighteen points outdid the fourteen points of the Buccaneers.

For some reason, the Buccaneers won the Super Bowl instead of the Raiders. Despite outscoring the Buccaneers 18-14, apparently that was not enough to override the first three quarters of the game, in which the Buccaneers squeaked past the Raiders 34-3. The Raiders closed to within 34-21, and then lost 48-21.

As painful as this Super Bowl was, it is almost as painful listening to Hillary Clinton explain to us why facts do not matter and numbers are mere inconveniences.

She gave a "victory" speech after her win in Kentucky. She was thrashed in Oregon and many other states across the country. She did not count those for various reasons. In her world, the last few minutes can make up for the first three quarters.

At least this woman was consistent. She was ready to lie on day one. Why would she not be? She had experience lying for thirty-five years.

"I am thinking about why we are all here. It is not just to win a primary, or even just to win an election; what propels us is the struggle to realize America's promise."

While this is harmless blather to some, somebody ought to tell Hillary that most people do not struggle with this issue. They already appreciate America for what it has been for more than a couple of centuries.

If this was the worst one could say about Hillary, it would not be that bad. It is not even close, which is why she is that bad. She spent much time making the obligatory comments praising Ted Kennedy, which was fine. He was supporting Barack Obama, not her. She does not have to mention this, but it is worth noting.

"It is not just Kentucky bluegrass that is music to my ears."

Hillary has loved Kentucky bluegrass all her life. She has also been a lifelong New York Yankees fan.

Does Hillary know the name of one bluegrass artist or song?

It is not about music. It is about insincerity and a patronizing nature.

It is one thing to thank people. It is another to claim kinship. Hillary is a wealthy woman from a privileged background that somehow managed to position herself to the right of Barack Obama.

"Some have said your votes didn't matter, that this campaign was over, that allowing everyone to vote and every vote to count would somehow be a mistake."

Nobody of any credibility said that. Hillary loves to play the "us against them" card.

"This is one of the closest races for a party's nomination in modern history."

Triple H stands for horseshoes, hand grenades and Hillary. Close means zilch.

"We're winning the popular vote…"

No you were not, Hillary. You turned into Al Gore's evil twin. The real fun will be those who still think Gore won in 2000 trying to explain why the rules were different this time. Sometimes I think liberals would even cheat at Monopoly. Then I remember that they would refuse to play it because some people get wealthy, making the game unfair.

"Though we have been outspent massively…"

As much as I hate using pop culture references, Justin Timberlake was right to tell Britney Spears to "Cry me a river."[104] Hillary was outspent because more people liked Barack Obama. Hillary loves the little people defeating the behemoths except when she is the behemoth. His supporters and their $25 donations beat out her fat cats and their $100 thousand donations.

Hillary does not understand that rich people have a right to be rich. Obama played by the same rules of raising money. He won fair and square. He became a complete hypocrite when he inevitably started bashing the rich, but that was expected. Life is not fair, no matter how desperately Hillary tried to spread the misery of equality. Obama spent into the stratosphere, as was his right.

(That was his money. Bankrupting America is wrong because he is spending our money.)

"We have to select a nominee who is best positioned to win in November, and someone who is best prepared to address the enormous challenges facing our country in these difficult times."

The "electability" argument is pure fraud. The rules cannot be undone. John Edwards (pre-bimbo eruptions), Bill Richardson (ditto) and Joe Biden (He is a bimbo eruption) were all more electable. The road is littered with candidates who would have been strong in a general election if only they did not have to go through the pesky nuisance of a primary. Rudy Giuliani in 2008, John Edwards and Joe Lieberman in 2004, and John McCain in 2000 all tried to play to the center. This is admirable, but passionate bases have every right to make their voices heard. Moderates troubled by this should speak up more forcefully. I detest activists, but respect the fact that they are motivated and get things done. Hillary was rejected by a majority of voters in her own party. Barely being rejected is no different than a landslide rejection. A close loss is a loss.

"Now, I'm told that more people have voted for me than for anyone who has ever run for the Democratic nomination."

That is also a lie, Hillary. Stop manipulating the numbers. You may have turned $1 thousand into $100 thousand playing commodities, but in this game, two plus two still does not equal five.

It must be repeatedly reinforced that even if she did win the popular vote, that would be a meaningless symbolic victory from an electoral standpoint.

(The talk before the 2000 election was Al Gore losing the popular vote but winning the Electoral College. His supporters were fine with this. His campaign's last minute hit job about his opponent's drunk-driving scandal almost made their concerns moot.)

"(This election is about) whether or not we will have a president who will rebuild the economy, end the war in Iraq, restore our leadership in the world and stand up for you every single day."

The economy was actually doing well. There was a chance that we would not have had a recession at all. Liberals then talked down the economy and allowed politically correct lending to create a mess because they hated President George W. Bush more than they liked a healthy economy. As for restoring our leadership in the world, Europeans are supporting conservative leaders in droves. Even if this was not the case, John Kerry's "global test" is as useless now as it was in 2004. As for ending the war in Iraq, if support for the war had upticked again, she would then be for the war since the beginning anyway.

"For too long, too many Americans have felt invisible in their own country. Well, you've never been invisible to me. I've been fighting for you my entire life."

Most people want to be left alone to make the most of their own lives. They are only invisible to the elites like Hillary who consider them "flyover country." Just because Obama was even more condescending than she was does not make her the champion of ordinary Americans. The people who make this country great, who shop at Wal-Mart, like NASCAR, go target-shooting… Hillary has utter contempt for these people.

We are in this race because we believe everyone deserves a shot at the American dream, the opportunity to work hard at a good job to get ahead, to save for college, for a home, for retirement."

This would be true except for the fact that Hillary wanted to raise capital gains taxes, which would decimate retirement accounts. Only people making less than a certain amount can open up IRAs. Hurting retirement accounts hurts the rich least. She also wanted to tax profits of legal businesses, which would cripple shareholders of these companies. The female version of Robin Hood would wreck a family owning a few shares of stock to teach rich powerful producers a lesson.

"(We need) a president with experience representing the people of the United States in more than eighty countries to restore our leadership and moral authority in the world."

I drank Coca-Cola in many places worldwide. I am therefore a world-renowned food and beverage expert who should be the CEO of Coca-Cola. I also own stock in Coca-Cola, which makes me part owner. Using Hillary's math, I should be the Chairman of the Board. My shares were bought recently, invalidating the millions of shares that the current CEO owns.

"This country needs our combination of strength and compassion to help people struggling with their bills."

Democrats love using words like "toughness" and "strength" everywhere except where it matters. Barack Obama has a meaningless phrase known as "tough diplomacy." John Kerry wanted a "stronger America."

Republicans don't have to announce how tough they are. It is taken at face value. (I wish Republicans would promise to never again try to run on compassion. It makes me ill).

As for my bills, I have student loans. I do not need nor want Hillary's help. I want my taxes low, so I can pay the loans myself. Period. Exclamation point. Let me keep my money. Mind your own business, Hillary.

"I'm going to keep standing up for the voters of Florida and Michigan. Democrats in those two states cast 2.3 million votes and they deserve to have those votes counted."

No. They do not. The rules were crystal clear.

"Who is ready on day one to lead?"

194

John McCain was. He actually had a record of accomplishment, despite his not attending coffee klatches and ribbon cutting ceremonies across eighty nations.

"Just this week, I met eighty-nine-year-old Emma Hollis, an African-American woman. She's seen so many barriers crumble and fall in her lifetime, but she is not finished yet."

This is the obligatory sop to a random black woman. While this is harmless, Obama was winning over 90 percent of the black vote, including black women. Hillary is cherry picking. There might be a white male gun owner watching football who likes Hillary. In statistics this would be called an aberration.

"I'm thinking about Andrea Steagall, a strong and composed young woman, twenty years old, who drove across Kentucky to meet me. Her husband, Justin, is deployed in Afghanistan."

This is another aberration. John Kerry lost 75 percent of the military vote. Al Gore tried to have their ballots invalidated, since "counting all the votes" was only meant for his supporters. Hillary claimed every left-of-center military person aching for a photo op and a cushy Pentagon job. The rank-and-file were behind war hero John McCain.

"I'm thinking again about Dalton Hatfield, the eleven-year-old from Kentucky, who sold his bike and his video games to raise money to support my campaign."

This was one time I hoped Hillary was lying. If this story is truthful, then I am appalled. I will not blame Hillary, but I will say that the boy's parents are most likely disgusting human beings. Eleven-year-old children are apolitical unless their parents indoctrinate them. Good parents who truly care about their children would prefer their child keep his bicycle and video games. The left "cares" about the children.

"The state motto of Kentucky is, 'United we stand, divided we fall.'"

Hillary is all about division. She pits groups against each other.

"We won't just unite our party; we will unite our country."[105]

Her life is bashing Republicans. To make sure I understand, she is a fighter who prides herself on defeating enemies and a healer who will bring us together.

Hillary, with all respect to the people of Maxwell House Coffee, you truly are consistent in your insincerity. You are good to the last drop.

The percolator has been turned off. Now all we see is a drip.

I would not even let her iron my shirts.[106] I know more about domestic life than she does. Perhaps her servants can show her how to do it.

Enough, Hillary. Even Democrats, who will believe anything, do not believe you. The most gullible have seen through you.

It is easy to see through when there is nothing actually there but a blank space.

More Democrats found substance in Barack Obama than in Hillary.

While that makes me laugh, they have every right to nominate whoever they wish.

Hillary, enjoy your existence sipping tea with despots while accomplishing nothing. Enjoy taking orders from a man you still consider beneath you. Just do it silently.

Hillary, the last drip has dropped. The last drop has dripped. The faucet has been turned off. The lights have been turned out.

It is time for you to do the same.

eric

Chapter 14:
Religious Islamofascist Jihadist Violence

Offering platitudes about why and how we need to defeat Islamofascist monsters is not necessary. Every word on my blog, in my books, and out of my mouth is devoted to winning this struggle. My contempt for the left on this issue makes elaborating unnecessary. Put the liberal children to bed and let the adults handle this. It's only life and death.

9/11/7…Flying to New York

September 11th, 2007…a Tuesday…only one thing to do…

GET ON A PLANE!

On September 11th, 2006, I flew from Los Angeles to Oakland. I wanted to fly to New York, but business took me there a week earlier.

September 11th, 2007, at 8:46 AM, had me en route to New York.

I was not scared. I was emboldened.

I am not a hero. Heroes are people who serve our military worldwide. I am just an American. I remain forever enraged at the brutal murder of three thousand of my fellow New Yorkers.

If we refuse to fly, the terrorists win. If we let fear defeat hope, the terrorists win.

I will not back down. I will not give in. While I might not die on my terms, it will not be on the terms of savage barbarians.

Upon landing at the airport, I visited my grandmother in Brooklyn. She lived three weeks shy of one hundred years, and was strong to the end. Then I conducted business on Wall Street before making my way to Six Flags Great Adventure for Sean Hannity's Freedom Concert.

Lee Greenwood headlines the annual concert. The proceeds go to the orphans of 9/11 victims and fallen soldiers.

I wore my t-shirt with the photo of Iwo Jima on it that says, "These Colors Don't Run…Or Burn."

My 9/11 necktie has the three soldiers on it. I wish I could meet these men and thank them myself.

On September 13th and 14th of 2007, I celebrated the Jewish holiday of Rosh Hashanah. On September 14th I left temple for a few minutes to go to Ground Zero. I looked to the sky, and quoted President Bush. "I hear you, the rest of the world hears you, and pretty soon the people who knocked down these buildings will hear from all of us."[107]

On September 20th, 2001, the president promised us that, "We would not falter, and we would not fail."[108] He urged people to fly. I urge everyone to do the same.

For people facing delays at airports, take a deep breath. Remind yourself that delays are caused by people. Longer delays are caused by larger amounts of people. I prefer that flights start and end on time, but I do not mind waiting if thousands of my fellow Americans are exercising their God-given right to be free...and fly.

Let the eagles soar. Let every day including September 11th be a day when America shows its resolve.

Bring it on. I am ready to fly.

eric

My Interview With Colonel Ralph Peters

I had the pleasure of interviewing Lieutenant Colonel Ralph Peters.

At the time of the interview, I had not yet met Colonel Peters in real life. The interview was conducted by e-mail. What I can say is that beneath the occasionally tough persona Colonel Peters displays on television and in print, he is a deliberate and thoughtful man who possesses genuine warmth.

In addition to having a distinguished military career, the Fox News military analyst and *New York Post* columnist is also an accomplished author.

On military matters, Colonel Peters holds a place in the recently created *Wall Street Journal*/Charles Krauthammer Index of Intellectual Titans.

With that, I present the brilliance of Ralph Peters.

1) What is the Lieutenant Colonel Ralph Peters story?

I'm a coal-miner's son. My family had dramatic ups and downs. I was a wild kid. I joined the army as an enlisted man in 1976. The army straightened me out. I became an officer through OCS. I picked up a couple of degrees along the way and started writing essays and novels while still on active duty. After serving as a Military Intelligence officer in conventional units, I became a Foreign Area Officer specializing in the dying Soviet Union and the "new" Russia. I got tapped as the army's global scout and found myself in dozens of different countries, from Bolivia to Burma. My job wasn't to pull triggers, but to observe other countries in crisis and report back. It was a fascinating chance to see just how ugly humanity can get, from refugee camps to roadblocks manned by drunken thugs.

I loved the army and serving our country, but I chose to retire in 1998, shortly after promotion to the rank of lieutenant colonel, since I was outraged by the Clinton administration's passivity in the face of various threats–not least, terrorism– and wanted to write freely (Serving officers cannot and should not criticize our president, no matter who he or she may be). On September 11, 2001, I regretted having retired–but we make our choices in life and must live with them. So I do my best to support our troops and our country by writing my columns and books, and by speaking out.

Oddly, I never thought I'd have anything to do with journalism, beyond a few military articles. Yet the phone started ringing as soon as I retired. I think what appeals to editors and readers is that I always turn in clean, clear "copy," I don't waffle, and I tell the truth as best I can determine it, no matter the consequences. This doesn't mean I'm always right–only God is perfect–but I tell folks that, well, if I'm wrong, at least I'm honestly wrong. I pay the bills with my pen and don't take any political or industry back-door funding.

I am happily married, love hiking and Shakespeare (all the Elizabethans and Jacobeans), and the thing that would most surprise people who know me only through my "warpath" public persona is that I'm actually a very happy person who delights in every God-given day. Despite all of our troubles these days, it's a wonderful thing to be an American citizen in 2009 (or any year).

2) What can ordinary citizens do, besides donating money and buying your books, to help win the War on Terror? What obligations do we have, and how can we help?

Buying my books won't help win the War on Terror (my publisher's grateful, though). Anyway, it's fine with me if people get the books from the library—I'd just like them to read them. I'm especially anxious for folks to read the new novel I have coming out on September 15 (2009), The War After Armageddon. It's set after—yes, after—the nuclear destruction of Israel, when a battered US military has to return to the Middle East. It's a fast-paced story, thrilling to read, and I chose fiction to drive home the risks Israel faces simply because more people read fiction—and, if you tell an exciting story, you reach them on an emotional level. Although I'm not Jewish myself (I'd be proud of it, if I were), I feel a deep bond with Israel and am horrified by the Obama administration's conviction that, somehow, Arab terrorists and Israeli kindergarten kids are equally guilty for the region's problems. Anyway, I do want to scare people—because the reality is terrifying.

What can we all do to help defeat terrorism? I'll resort to platitudes, because the platitudes are true: Support our troops. Vote. Fight political correctness. Tell the truth. Be a good citizen. Don't let the establishment media tyrannize you. Don't vote party lines—for either party. Hold politicians individually responsible. Love your neighbor, smite the wicked, and salute the flag.

3) Many people say they support the troops, but what can and should Americans do to make that more than a slogan? What are the very best ways ordinary citizens can help our soldiers?

One of the best ways to support our troops is just to think for yourself and not let the establishment media sell you a bill of goods. Freedom of thought and expression is elementary. The extreme left loves the First Amendment—as long as it only applies to them. When you believe the media are lying, talk back, write back, and fight back.

On a practical level, there are some very good charities that help our gravely wounded soldiers and their families. I won't favor any one of them here, but just say "Check before you donate," of course, because there are always vicious characters who'd steal from anyone. But some of these soldiers have multiple limb losses, devastating burns, memory loss, blindness…they gave all they could to us.

Let's help them in their recovery and transition back into our society. By the way, one of the things I'm proudest of as a journalist is that, with the New York Post team, I was able to raise over a million dollars for a re-integration facility for our veterans in San Antonio. Oh, and one other thing: When you're traveling or just out and about...if you see a soldier, walk up and say, "Thank you!" They appreciate it.

4) With regards to Iraq, what have we done right, and what have we gotten wrong, in the last six years, and what steps need to be taken to improve the situations that require improvement?

What did we do right? We deposed Saddam Hussein, a monstrous dictator responsible for over a million-and-a-half deaths, and we gave one vital Arab state a chance to become a rule-of-law democracy. What did we get wrong? Trying to do the occupation on the cheap. In warfare—the most complex of human endeavors—some few things are straightforward. One clear thing is this ironclad rule: "He who is unwilling to pay the butcher's bill up front will pay it with compound interest in the end." Iraq wasn't inherently hard. We made it hard by trying to do it on the cheap and violating fundamental principles. Secretary of Defense Donald Rumsfeld, especially, was a disaster. But, despite the tragic errors, it's to President Bush's credit that he didn't quit. Today, Iraq looks like it has a chance to succeed—imperfectly, but wonderfully by the standards of the Arab world. It won't be Iowa, but it still may be a democratic beacon for its neighbors—and we've already seen the Iranians next door out in the streets, crying out for honest democracy. I believe it was Bush's tenacity, not Obama's disgraceful apologia in Cairo that made the difference.

5) With regards to Afghanistan, what have we done right, and what have we gotten wrong, in the last eight years, and what steps need to be taken to improve the situations that require improvement?

What did we do right? We promptly struck back, stunning al-Qaeda and punishing the Taliban for hosting the terrorists. What did we get wrong? We stayed. Afghanistan wasn't the problem. Al-Qaeda was. Afghanistan is a black hole. Trying to turn Afghan elders into good Americans is a hopeless cause. We should never tie our troops to "real estate" and feckless nation-building efforts. We need to concentrate on killing terrorists, not teaching hygiene to Afghan hillbillies. Let me be perfectly clear: In and of itself, Afghanistan is worthless. And nobody in Washington can give a convincing rationale for our continued presence. We don't have a strategy, just sound bites. And no American soldier should die for a sound bite.

6) With regards to any other foreign policy hot spots, what have we done right, and what have we gotten wrong, in the last eight years, and what steps need to be taken to improve the situations that require improvement?

We promoted democracy, which was wonderful. Then we backed away from promoting democracy, which was tragic. Our foreign-policy principles should be based upon our values and security needs, and they should not bounce back and forth between administrations. Our face to the world should wear a constant expression of vigilant good intentions. One terrible mistake, though, that Bush and Obama both share, is the belief that strategic progress is all about personal relationships. It's not. It's about interests. It doesn't help to make nice with Putin or Chavez. We need sober policies based upon our strategic interests—not on weekend getaways or bear-hugs with dictators.

7) How does the Obama Doctrine differ most consequentially from the Bush Doctrine? What aspects of the Obama Doctrine are an improvement, and what aspects are a regression?

As near as I can tell, the Obama Doctrine is simply "America's guilty." Bush's corresponding doctrine was "America's a force for good in the world." Take your pick.

8) Our country is incredibly polarized. Outside of another 9/11, is it even possible to unite Americans? What can be done to help reduce the acrimony among Americans today?

I believe that most Americans are still in the middle. But middle-of-the-road views don't make for exciting television or radio shows, or for dramatic headlines. Extremists—hardcore extremists—on either end of the political spectrum are bad for our democracy. Unfortunately, the blogosphere does a great deal to empower irresponsible extremists, the really good haters. Speaking of the blogosphere, my rule is simple: I don't trust or take seriously anyone who lacks the guts to sign his or her own name. Now, I'm not talking about people having legitimate fun—I'm talking about the obscenity-laced rants. "Anonymous" is a synonym for "coward."

9) Who are your three favorite political leaders of all time, American or worldwide?

Abraham Lincoln, George Washington and Oliver Cromwell.

10) Who are your three favorite military leaders of all time, American or worldwide?

Joshua, Ulysses S. Grant, and Dwight D. Eisenhower.

11) What America refers to as 9/11, Israel refers to as every day life. What did America get right and wrong in its relationship with Israel during the George W. Bush administration? What about so far in the Obama administration?

What do Israel and Mexico have in common? They're both vital to US security; they were both high on the Bush administration's agenda on inauguration day; and they were both victims of 9/11. Despite some fussing about, the Bush administration simply had other priorities than Israel—which wasn't all bad, since Bush didn't force any genuinely stupid polices on Israel. As for the Obama administration, well, I believe our president's world-view is much farther left than he consciously realizes. You can't spend twenty years listening to the Rev. Jeremiah Wright spew anti-Jewish hatred, or hanging around left-wing activists, and not absorb some of their bigotry by osmosis. Sad to say, I fear that Obama came to office with a huge anti-Israel chip on his shoulder, along with a lot of phony Third-World free-the-poor-Palestinians b.s. Well, as I point out to folks, the other Arabs never really cared about the Palestinians, except as a cause, and the Palestinians could have much greater freedom, mobility and prosperity if they stopped murdering Israeli children. Obama just doesn't get the fundamental difference between Israel and its enemies: Israel is willing to live in peace, while Israel's enemies want every Jew dead. I hope Obama will figure things out, but I worry about him doing great damage to Israel.

12) Can the issue of Iran be resolved through diplomacy, or are we at the point where military strikes are necessary? If strikes are needed, should they come from Israel or America?

No. Almost. America.

13) Do you support coercive interrogation techniques? If so, is there a specific example where they have been proven to work?

Generally speaking, violent coercion in interrogations isn't productive. But there are always exceptions. The master interrogators I've known much prefer a methodical, non-violent approach that plays to the captive's ego. But sometimes you don't have months. And—while I do NOT condone torture as normative behavior, if it could keep Americans alive, I'm not sure I'd stop at any means. I'm ultimately more concerned about the human rights of the innocent than I am about the rights of terrorists (the left takes the opposite view).

14) Should Guantanamo Bay stay open? If not, what should we do with the detainees?

Yes. Period.

15) Without delving into your personal life, what would you want Americans to know about Ralph Peters the person? One hundred years from now, what

would you want people to remember about you, and what would you hope the history books say about you?

I would just like them to know that I have never knowingly written or said a false word when speaking to the American people. As I said at the outset, I may be wrong, but, if so, I'm honestly wrong. I believe that integrity is a fundamental value—and that, if a person has the privilege to speak to his or her fellow Americans through the media, he or she has the obligation to be honest. No excuses. As for how I'd like people to remember me one hundred years from now, my vanity isn't that great. I want to continue to live a good life; thereafter, it's in God's hands. Rather than remembering me, I want future generations to remember that, despite a national crisis of convictions in the early twenty-first century, Americans came through, made the right decisions, and continued to lead the world toward freedom and human dignity.

I would like to thank Colonel Peters for his time, and more importantly, for his service. He is too humble to say it, so I will say it for him. He is a great man.

I wish Colonel Peters well always, and eagerly await his next analytical report.

The only thing left to say is what all Americans and freedom loving people world wide should say to him.

Thank you Colonel Peters. Thank you, and welcome home.

eric

We Are At War...Torture Early, Often and Repeatedly

Many people claim to be against torture. When pressing many of these people on specifics, they respond with the nonsensical notion that torture is torture, period, and that it is always wrong. Liberals get indignant for being portrayed as Kumbaya-loving, hand-holding jellyfish who wish to take al-Qaeda operatives and send them to bed without supper (no dessert anyway). Their stubborn refusal to consider torture methods allows them to be defined as weak. Rather than lump all torture together, looking at various methods provides for a more complex issue than meets the eye.

There are people who practice beheading, thumbscrews, ratchet sets across the testicles, burning people with cigarettes, and throwing acid on faces. These people are al-Qaeda. They do this. We do not. I have yet to meet an American that advocates this. Yet not every form of coercive interrogation, or even real torture, should be out of bounds. Even beating somebody with a whip (Ironically, dominatrixes make a good living. How can something be too tough on terrorists when business executives pay to receive such treatment?) could be appropriate.

Sleep deprivation—if this is illegal, college campuses should be shut down. Any student trying to get through final exams has put through all-nighters. Manuel Noriega was brought down in Panama through blaring rock music from groups such as Def Leppard (had it been Barbra Streisand I would have cracked in five minutes). While children have been torturing their parents by listening to everything from gangsta rap to hard rock, at no point has loud music been considered too cruel to deal with al-Qaeda.

Altering the room temperature—Whether making it ice cold or uncomfortably warm, terrorists are not entitled to a room temperature room containing a fridge stocked with miniatures. They are supposed to be uncomfortable. If this is out of bounds, then Vince Lombardi should have been jailed for coaching in the Ice Bowl in 1967. The Green Bay Packers and Dallas Cowboys survived the cold. Cave dwellers like Osama can cope.

Forcing terrorists to stand up in uncomfortable positions—Has anyone ever worked as a bank teller? Wells Fargo initially did not give their bank tellers chairs. They stood for hours on end. Where does it say that Al Zawahiri or Zarquai or Saddam Hussein must have a Sharper Image massage chair? Maybe we should fluff their pillows as well.

Waterboarding—This is not to be confused with motorboarding, which is one of the world's great pleasures (when a guy places his face in a woman's yummy bouncies). Waterboarding is when terrorists are made to feel as if they are drowning. They do not actually drown. They merely gasp for air when submerged. It scares them. That is the point. They are supposed to be scared.

Deporting them to less "civilized" nations–This option is fabulous. Liberals are constantly carping (again, redundant) that America tries to impose its will on other nations. We should back off and let other nations govern as they see fit. If we capture an al-Qaeda leader in Pakistan, we should turn him over to the Pakistani authorities (although we should stay outside the prison door as observers). What if Pakistani authorities plan to use severe interrogation techniques such as shooting bad guys in the legs and arms? Oh well. It is not our place to tell them how to run their judicial system. If liberals would feel better with us offering statements of horror at how barbaric this other nation is behaving, we can wave our finger at them and yell "shame, shame," before taking their leaders out for steaks and drinks.

Some would argue that we cannot sink to the level of the terrorists. Not only can we...we must. Being noble and murdered is a less desirable outcome than getting our hands dirty but being alive.

When I was fourteen, I thought my dad was torturing me when he grounded me, no television for a week. Being forced to get up at 5:00 AM can be torture for some. If our enemies were fourteen-year-old stockbrokers in Los Angeles, both of these techniques would win the War on Terror. If Osama was eight years old, we could run our nails on a chalkboard and then send him to the principal's office.

Adult issues require adult methods of communication. Liberals see torture as the methods that al-Qaeda uses. The solution is semantics. People against gay marriage often support civil unions, which is basically saying "I will give you everything you want provided you call it a different word." Some people are tortured by the word torture. We should engage in coerced interrogation, but not call it torture. Then the only thing that we will be torturing is the English language.

I am more concerned with winning the struggle of civilization vs. barbarism than winning the war of linguistics and semantics. The answer is pure, unadulterated torture. Terrorists should be tortured early, often and repeatedly. If they don't like it, they can simply stop being terrorists. Asking them to stop nicely is not working.

Abu Gharaib was behavior found at college fraternities. It is called "Rush Week," also known as "Pledge Week." Guantanamo Bay is Tampa Bay without football. Haditha was hijinks. Al-Qaeda beheads people. We should not lose an ounce of sleep over denying them a peaceful night's sleep. The war ends when we crack the torture whip, and they just crack. We should do this now, before there is no one left on our side to stop them.

eric

Chapter 15:
Religious Leftist Jihadist Violence

Dealing with Islamofascists is easy. You kill them. Dealing with leftists is tougher. It is tempting to want to waterboard environmentalists, animal rights zealots, and other perpetually aggrieved activists. The Constitution that they are helping undermine allows them to be as defective as they are. A right to live does not give them a right to live unchallenged. Every time they open their mouths, they need to be silenced with piercing logic and swift reasoning. If that does not work, use their tactics against them. Humiliate them in the town square until they are afraid to leave their homes for fear of being ridiculed. Do it legally, since they have access to leftist and jihadist-loving attorneys.

Al-Qaeda vs. Al Gore

Mr. Alex Trebek said the following words: Iowa, New Hampshire, Al Gore, and Britney Spears.

I raised my hand and asked, "Alex, what are things that nobody in their right mind should care about, and are not worth any media coverage?"

To quote Paul Simon, (the singer, not the late senator), "If I can call you Betty, you can call me Al."[109] The only pair of Als who irritate me more than Al Sharpton are al-Qaeda and Al Gore. Compare for yourselves.

Al-Qaeda: Power obsessed individuals who want to destroy the world.

Al Gore: Power obsessed individual who wants to convince Americans that they are destroying the world so policies can be enacted that will destroy the world economy.

Al-Qaeda: Shave their beards to avoid being captured by U.S. Forces.

Al Gore: Shaved his beard to remain politically viable.

Al-Qaeda: Hates Republicans and President Bush, earning a runner-up position as Time Magazine's Person of the Year. He was denied the top position solely due to fear of people canceling their subscriptions.

Al Gore: Hates Republicans and President Bush, earning a runner-up position as Time Magazine's Person of the Year. He was denied the top position solely due to fear of people canceling their subscriptions.

Al-Qaeda: The people who knew them best and initially supported them eventually turned against them, as the surge worked and Sunni Muslims got tired of being murdered.

Al Gore: The people who knew him best and initially supported him turned against him, as a surge of Tennessee votes for George W. Bush cost Al Gore his home state and the election.

Al-Qaeda: Refers to America as the Great Satan, and blames America and President Bush for all the evil in the world.

Al Gore: Blames America for destroying the environment, and maniacally screamed that President Bush betrayed his country.

Al-Qaeda: Tried to overthrow a fledgling democracy in Iraq by any means necessary, with ten thousand suicide bombers.

Al Gore: Tried to overturn an election in an established democracy by any means necessary, with ten thousand lawyers.

Al-Qaeda: Bin Laden's own family has distanced themselves from him.

Al Gore: His former boss President Clinton has distanced himself from him.

Al-Qaeda: Recruits suicide bombers over the Internet.

Al Gore: Invented the Internet.

Al-Qaeda: Against waterboarding.

Al Gore: Against waterboarding.

Al-Qaeda: Uses murderers such as Khalid Sheik Mohammed to intimidate others to drop their opposition to him.

Al Gore: Used murderer Willie Horton to intimidate Michael Dukakis to try and remove him as political opposition.

Al-Qaeda: Trying to establish a society with one religion, where we bow down to the Islamic Caliphate.

Al Gore: Trying to establish a society with one religion, where we bow down to the Earth Goddess Gaea.

Al-Qaeda: Failed to prevent the 2004 election win by George W. Bush. Bin Laden had almost no influence in 2008 despite his insisting otherwise. He is sliding into irrelevance.

Al Gore: Failed to prevent the 2000 election win by George W. Bush. Gore had almost no influence in 2008 despite his insisting otherwise. He is sliding into irrelevance.

Al-Qaeda: Lampooned brilliantly on *South Park*. Terrorists hijacked our imagination, and Osama has fartypants.[110]

Al Gore: Lampooned brilliantly on *South Park*. Terrorists hijacked our imagination, and the search for ManBearPig.[111]

Al-Qaeda: Osama speaks in a tongue only Arab terrorists can understand. Normal Americans tune him out and find him grating.

Al Gore: Speaks in a tongue only liberal elitist snobs can understand. Normal Americans tune him out and find him grating.

Al-Qaeda: Bill Clinton helped elevate them to power by doing nothing to stop them.

Al Gore: Bill Clinton helped elevate him to power by rescuing him from the ash heap of failed presidential candidates.

Al-Qaeda: Worth hundreds of millions of dollars while railing against American capitalism, through drug-running, gunrunning, prostitution, and gambling. Bin Laden initially inherited the money from dad.

Al Gore: Worth hundreds of millions of dollars while railing against American capitalism, mainly through gambling in Google stock. Junior initially inherited the money from dad.

Al-Qaeda: Blows up airplanes, wants to disrupt the world supply of oil.

Al Gore: Flies on private jets, eating up fuel and jacking up the price of oil.

Al-Qaeda: Will be with us forever. They refuse to go away.

Al Gore: Will be with us forever. He refuses to go away.

Al-Qaeda: Like most terrorists, can be brought to their knees with America staying on offense in the War on Terror.

Al Gore: Like most liberals, can be brought to his knees with a phone call from Al Sharpton or Jesse Jackson.

Al-Qaeda: If only General David Petraeus had stayed home and wrote books.

Al Gore: If only Hillary Clinton had stayed home and baked cookies.

Al-Qaeda: Wants to destroy all Jews including Weird Al Yankovic.

Al Gore: Destroyed Weird Al Yankovic on MTV's *Celebrity Deathmatch*.[112]

Life is momentarily peaceful, but we cannot be complacent. At this very minute, al-Qaeda and Al Gore are plotting to get our attention and dominate our news cycles.

eric

Climatological Criminality

The climate may or may not be warming, but the most ardent global warming proponents are doing a slow burn themselves.

The planet may or may not be warming, but several scientists are seeing their careers, theories, and everything they claim to believe in go up in flames.

There is plenty to say about what appears to be climatological criminality. What chaps my hide (global warming does that, but so does Mistress Evil) is that this reverberates beyond anything having to do with environmental issues.

This reminds me of Alex P. Keaton, played by Michael J. Fox on *Family Ties*.

(Stick with me, I will eventually get there.)

While I developed my politics from my parents, Alex P. Keaton made Republicanism cool. More importantly to me, I think that show made me at age eight want to be a stockbroker. If there is another explanation, I can't find one. Nobody in my family knew or talked about finance or the stock market. That character was who I idolized as a boy. One particular episode stands out. I had not thought about it in twenty years, but I wish I could go watch it again.

Alex was in line for a very prestigious award. His professor was going to publish a brilliant paper. As the understudy, Alex would reap some benefits. Days before the ceremony, Alex was up at 3:00 AM frantically banging away on his calculator. His parents wanted to know what was wrong. He looked at them and said, "The numbers don't add up."[113]

He calculated several times, but the entire paper the professor was going to submit was based upon assumptions that were wrong. Everything was wrong.

In one of the funniest scenes, his parents asked him if maybe he had simply added the numbers wrong himself. He gave them a look that I have given my parents on occasion. I am a stockbrokerage professional. They are retired schoolteachers. His parents then realized that in Alexworld, Alex is never wrong. The numbers did not add up.

Alex told this to his professor. After Alex left his office, the white-haired professor made a phone call, happily letting others know that everything was fine and that he looked forward to the ceremony.

When Alex learned about this, he confronted his professor. The professor explained what it was like to be old, at the end of your career, and feeling like none of it matters. In the middle of the ceremony, the professor breaks down, and does the right thing. He says, "I was willing to submit a fraudulent paper to keep my job."[114] He spoke about how he did not want to become a dinosaur, and how he would rather have his integrity than any award.

The climate scandal is not just about environmentalism. It is about every step we take, every action we engage in, and every consequence and subsequent reaction that emanates from the original information we process.

We go to the doctor, and take for granted that the doctor has our best interests at heart. The doctor gives us a pill or a spray. What if the drug company called their study of the pill a double-blind test when the truth is it was not so? What if the doctor is given commissions for recommending a certain amount of a drug?

We buy a stock after reading "reports," and paying attention to analysts who do "research." How can we do this when companies "manage earnings," and "massage the numbers?" How can we know that the Chinese Walls set up were not broken? Are the investment bankers putting pressure on the analysts? Are the accounting practices honest?

We hear that a president lied to get us into a war. Why are people so cynical? In the 1960s, LBJ did this. He deliberately lied to congress so he could escalate Vietnam. People have not trusted their government since. Nobody gets the benefit of the doubt.

Politicians say they are there for the public trust. Then many of them commit adultery and lie about it. This corrodes our souls, as hysterical accusations are given credence.

Airlines want us to trust that everything is safe. Then we find drunken pilots, mechanical problems, and other avoidable issues that can be fatal.

This is so much more than environmentalism.

Some will say that the scientists in the current scandal acted with deliberate malice. I am going to be perhaps more charitable than I should be, knowing that they would not be that generous with me.

I am putting myself in their shoes.

As a stock trader, I spent time doing research. The boss would then look at his traders and remind us of a very simple credo.

"Do what the stock tells you to do."

This means reading the ticker tape and watching. It also means being neutral. If one comes in thinking that the news means that the stock "has to" go up or down, the trader will look for signs that confirm the original bias and discount contrary evidence. This leads to losing. As a rookie trader I remember trying to tell the stock what to do. It "can't possibly" go any higher or lower. Yet it can.

The thing a trader must do is realize that they can, and often will be, wrong. The best traders are wrong 80-90 percent of the time. They realize this quickly. The 10-20 percent of the time they are right, it compensates.[115]

Now picture something much more serious than trading stocks. Try curing cancer.

You sacrifice your social life to get a 4.0 GPA so you can get into the best school. You spend over a decade in medical school and residency. You put in what seems like twenty-hour days for the right to be a glorified lab rat.

You spend years in the lab, and then it happens. You find the cure. You picture a world of fame, fortune, hot assistants, and a larger lab. You win awards and are universally praised. Oprah interviews you.

Then one day you find out that you were wrong. You were wrong in a way that can kill people, like NASA being off by a fraction of something smaller than an Amoeba's little kid. Instead of being blatantly wrong, in another scenario you might still be right with a statistically small chance that you might be wrong.

So what happens?

You look people in the eye, and tell the entire scientific community, "I might be wrong. More testing is needed."

You don't let people keep believing something that may not be right.

I am not an expert on climate issues. I wrote a column awhile back entitled "Are the Greeniacs Wrong?"

It was a question, not a statement of certitude. I am not a "denier." I am simply Socratic.

Some will argue that despite the scandal, the theory of global warming could be true.

"Could be" is not good enough.

The climatologists were willing to do anything to preserve their reputations. Now look at them. Their reputations are shattered. The public backlash is under way.

While this could have been a deliberate conspiracy, it was more likely the same thing that destroyed LBJ. It is called "escalation of commitment."

People "double down" at the Blackjack table. Stock traders stubbornly refuse to face the changing market conditions because ego gets in the way of accepting being wrong and cutting losses.

Another television show featured a police officer who accidentally killed an innocent man. Defiant for most of the show, he screams at his partner, "The man was guilty." When the partner asks why, he responds, "Because I killed him."[116] Then he goes behind a tree and cries, realizing that he made a horrendous and irreversible but honest tragic mistake.

The scientists at the heart of the climatological scandal need to stop lashing out. They need to stop closing ranks. They need to get out in front of this, and say what they will do to improve their procedures.

They can start by having anybody who destroyed evidence be fired. Then an independent investigator should be allowed to find out how dissenting opinions were suppressed.

People no longer trust newspapers. At this rate, medical journals will be discredited.

The scientists need to decide if they care more about getting to the truth or saving their bacon.

Is this about science or adulation?

I don't know about climate change. I do know that those who are right do not need to resort to such behind-the-scenes machinations. Certitude makes open disclosure easy.

It has been a long time since Alex P. Keaton was on television. It has been a long time since people believed that those they trusted would do the right thing.

That is the real criminal shame of this. "Experts" went to Copenhagen to double down. They are still making statements. This will not stop the swirling questions.

It is not about being right. It is about doing right.

eric

Radical Gays Are Aggressors, Not Victims

Radical gays need to get back in the closet. Then the closet needs to be locked. Then the room needs to either be flooded with water or set ablaze.

(Fine, I do not want to take it that far. Yeah, the hyperbole train went off the track. Yeah, I am deliberately provoking those that deserve it. No, I don't want God to strike them down. I just wish he would give them laryngitis.)

Either way, I never want to hear from another radical gay lunatic ever again.

I supported gay rights and civil unions. I was neutral on gay marriage, vowing to follow the law, whatever the eventual decision.

That is not enough for radical gays. They will not be satisfied until they successfully terrorize every person that disagrees with them. Their bigotry is hurting non-radical gay Americans who do wish to coexist.

All bigotry is wrong. Being the victim of past bigotry does not excuse current bigotry, whether it be reverse racism, reverse sexism, or reverse sexuality.

Radical gays celebrated when Dr. Laura Schlessinger had her television show canceled before it began. All Dr. Laura ever did was express disagreement with gay marriage. She passed no laws.

Now the radical gay community has affected the Miss USA Pageant.

Miss USA was supposed to be a beauty contest. Then they added stupid talent contests as political correctness increased and ratings nosedived. Then overt politics was interjected.

Perez Hilton, who is basically famous for being gay and obnoxious, decided to ask Miss California Carrie Prejean what her views were on gay marriage. Miss California stated that she was against it.

Why the heck was this question asked? What does gay marriage have to do with being Miss America?

Miss California's answer may have cost her the crown. Perez Hilton smugly seems to think so.

I want to know why this question was asked. Why was Perez Hilton, an untraditional person to say the least, allowed anywhere near a traditional forum in a speaking role?

This was thuggery, not equal rights or tolerance. This was the verbal equivalent of what was done to Matthew Shepherd. Miss California was ambushed and savagely beaten.

I was neutral on gay marriage. No more.

The agents of intolerance are not those against gay marriage. 70 percent of black Americans and an almost equal number of Hispanic Americans in California would be intolerant, and we know that minorities are always tolerant.

The bigots are the radical gays.

I have friends who are Log Cabin Republicans. They are embarrassed by liberal gays.

The intolerance is not even an accurate reflection of all gays. It is a completely accurate reflection of liberals.

This is why I claim that liberals spread ideological bigotry. They just cannot stop the hate. They are diseased.

The next time somebody supporting gay marriage preaches to me about tolerance and equality, I will tell them that until radical gay America stops trying to bully innocent people for feeling and thinking differently, they will not get my support.

U.S. Supreme Court Justice Antonin Scalia is not a bigot. Congressman Barney Frank is a bigot.

When anybody questions Barney Frank for being corrupt, he plays the gay card. Ask him about why he let his boyfriend run a prostitution ring out of his home. Ask him why he let another boyfriend run drugs out of his apartment. Ask him why he was one of the leading culprits behind the 2008 financial crisis. Ask him why he had a sexual relationship with an employee of a company that his committee was supposed to be regulating (Has any relationship he ever had been non-criminal?).

Then expect to be called a bigot.

Governor Jim McGreevey was not fired for being gay. He was fired for being corrupt. The only person who used his sexuality as a weapon was McGreevey himself.

If the gay community wants to blame innocent people for their problems, then perhaps everyday Americans should just stop putting up with the abuse.

The next time I am presented with a leaflet from a gay marriage supporter, I will set it on fire right in front of them.

I have utter contempt for these bigots.

They have civil rights. They are not victims. They are aggressors.

Aggressors are bullies. Bullies need to be decked between the eyes.

Call me intolerant. I don't care.

I will side with whoever wants them to shut up.

Unless the gay community, outside of the Log Cabin Republicans, condemns Perez Hilton, then they are just as culpable.

They should also condemn him for calling Miss California a "dumb b*tch."

No Mr. Hilton. You are a dumb b*tch and a bigot.

Until the gay community condemns this bigotry, my advice to the gay community comes with even more anger than when they tried to declare "gay day" and skip work.

Gay America needs to do what straight America has been doing for years.

Gay America needs to shut up. Just shut up. For the love of God, shut up.

I want gays and straight people to be treated equally. Straight people shut up and go to work. Gay people should do the same. People wanting to be treated equally need to act equally.

Otherwise, I will be happy to take up the cause of gay rights. I will break my neutral stance. I will join the gay marriage opponents.

After all, somebody has to stand up for the innocent victims of ideological bigotry.

eric

The Animals Had It Coming

I have never accused activists of being guilty of logical reasoning or thoughtfulness. They value trees, mosquitoes and dirt more than human beings. At some point the hyperbole train needs to avoid going off the rails.

For liberal activists, being off the rails is a way of life. They evoke the Holocaust when Colonel Sanders kills a chicken. They evoke the pain of slavery when a bunny rabbit becomes Hossenfeffer (to quote my favorite Bugs Bunny cartoon). Chanting, "Meat is murder," they truly can compare Jeffrey Dahmer with the woman taking her children to McDonalds. The way those bloodthirsty children play on the slide after devouring a dead cow is just sinister. They are future killers in waiting.

Rather than try and teach a pig to sing, which wastes time and annoys the pig, it is easy to use these "lacktivists (activists usually lack everything normal people possess)" as a foil to entertain normal people. Lacktivists tend to be intolerant. In some cases they are lactose intolerant, but Jewish law prohibits mixing milk and meat, so I will leave milk out of this discussion.

Denis Leary crystallizes it perfectly when he claims, "We only want to save the cute animals." Here is a segment from his routine.

"What are you?"

"I'm an otter."

"What do you do?"

"I swim on my back and do cute things in the water."

"You're free to go."

"And you, what do you do?"

"I'm a cow."

"Get in the truck!"

"But I'm an animal."

"You're a baseball glove, get in the truck!"[117]

I encountered one lacktivist on Michelle Malkin's Web site. I redacted their name for privacy and part of the screed itself for length and coherence without altering the context.

"I am also a longtime member of PETA and been veg for about 22 years. I think refraining from eating meat is a noble act. It takes thoughtfulness, restraint and discernment. It means you have standards. It's not the only noble act we can do in this world, but it's a significant one. Meat eating is destructive on many levels, not only to animals themselves but to humans as well. If you want to eat meat, fine, do it, but don't embarrass yourself by putting down others who actually have a higher standard than you. It only shows your insecurity (can you say 'tallest poppy?'). Most of all, those who care about this are *thinkers*. I just read a study that said vegetarians, as a whole, have a higher Intelligence than the general population. Go ahead and Google it…and find out for yourselves. It just means you care about the horrible suffering of innocent animals at our hands. Caring about animal suffering is sweet, noble, and kind. These are ideals that conservatives should, at least theoretically, embrace and admire."

I should return my advanced degree, since apparently my eating meat means I am too stupid to grasp concepts that enlightened lacktivists can understand. I did not go to a Poison Ivy League school, so I thought my degree was worth something. I feel a little levity is best when dealing with lacktivists. I contemplated a burger and then responded.

"Who says these animals are innocent? I have it on good authority by a well respected anonymous moral authority that many of these animals had it coming. Their parents were awful animals, and their kids would have been awful animals.

I know I am right because the anonymous study I cite is beyond reproach, because it agrees with me, which confirms I am right.

Hail to the lord of circular logicians everywhere!

Time for Monday Night Football and a burger."

Apparently humor is lost on lacktivists. I suspect we could make the left and the right environmentally happy if we could just remove the wooden sticks that lacktivists have up their rumpuses. The right would be pleased that leftists would be less self-righteous. The left would be happy to find another tree. Perhaps the proctologists and environmentalists can unite to work on this. Until then, the lacktivist missed my point.

"Vegetarianism and, even better, veganism is a higher choice *morally* and *ethically* because it takes into account the effects meat eating has on animals and the planet. Blackty Grrrrr the animals that have to live in factory farms and face a gruesome end in the slaughterhouse certainly didn't ask for it. They did nothing but were found in hapless circumstances. I can't believe you said such a thing…I've never, in all my years of arguing this issue, have I heard *anyone* say that animals deserve such abuse and had it 'coming to them'. Just proves that we humans will and can rationalize almost any habit, no matter how little substance we can give for it."

I can't make this stuff up. Liberal lacktivists are the gift that keeps on giving. I offered one last response.

"You may or may not be the only person on this site who did not realize I was kidding. Reread what I wrote above.

Personally I have nothing against animals. Dogs can't raise my taxes. Felines can't block traffic with protests about nonsense. Iguanas can't screw up public schools.

Liberals mess up society more than animals ever could, which is why I rooted for the Cincinnati Bengals to defeat the New England Patriots on Monday Night Football.

Unfortunately, humans, even liberals, are superior to animals, even tigers... Patriots 34, Bengals 13. The Pats ate the Bengals for dinner! Somebody call PETA now! It wouldn't be the first time this year they harassed the NFL, but I won't go there."

Let me explain it to the lacktivists one last time.

Lacktivists...nobody likes you. You talk to each other. The rest of the normal American population wants to get to their car without being burdened with leaflets. It is not your cause that bothers us as much as the leaflets. Attending peace rallies and engaging in violent shouting matches defies sanity. Trying to destroy the global economy for a greater good is nuts. Criticizing terrorists for eating meat would be great if you also criticized them for killing innocent human beings. Lastly, just because Adolf Hitler was a vegetarian does not mitigate other bad things he did.

How I live my life is my business, but I grew up around wild kingdom. I had dogs, cats, birds, iguanas, and fish. I loved them all. I miss them all.

They are in heaven, where they are enjoying peace and quiet. A world without lacktivists...of course it is peaceful.

I just need to relax and enjoy my own peace and quiet, in a place where humans reign supreme and animals have no say. I will have a burger for dinner while watching another animal slaughter on television.

What kind of human being takes joy in watching animal slaughters? I do.

The Dallas Cowboys will eat up the Buffalo Bills. Let the lacktivists protest all they want. Barring an upset, a good old-fashioned rodeo steer roping... excuse me, bison roping...will round out the day.

Besides, if one day I am wrong, I will stand before God and sing, "I'm just a soul whose intentions are good. Oh lord, please don't let me be misunderstood."[118]

That 1960s song was done by…you guessed it…The Animals.

eric

Quarantine the Mentally Ill

Every once in awhile I need to light myself on fire.

I need to take the bullets, slings and arrows so that other people can breathe easier.

I need to say things that need to be said. You know that many of you are thinking it. I am going to say it and face the wrath and consequences.

Mentally ill people need to be quarantined.

Drug them up. Lock them up. For the love of God, just shut them up.

I am a compassionless, heartless b@stard. So what? When mentally ill people are not around, I have something that is more priceless than platinum. I have peace of mind.

I was not born with this hostility. It has taken a lifetime for me to want to take these people and rip their tongues out so that they cannot utter another bat spit crazy word.

I was not born wanting to hack their hands off so they could never send another angry text message at 4:00 AM.

I was not born wanting to be a vigilante because these mental lunatics have lawyers who want to trumpet their causes. They sue because they are angry about something, even if they are not sure exactly what and why.

As a productive worker, I have seen truly deranged people force my firm to spend legal bills defending junk lawsuits while refusing to say exactly what they want. Even al-Qaeda has a list of actual demands.

Legal Aid lawyers take these cases. Thousands of dollars later my firm still has no idea exactly why the other side is angry. They have doctor's notices. This has nothing to do with us.

Even when they do not sue, they call in and complain. One woman screamed at me for ten minutes because her husband was cheating on her. She did mention her "condition." Finally I had to ask her exactly what that had to do with our company.

Apparently we randomly cold-called him. She was checking all of his messages to see who was on his cell phone. I finally convinced this nutcase woman that we had never met, spoken to, or done business with him. I will never get those minutes of my life back.

It is not just work. One woman I went to college with blew up at me as I was planning her birthday party. She had just seen the movie "Thelma and

Louise," and it put her in an angry mood toward men. She had "issues." I was in the wrong place at the wrong time.

Eighteen years later, this woman sent me hate mail because she did not like one of my columns. That hate mail became an entire column in itself. She threatened to sue me if I published it, even though I told her the names would be redacted. Needless to say, her language was as uncivil as her brain was fried. Of course I published the rantings.

These are not aberrations. Some people are just certifiable.

An ex-girlfriend of mine was very troubled. When I say troubled, I mean unstable. When I quickly broke it off, the hostile phone calls kept coming. I had to call her mother, who apologized for her daughter's behavior, and promised to make her cease. She did.

All of these nutcases were women. Men get no exemption.

Twice in my life, I have had roommates that were simply not mentally all there. They hid it well in the beginning.

They would fly into rages over politics, especially when failing to take their medication.

Every one of these people mentioned was hard left politically.

I did not start these political conversations. I would be watching television, minding my own business, and they would start yelling. You cannot win an argument with a lunatic. You have to wait until they burn themselves out. It is truly like being subjected to domestic terrorism.

I am not implying that being a liberal makes one mentally ill. I am sure there are non-liberals who have mental illnesses. I have just been lucky enough to not meet them.

I will at some point try to analyze why the correlation between mental illness and far leftism is so strong, but not now. My suspicion is that leftism teaches people to rail against perceived injustices. Easily susceptible people then consider every possible real or imaginary slight to be an injustice. They become crusaders. Railing against the rich and the powerful is just an extension of railing at random inanimate objects on the street.

My analysis is not environmentally scientific, meaning it has credibility. Anyway, back to the crazies.

Two members of my family are mentally ill.

The good news for me is that neither one of them are my mother or father. The bad news is that my parents want me to be more "compassionate."

No. I am done. I gave at the office. Repeatedly.

I am tired of being let down. I am tired of having to tolerate bad behavior. I am tired of being told that these people are "not well," and that "they can't help what they do."

Yes they can. They can check themselves into treatment centers. If they won't, then their caretakers should forcibly enter them.

Some say the law will not allow this. The law needs to be fixed. Do we have to wait until these people boil a bunny rabbit or kill a productive human being before we realize that something should have been done? The Son of Sam may have been a lovely child. If a dog is telling him to kill people, either shoot the dog for telling him to do it, or get rid of him for listening!

Some say that a major problem in this society is that we do not give mental illness the same respect that we give physical illnesses. There is a major difference.

Nobody used cancer or heart disease as an excuse to make my life miserable. The physically ill do not drag down healthy people.

Mentally ill people are a threat to the very survival of people who have a chance at success and normalcy.

I experienced years of trying to love "sick" relatives only to be violated repeatedly.

I cannot be pulled out of a business meeting where serious issues are on the line because somebody is having a breakdown and crying because that is what they do.

My parents have told me to turn my phone off. No. I leave it on in case of an emergency.

This gets to the heart of what I freely admit is rage toward these people. It is not the normal people that should be forced to adapt. It is so easy to tell productive and sane people, "Just change so the behavior of ill people will not interfere."

I don't have to change. The people screaming at inanimate objects need to change.

"They can't help who and how they are."

That does not mean I have to tolerate these people. Get them away from me.

One day I plan to have kids. I cannot endanger my family. Safety comes first.

What if one day I gave birth to a mentally ill child?

I would be crushed, angry, bitter, and would still love my child. I would not let them be unleashed on society to wreak havoc. I would get them the appropriate treatment.

Those who are responsible for mentally ill people, be it their parents or their government, must force these people into getting better. If a parent of a mentally ill teenager does not get them treatment, and the mentally ill teenager goes and kills somebody, the parents should be arrested immediately.

"You can't try the parents. They have suffered enough."

No. The people who had their family member killed by a lunatic are the ones who suffered. The parents enabled this. Behind every act of violence by one of these monsters is a person or people who did nothing to stop it, preferring excuses over corrective actions.

Don't be fooled by feel-good Hollywood garbage. In real life Forrest Gump is not charming. He is not a hero. He is a babbling psychopath that most likely is wielding a knife while yelling about "The eye of the dog of the drum of the morlock of the power broker of the king of Henry the Eighth I am!"

I have the right to life, liberty, and the pursuit of happiness.

I have a right to walk down the street safely. I have the right to watch television without being verbally assaulted. I have the right to get through a business meeting without "emergencies" that are not actual emergencies getting in the way. I have the right to not be inundated with text messages at 4:00 AM.

I have the right to not have to deplete my savings because others who failed in their financial obligations will continue to fail forever and ever. A 0 percent success rate is a pretty reliable statistic to predict future failures.

I have the right to be left the heck alone.

I really don't care how many people get hurt by these words.

Call me every name in the book, but I honor my responsibilities.

When you have pets that are wild and out of control, you get them spayed or neutered. If people are willing to get their animals treated so that society does not suffer, then surely people deserve no less.

Drug them up. Lock them up. Do what it takes. Just shut them up.

If we don't do this, we will all eventually be driven to that level of insanity. Nobody will be left to produce.

If any one of us sane people snaps and kill one of them, we can always just claim we are crazy and be absolved of all responsibility.

It works for both of my relatives. They attack everybody and answer to nobody.

I am done trying to help people who only hurt others. I would be willing to stick them in Guantanamo Bay before it gets shut down for good. Maybe they can make the al-Qaeda crazies even crazier. It would be interesting to see who surrenders at that point.

Mentally ill people turn into verbal terrorists. They become verbal (unless they cross over into actual) suicide bombers. The only solution is to break them in half. Indulging them does not work. Enabling them emboldens them.

Like other terrorists, the solution is force.

I pray that the various people I have cited, including my relatives, get forcibly dragged into appropriate treatment facilities. I hope they get drugged against their will until they stop being threatening.

I have the right to live in peace and tranquility.

Until the streets are cleared from these dangerous people, none of us are safe.

"They can't help it."

Well make them help it.

I can't help it anymore. I shouldn't have to help it. I gave at the office. Then they interrupted a critical meeting and demanded that I give even more.

It's them or me. It sure as hell won't be me. I worked too d@mn hard.

eric

Chapter 16:
Rancher Violence

Batman had his cave. Ronald Reagan and George W. Bush had their ranches. While a bunch of spoiled ungrateful brats carped and complained, they went about their business, did their jobs, and saved the world. I spend very little time praising Ronald Reagan because such praise is universal. Everybody loves the man, as they should. George W. Bush has not been given his due, and it is high time people start getting it. In college he branded a guy. Then he went to Iraq and did everything but brand a "W" on Saddam's @ss. Now the only branding required is the marketing kind. For those who love freedom, the George W. Bush brand is as great as ever. Those who disagree can go crawl into the spider hole where we found Saddam and stay there until the adults are done handling the business of keeping us alive.

Liberty is Life

Pop singer Prince was off by ten years. The Germans partied like it was 1989.

Included in the festivities was the German rock band "the Scorpions."

Their song "Wind of Change" was specifically dedicated to the fall of the Berlin Wall.

"The world is closing in/but did you ever think/that we could be so close/ like brothers."[119]

In a world where much has gone mad and wrong, this was a celebration of everything decent and right with this world.

Ronald Reagan told Mr. Gorbachev to "Tear down this wall."[120]

For those who need to be reminded of what can happen when true greatness dares to dream, go read President Reagan's entire remarks.

Twenty years ago the Berlin Wall came down.

Within months, millions of people who had been living in captivity were given the God-given gifts of freedom and liberty.

Some have said that without love, there is no life.

Perhaps. Without liberty, there is nothing at all.

While we rightly celebrate Ronald Reagan's greatness, the best way we can honor his memory is by continuing what he started.

Some say that George W. Bush was evil. Others say he was well-intentioned but wrong.

I loudly stand up and say that he was…and still is…right.

He is right because liberty is right. It is right morally, politically, and strategically.

Strategically we know that free nations do not attack each other. Nations basking in liberty do not bomb each other or kill innocent civilians. Never in history has any true democracy ever attacked another one.

Politically we know that leaders who free people from slavery and bondage are treated as heroes. Moses led the Jews out of Egypt. Nelson Mandela ended Apartheid in South Africa. Abraham Lincoln gave the Emancipation Proclamation. Ronald Reagan gave real hope to Eastern Europe. George W. Bush liberated two nations in the Middle East.

Freedom was not gained through flowery rhetoric, since neither Moses nor George W. Bush possessed the eloquence of Lincoln or Reagan. Liberty spread through noble deeds by men with noble hearts.

They did not need polls or focus groups to tell them what people in every corner of the world know.

Every human being is a creature of God. No human was meant to own another human.

We were meant to have dignity, which can only come with freedom and liberty.

It is worth dying for. Ask the survivors of Germans killed trying to cross over the wall.

Twenty years after the fall of the wall, we are at a critical moment in history.

Will we as Americans continue to fight for liberty, or will we give up?

Will we "bear any burden, pay any price?"[121]

Are we up to the challenge?

We have to be.

Millions of people world wide are standing up.

We are at our best when we stand with them. Yet we have not always stood up.

We stood down when Tiananmen Square happened. We stood down when the Kurds needed us. We initially stood down when we allowed blacks to be seen as three fifths of a human being.

Most of the time, we get it right. It just takes leadership that believes in liberty. Abraham Lincoln freed the slaves. Ronald Reagan won the Cold War. George W. Bush will one day get credit for bringing liberty to the Middle East.

Iranians are standing up. They want to be free of the mullahs. Will we stand up?

Iraqis are waving their purple-stained fingers. Will we stand up?

Afghanis hate the Taliban. They want to be free. Will we stand up?

We stood up against slavery, Communism, and Nazism. Islamofascism is not insurmountable. It will be tough, but as Ronald Reagan reminded us in his inaugural address, we are up to the challenge. He summed it up in three words.

"We are Americans."[122]

The road ahead to spread liberty will not be easy. Being American is not about doing what is easy. It is about standing tall and doing what is right.

Liberty is right.

Tyranny kills. Liberty breathes life into people.

Liberty gives people their humanity. It is every bit as vital to the human as blood, water, and plasma.

Twenty years ago Europe saw the beauty of liberty.

Middle Easterners are human beings loved by God. They deserve liberty as well.

Twenty years from now, they will love us the same way that Eastern Europeans and most Americans love and admire Ronald Reagan.

L'chaim to liberty. L'chaim to life.

eric

The Many Reasons Why I Like President Bush—A LOT!

A gentleman from Britain asked me in 2007 how anyone could possibly like President Bush, and that he did not know anyone who did. I pointed out to him that liberal Manhattan columnist Pauline Kael did not know one person in 1972 who voted for Richard Nixon, even though he won forty-nine states.[123] This British fellow watches BBC. Normally I would not bother to engage him, but he was so incredibly polite and sincere in his effort to hear a dissenting viewpoint that I felt compelled to respond. I am about promoting healthy dialogue and debate. This fellow, while being on the left, was quite reasonable. My response to him is longer than Tolstoy's War and Peace, because my reasons for liking the president a lot are numerous. Now, my ode to "The Dub."

Sir,

Although you said a mouthful, I will do my best to respond only because you come across as very thoughtful. I will not be giving you an unbiased perspective, because I am quite biased. I am a conservative, and my heroes include Ronald Reagan and Margaret Thatcher. My opinion is mine alone. You could ask other Americans, and they would disagree with me. I will do my best to answer your questions. You come across as very likable. I am happy to disagree with you while not being disagreeable.

The BBC is left-wing. So are the New York Times and MSNBC. CNN is to the left, although less so. Fox News is considered center-right, but the left likes to call it right-wing. Fox News bothers the left, but the truth is Fox News does not stifle debate. Without Fox News, there is no debate. The left has ABC, NBC, CBS, PBS, NPR, etc...The left in America is angry that the right has any voice at all. You should watch Fox News, not because they are always right, but because it is a perspective that you will never get on BBC or the others. Other fabulous sources are the *Wall Street Journal, Investors Business Daily*, the *New York Post* (NOT the *NY Times*) and *RealClearPolitics*, which links to sites on the left and right.

One funny thing about Americans is that we reserve the right to fiercely criticize our leaders, but get enraged and rally around them when others do so...especially the French. In fact, the election of 2004 came down to Ohio. Some citizens in one town in England decided to adopt one town in Ohio as their "sister city." They wrote letters to these Ohio citizens asking them to support Kerry. It backfired. This town, normally pretty centrist, voted overwhelmingly for President Bush even as their surrounding cities split evenly. They resented the foreign interference.

Here are several reasons why I like the president.

1) His economic policies are FABULOUS. The U.S. economy was good during the Clinton years, but it is even better now. Respected economist Larry Kudlow calls the U.S. economy "The Greatest story never told."[124] The war in Iraq overshadows everything, and I understand that. However, the economy right now is doing well. One main reason for this is the president's 2001 and 2003 tax cuts. I support supply-side economics, which is the heart of Reaganomics. Respectable people can disagree on whether supply-side theory works. I believe it does. The US stock market (no longer for the rich, now many small investors own stock) has never been higher, inflation is low, unemployment is low, etc. The media will not talk about this good news because good news does not sell, and Republicans are hated by the media in this country outside of Fox News.

(While the economy turned down hard in September of 2008, liberals that prayed for rain and finally got it still give Clinton high economic marks despite the fact that President Bush inherited a collapsing economy and stock market in 2000.)

2) I am Jewish. My father is a Holocaust survivor. The president is the best friend Israel has ever had. Now the BBC is almost as anti-Israel as Al Jazeera, but for anyone who cares about Israel and Jews, President Bush is fantastic. When other nations are attacked, they fight back. When Israel is attacked on a daily basis, they are told to exercise restraint. This is nonsense. George W. Bush let Ariel Sharon run wild, and I will forever be grateful for that. Diplomacy does not work with genocidal lunatics. Force is the only solution. 70-80 percent of Jews are Democrats, but that is because they tend to care more about social issues such as abortion than Israel. They are liberal first and Jewish second. Also, most Jews are secular. Secular Jews and Christians vote Democrat, religious Jews and Christians vote Republican. I am not saying Democrats are Godless, but by and large the more one goes to church/synagogue/mosque, the more one votes Republican.

3) I am an unabashed, unashamed supporter of the War on Terror, and believe the Iraq War was the right thing to do. One day I will have to answer before God, and I pray I am right. As of now, I will go to my grave believing it was and is right. To avoid spending hours on this topic alone, please read the article on my blog entitled "The Iraq War–Legally and Morally right then and now." I do not expect you to agree with me, but I break down why I feel this way point by point.

4) I like his trade policies. I believe in Free Trade, such as NAFTA and CAFTA. Isolationism and protectionism are wrong. Tariffs and quotas are

a mistake. I believe in an international global world with very few trade barriers.

5) I support the NRA. I know Europe does not like America's gun culture. In America, the areas with the strictest gun laws have the highest crime rates, and the areas with the loosest gun laws have the lowest crime rates. Gun control does not work because criminals do not obey laws. When you disarm law abiding citizens, crime goes up. President Bush understands this.

6) His choices for the U.S. Supreme Court have been superb. To me whether a justice is liberal or conservative is less important than that they are the finest legal minds. Past presidents Republican and Democrat have picked choices that were not the very best. President Bush picked Sam Alito, a very bright man. His choice for Chief Justice, John Roberts, is one of the finest legal minds in American history. Intellectually, the guy is a heavyweight, the top of the legal food chain. He did pick someone else that was seen as a lightweight, but she was not confirmed, so no harm done. He truly has helped make the Supreme Court a deliberative body of legal excellence.

When I say I could care less that the rest of the world hates us, what I mean is that a leader of America has to lead America. We cannot let the fact that other nations disagree with us force us to alter our policies. I will even take it a step further. Even if 51 percent of the people disagree with the president, he should not automatically abandon his position. Bush's critics call him stubborn, but I see him as resolute. Stubborn is when one is wrong and refuses to change. Resolute is when someone is right and refuses to change. Bill Clinton was popular because he followed popular opinion. That is not leadership.

Lastly, and this is not to make excuses, Bill Clinton was president during an inconsequential time. The Cold War had ended, and 9/11 was far away. Anybody could have led America in the 1990s. President Bush is a war president. He has made unpopular decisions. Reevaluation is acceptable, but not to the point of vacillating. I understand a lot of the world is against the Iraq War, but President Bush cannot use that as his guide. Also, France and Germany have elected conservative leaders to go along with John Howard as staunch U.S. supporters. Aznar in Spain and Berlusconi in Italy backed Bush when they were in power. I have traveled to Thailand and Singapore. They were very pro-American. Again, the BBC is not a good source in terms of unbiased news.

Anyway, I will visit your nation one day, if for no other reason than I find British women to be the hottest, classiest women in the world. If I found one who is a Tory, and Jewish, I would marry her tomorrow.

Oh, and I loved Whitesnake and Def Leppard, and Dangermouse was my favorite cartoon growing up. American football is my biggest passion, and the very first game in England will be played October 28th. I hope you enjoy it.

Be well good sir.

eric

From George W to George W

He was saddled with a controversial war that had the potential to split the country. He was roundly criticized at the time for leading America to its destruction. Any number of mistakes could have caused America to cease existing as a nation. George W was doing irreparable damage.

No, not George W. Bush…George Washington.

Happy Presidents Day. More specifically, Happy Thankless Job Day to the leader of the free world. I truly wonder why anybody would want this job.

The reason why we celebrate Presidents Day is because Americans have gotten cheated out of separate birthday holidays for George Washington and Abraham Lincoln.

George Washington was the father of his country. Yet the Revolutionary War was not popular when it started. Most Americans did not want to break away from England. After several high profile military defeats, enlistment levels were down, and morale was low. A critical battle at Saratoga in New York turned things around.

Abraham Lincoln was not universally beloved while he was alive. He was certainly not happy in his marriage to a dominating shrew who had a habit of hurling vases. If Lincoln were alive today he might be helping Mrs. Lincoln become president just so he could get the peace and quiet that eluded him while he was in office. During his presidency, he was seen as a bumbler who had incompetent generals. The eventual Union victory in the Civil War did not change the fact that many carped about why it took so long to get the right general to begin with.

I cannot recall any president who was universally loved while they were in office. There were ones that "did not harm." They presided over peaceful times, and failed to make matters worse. That assessment is often given to Calvin Coolidge in the 1920s, Dwight Eisenhower in the 1950s, and Bill Clinton in the 1990s. Some people considered these men to be peripheral. Others saw them as merely ignoring serious issues that their successors would have to deal with.

We deify men like John F. Kennedy. At the risk of slaying a sacred cow, Kennedy the myth was much more significant than Kennedy the man. He was an undistinguished senator who won an election riddled with fraud. He spoke well, but did not have any concrete achievements. He died a tragic and untimely death, and became a hero in the mold of Marilyn Monroe, and later on, Elvis Presley. While his words often did eventually ring true, such as putting a man on the moon, his actual presidency is mostly myth devoid of results.

JFK is not the only one to be lionized. Harry Truman is romanticized as an honest and sincere man, which he may have been. In office, he was seen as a bumbler.

Even presidents who truly did change the world were beleaguered while in office. Ronald Reagan won the Cold War and brought down the Berlin Wall. By the end of his second term, he had lost congress, and was mired in scandal.

It is through this lens of history that I maintain that we will not know for another three decades what will become of the Presidency of George W. Bush.

Many individuals hate his guts. They hated him before he was ever sworn in. They believe he stole a close election. They never speak likewise about their God JFK defeating Richard Nixon in 1960. That was a stolen election.

George W. Bush's detractors hated him not for his deeds, but for his existence. He is in favor of something, so his critics have to reflexively be against it.

With George W. Bush having left office, I can safely say that the opinions of him now do not matter. Today is a vacuum. Anybody can judge things in a vacuum. The only thing that matters in the long run is the judgment of history. I maintain that the history books will be kind to George W. Bush.

Everything will depend on the War on Terror, with Iraq being the central front. If Iraq succeeds, which it may be on the verge of doing, then the honorable goal of making the world a better place will have been achieved. Saddam Hussein is already dead. Slowly but surely, Iraq is on the upswing.

Some would say that if Iraq were to fail, the legacy of George W. Bush would be that of failure. This would be an overstatement. The Berlin Wall fell when George Herbert Walker Bush was president. The seeds began during the Reagan Presidency, which is why the Gipper is properly given the credit.

Lyndon Johnson actually did pass civil rights legislation. JFK is given the credit. Some say Kennedy put the idea in motion, but others say his words were lip service, and that he did not have the same passion for civil rights that his brother did.

We can dissect every aspect of George W. Bush, but the truth is that we need time to see how his deeds affect the world after he leaves office. From Chief Justice John Roberts to General David Petraeus to treasury secretaries to the next president, the George W. Bush story has not been written yet. Some

238

had it written before he took office, but those without the fancy 3-D glasses they sell at 7-11 can be open-minded enough to admit that stories take time to develop.

On Presidents Day, I can only look at George W. Bush and feel sympathy for the man. He came into office expecting to focus on economics, and history dealt him a situation that nobody is ever prepared for. Thrust into a war that nobody except the terrorists wanted, he had to be a steely-eyed leader. If he failed at this task, an American collapse would not be unthinkable.

I remember how young and vigorous George W. Bush looked in 1999. He looks much older now. War takes its toll.

George W. Bush was not destined for greatness. If anything, he was destined for mediocrity. For some reason, history thrust a situation upon him. Those who believe he met the historical challenge will see him as a great president. Those who feel he failed to answer history's call will see him as a disaster. Either way, there most likely will be no middle ground. No matter what, unlike his predecessor, he will be seen as relevant. He cannot be average. He will either be among the best, or the worst.

Some judge a president on their ability to elect their successor. Ronald Reagan was successful in this endeavor. Bill Clinton was not. George W. Bush's successor is actually Dick Cheney. If John McCain had won, would President Bush have gotten credit? Does President Bush get blame for McCain's loss?

When all is said and done, the main criteria for evaluating presidents should be whether or not they made America better.

With some presidents, evaluation is simple. Thomas Jefferson doubled the size of the country with one purchase. He was a success. By almost every possible conceivable metric, Jimmy Carter was a failure.

Most presidents are more complex.

George W. Bush is not universally beloved at this moment. He is beleaguered.

Thirty years from now, when Presidents Day includes several more presidents, we will remember that in the same way we now see critics of George W. Bush, we saw much worse way back when.

George Washington and Abraham Lincoln did just fine in the long run. In the long run, all there is, is the long run.

May Presidents Day bring us one day closer to world peace. May it bring peace of mind for George W. Bush. Everybody needs a respite from the worries of the world.

After all, presidents are people too.

eric

Dear President George W. Bush

Dear President Bush,

As you prepare for your final day in office, it almost seems unfair that you have to share it with Dr. Martin Luther King Jr. Given how incredibly gracious you are, I suspect you would let us know that you would be honored by this, so I will accept that speculated explanation.

Dr. King was a much better speaker than you. His oratory soared. Even he would admit that while powerful words matter, deeds are what count in the long run. Despite attempts by some who try to rewrite history for their own gain, I want to thank you for your many accomplishments. We could begin with everything you did to secure Dr. King's vision of a truly colorblind society.

Nobody hired as many black Americans to as many prominent positions as you did. You made Colin Powell your secretary of state. You appointed Dr. Condoleezza Rice to be your next secretary of state after a stint as your national security advisor. You hired Larry Thompson to be your deputy attorney general under John Ashcroft. Rod Paige was your secretary of education.

These people were not hired because they were black. They were hired because they deserved the jobs based on merit. You did not make token appointments. You hired good people who happened to be black. That is colorblindness.

Many people blame you for the housing crisis, which hurt black people disproportionately. What these people fail to mention was that for most of your presidency, black home ownership was at an all time high. Black Americans were a larger than average share of new homes. It would be totally statistically normal for them to get hurt in larger percentages when the economy changed. What will not ever change is that you gave them access to the American dream. It is hypocritical that some blame you for the fall while refusing to credit you for the rise.

Some will forever blame you for the perceived slow response to Hurricane Katrina. That was an unprecedented crisis. As you mentioned, nobody seems to give you the credit for the thirty thousand people rescued off of rooftops. A rap singer even stated that you did not care about black people. You were too dignified to give that the response it deserves. I will say that the claim is baseless garbage.

You looked past skin color to try and enact policies that helped all people. You did not care about the skin color of the people you helped. You considered that to be irrelevant, which is exactly what a colorblind society demands.

The left deliberately misrepresents your economy. It was not eight years of failure. Your economy was very good from 2002 through 2007. 2008 featured a spectacular collapse. That does not change the fact that for most of your presidency, the Bush economy was better than that of your predecessor. This led to the lowest levels of black unemployment in history.

Your insistence on tough crime policies was not racist. They reduced black-on-black crime. Decent black Americans, like decent non-black Americans, hate criminals. They want to feel safe. You sided with the rights of innocent victims, and not their tormentors.

Even your harshest critics now grudgingly admit that you were the best friend Africa has ever had. You committed billions of dollars to Africa to help fight AIDS, malaria, and poverty. You gave your word, and the continent of Africa knows that you kept it.

Your faith-based initiatives program was a godsend to religious institutions. Black Americans are more religious than their white counterparts. Black churches help strengthen black families in ways that governments cannot.

You were the president of all Americans. What benefits all of us will benefit black Americans. I would be remiss if I did not again thank you for helping all Americans where it mattered.

You rallied this nation after the worst attack on American soil since 1941, and perhaps ever. As you reminded us, others may have gone back to normal after 9/11. You never did.[125] You led two wars, and turned Afghanistan and Iraq from brutal dictatorships led by madmen into functioning secular democracies.

You freed women in Iraq and Afghanistan. They are no longer physically beaten for leaving the house unchaperoned. They even have positions in government.

You understood that freedom and liberty are gifts from Almighty God. Human beings want to be free. Black people fought through slavery and Jim Crow laws because no human being should ever be the property of another. Eastern Europeans fought and died trying to climb over a wall that eventually could not contain their human desires. Freedom gives people life. It gives them dignity. Millions of people in the Middle East are praying that your vision succeeds.

The War on Terror was not completely won during your presidency. It might not even be fully won in your lifetime, or even in mine. I am twenty-five years your junior. We have made astounding progress in a short amount of time. Some accused you of shredding the Constitution. What you did was help save all of our lives. Your vigilance gave your critics the freedom to criticize you at the top of their lungs. To me that sounds like democracy and liberty, not censorship.

You appointed first-rate judges. Justice Sam Alito is a fine legal mind. Chief Justice John Roberts might be one of the greatest intellectual titans the court has ever seen. Strict constructionists respect the Constitution the most, by simply obeying it.

As a Jewish person, I know that your support of Israel has never wavered. You also made sure that Arabs and Muslims in America were treated with dignity. Your support of Israel was more than just perfunctory acknowledgment of a democracy surrounded by dictatorships. You gave full-throttled support to Ariel Sharon to crush those that are spreading terrorism. Beyond the nation of Israel, you showed deep respect and warmth toward Jewish Americans. This was found in your annual White House Hanukkah parties and your warm wishes to us as we lit our candles.

Some said that you ruined our relations with the world, partly because of your support for Israel. This is completely false. The world does not hate us. The world's socialist, communist, and Islamofascist governments publicly hate us, while privately yearning to be us. They are already burning your successor in effigy. This tells me that the responsibility of the president is to do what benefits America, and only America. Our relations with Italy, Germany, France, Canada, Israel, Australia, India, and Japan were stronger than ever under your leadership.

I could spend hours praising your 2001 and 2003 tax cuts, in addition to your many fine qualities in terms of how you treated ordinary human beings.

To me you will always be the man that kept us safe. I will always see you through the prism of September 11th, 2001. I will always well up with emotion when I think of you standing with that firefighter on September 14th, three days after the attacks. I still hear your voice exalting Americans. "I hear you, the rest of the world hears you, and pretty soon the people who knocked down these buildings will hear from all of us!"[126] They heard us loud and clear.

I will go to my grave believing that the Iraq War was the legally and morally right thing to do. Reconstruction has been tough, but Saddam is gone. The world is absolutely better off. The collateral effects included Libya's Khadafi voluntarily giving up his weapons programs. This was a direct result of your leadership. You labeled Iran, Iraq, and North Korea as the "Axis of Evil."[127] You were right, and one of those three is no longer led by a dictator out to threaten the world. Your critics declared that the Iraq War was lost[128]. You doubled down, ordered a surge, and brought in General David Petraeus. Not only did you hire the best and brightest, you let them do their jobs and get those jobs done right.

On September 20th, 2001, you told us that America, "would not falter, and would not fail."[129] You let us know in January of 2009 that we "did not falter and did not fail."

If anybody wants evidence that America is still a beacon for the world to admire and emulate, just look at your successor. Only in America could his election be possible. As expected, your graciousness and kindness toward him and his family was sincere. Some said you were a divider and not a uniter. This is totally false. You reached out to your critics. They never accepted your hand of friendship. Your political enemies were the ones who polarized this nation. Your successor mentioned once that he thought you were a good person. Your critics need to hear this over and over again. Despite their obsession with division, you remained kind to the end. You were able to unite people who were willing to let decency override partisanship.

Some pointed to your low poll numbers, but it is easy to have high polls when consequential decisions are avoided. Your predecessor let the polls lead. That is the life of a follower. Leaders will always be controversial. History will vindicate you. As Winston Churchill said, "I will help write it."[130]

Part of this is selfishness. I believed in you. Vindicating your presidency will vindicate me. I was right to support you, and have zero regrets. You did not get everything right, but life is about getting the big things right. On what truly matters, the preserving of the lives of the American people, you got it right in a way your critics will one day be forced to admit. You got it right "big-time."[131]

Mr. President, I wish you, First Lady Laura Bush, and Vice President and Mrs. Cheney peace, happiness, and blessings always.

I shall continue to let my friends know how lucky they were that America was led by "The Dub," President George W. Bush.

As you leave, just know that while you are no longer leading the free world, you will forever be my president.

Luv Ya Dubya.

God bless you sir.

eric

Chapter 17:
2012 and Future Violence

2012 is more than an election year. It is our first chance to drag the First Sissy-in-Chief kicking and screaming into manhood. Watch for a change some time after the 2010 elections, as Mr. Obama rips off his ballet slippers and tutu and starts talking tough. I would rather get to know people who were tough when the cameras were off. For those wondering where the next Margaret Thatcher resides, visit Alaska and Minnesota. Oh, and these women are as hot and sexy as Helen Thomas is decrepit and repulsive.

Ideological Bigotry Part XXII–The Lynching of Sarah Palin

For those on the left who climax by taking decent conservative Americans and ripping their guts out, congratulate yourselves. First your failure to destroy Ronald Reagan led to Dan Quayle getting twice as much abuse. Now the failure of the left to rip George W. Bush to shreds has led to the stoning of Sarah Palin in the town square.

In a bombshell announcement, Alaska Governor Sarah Palin resigned.

While Minnesota Governor Tim Pawlenty declined to seek reelection in 2010 to focus on building a national presence for 2012, Governor Palin went a step further. She resigned altogether.

The press conference was unscripted and hastily read. When Sarah Palin was done speaking, her supporters and opponents had the same question. Why?

Is there a scandal building along the lines of an extramarital affair? Does she have a health problem such as cancer? Is there something wrong with her children?

Some described her move as politically shrewd. If she truly wants to be president, she needs to bone up on her foreign policy credentials. Mitt Romney and Mike Huckabee are already running. They have the luxury of flexible schedules. Mr. Huckabee has a built-in television audience. Mr. Romney is the wealthiest unemployed man in America.

Sarah Palin perhaps decided that she could not run a state and run for president. There is no shame in this. Bob Dole had to end his thirty-five year senate career because juggling became too much. Bob Dole also did not have to raise five children, one of them a special needs child.

Sarah Palin may be Superwoman, but even Superwoman never had to deal with villains as ruthless and vicious as the leftist smear merchants in America today.

The left needs to describe every powerful conservative as either evil, or as a complete imbecile.

Dick Cheney and Newt Gingrich were too intelligent to be seen as imbeciles. Therefore, they were evil. Dan Quayle was too nice and decent a man to be evil. Therefore, he had to be an imbecile.

Sarah Palin is a beautiful woman inside and out. She is also a religious Christian. Her election would destroy the feminist grievance-mongers in the same way Barack Obama has been the death knell for racial hustlers Jesse Jackson and Al Sharpton. Until feminists learn that a woman can be pro-life and still be a feminist, the movement will continue to be seen as a bunch of unattractive, over the hill, man-hating hags.

Sarah Palin is a hockey mom and a hunter. She eats moose stew. She is also a former beauty queen, another reason radical feminists despise her.

Sarah Palin also has something else in common with George W. Bush and Dan Quayle. She is a human being. She is a creature of God who simply wants to be treated with dignity. The concept of treating political opponents with dignity is totally lost on the left. The same bullies that took down Robert Bork took glee in Borking Sarah Palin.

Sarah Palin said that she stepped down as Alaska Governor because she had had enough. The abuse was relentless. Fifteen investigations, almost all dismissed, drained her resources. She can make more money in the private sector than she can running Alaska under the media glare. Maybe she saw her critics and thought, "Who needs this?"

If that is the case, she might wish to decline to run for president. Politics, as the cliché goes, ain't beanbag. If she is perceived as a quitter, she may be done.

The exact reasons of her departure from the governorship were initially shrouded in mystery.

What is no mystery is that the abuse she received went far beyond anything political. She was called a slutty flight attendant[132]. She was accused of being the mother of the child that is actually her granddaughter. Her daughters have been verbally assaulted for no reason other than that they love their mother.

Enough is enough is enough is enough is enough.

Sarah Palin is now a private citizen. I pray that she gets the peace of mind that all private citizens are entitled to receiving.

The lynching of conservatives must stop. The verbal suicide bombers on the left must stop.

The ideological bigotry must stop.

If it does not, payback against the liberals will be bloody, as they reap what they sowed.

eric

My Interview With Congresswoman Michele Bachmann

I had the pleasure of interviewing Minnesota Congresswoman Michele Bachmann.

I met her in May of 2008 in Washington, DC, at a Republican Jewish Coalition leadership meeting. She wowed the crowd, and is definitely a rising star in the Republican Party. At that event she agreed to an e-mail interview. Her staff was friendly, courteous, and responsive.

Before getting to the significant amount of substance that Congresswoman Bachmann brings to the political discussion in America, I want to offer one piece of apolitical frivolity.

The congresswoman is gorgeous. She might be the most beautiful woman in all of politics. I suspect she went into politics because modeling, while glamorous, does not allow for tackling world issues. I plan to start a rumor that Minnesota voters believe their state lottery is rigged because her husband won the lottery by being married to her.

Fawning aside, she is brilliant on the issues. She is an unapologetic conservative Republican who wears her conservative credentials with pride. The Republican Party has great ideas, but does not always market them properly. Congresswoman Bachmann is a highly effective spokesperson. The party will benefit in the long run from having given her a good speaking slot at the GOP Convention in her home state of Minnesota.

Now America will have to settle for her brilliance in this e-mail interview.

1) What is the Michele Bachman story? What made you decide to enter the political arena and congress?

I never longed to be a career politician, but an opportunity presented itself in 2000 to challenge an incumbent and not so responsive Minnesota State Senator. It turned out the numbers were on my side. I won then and again in 2004. In 2006, when Congressman Mark Kennedy decided to run for the U.S. Senate, I made a run for the U.S. House. Two years later, here I am in congress seeking a second term, and I couldn't be happier.

2) What can ordinary citizens do, besides donating money and voting for you to help win the War on Terror? What obligations do we have, and how can we help?

There are so many great organizations that exist who are truly proud to work with and honor the troops putting their lives on the line to preserve our freedom. I suggest that everyone find one of these organizations, such as Operation Minnesota

Nice or Homes for Our Troops, and learn how to get involved. You can learn more about local options at www.americasupportsyou.mil

3) It is one thing to ask people to have faith in God. It is much tougher to ask people to have faith in government. What does our government do right and what does it need to do better so people can start believing in their government again?

From the founding of this great nation, our forefathers have had heated debates on which policies are best for our nation. At the beginning it was Thomas Jefferson feuding with John Adams, today we have John McCain pitted against Barack Obama. What's most unfortunate about politics today is the deep mistrust and bitterness that political parties have for each other. You do not see as many cross-party friendships as previously and the sense of working together as one body has greatly diminished from years past. We need to look no further than this energy debate we're having now. With the exception of a handful of Democrats, it's the R's versus the D's, and the Democrats are not willing to work with us to hash out a comprehensive policy. If it's drilling they don't want it, and they aren't even willing to debate it. Americans deserve better.

With all that said, the mere fact that our country allows for so many differing opinions makes our nation a true model of government.

4) With regards to foreign policy, what have we done right, and what have we gotten wrong, in the last eight years, and what steps need to be taken to improve the situations that require improvement?

9/11 has changed America's foreign policy forever. We should support our military's efforts to combat terrorism, to ensure the safety of our country, and to further democracy in other parts of the world.

The most important vote I have taken in congress was for FISA to ensure that our intelligence professionals have all the tools they need at their disposal. Prior to 9/11, our intelligence community was at a great disadvantage as a result of the Clinton White House, and thankfully we've had a president who understands the importance of keeping our homeland safe and secure.

5) The American dollar seems to be in free fall, and homeowners are seeking a bailout at taxpayer expense. Should government get involved, and is this even a problem at all? If so, what needs to be done?

As a member of the Financial Services Committee, I've had the opportunity to take part in these discussions at the most basic legislative level. No matter how Washington spins it, the housing legislation it just passed does no good for America's homeowners. With this bill, congress is turning a blind eye to irresponsible borrowers and is, in fact, rewarding them with a federal program paid for by struggling taxpayers barely able to make ends meet. Proponents of the housing bill claim that it actually creates revenue because it forces Fannie Mae and Freddie Mac - currently in a very precarious financial position themselves - to pay a principal balance of each business purchase. But, in the end, this only puts taxpayers on the hook for even more money when Fannie and Freddie end up raising their fees to lenders in order to curb their increased costs. Simultaneously, the bill gives Fannie and Freddie billions of dollars of taxpayer backing to remain financially stable with no guarantee that they will never again overextend in this same way and require another taxpayer bailout. Our nation's housing market will recover more quickly if congress is more circumspect in its actions. Giving the government the privy to expand programs and increase oversight only stunts the growth of the free market, and forcing more taxes on innocent taxpayers is not a solution, it's a recipe for disaster.

6) What would be the main qualities and criteria you would look for with regards to potential Supreme Court justices? Could they disagree with you on major issues, and still be qualified? How do you feel about how they ruled on the DC Second Amendment case?

My ideal Supreme Court Justice is in the mold of Justices Scalia and Roberts, judges who do not view their position as an express lane to further their personal ideology and politics, but who are strict constitutionalists.

7) Do you support the Bush Doctrine of pre-emptive action? Do you feel that it may be necessary to take pre-emptive action against Iran? How does it differ from the Bachmann Doctrine?

We must do what we can to keep our nation safe. If there is compelling evidence that shows Iran is an imminent threat to the United States, we should act and act swiftly.

8) What Americans call 9/11, Israel refers to as every day life. Israel is then asked to show restraint. What is your view on Israel taking pre-emptive action, including a strike on Iran's nuclear facilities if necessary? What about with regards to the disputed territories such as Gaza? What about against Damascus, who funds Hezbollah?

I believe that Israel has the right to defend itself against hostile extremists. Israel has been the shining symbol of freedom and democracy in an area historically rampant with violence and oppression and has become an economic leader of the Middle East by proving to its people the rewards of capitalism, while also leading the region in other facets of a free society, including human rights and freedom of the press. Israel should do what's necessary to protect its citizens. I strongly urge my colleagues to stand committed to a free Israel.

9) Attempts to partially privatize Social Security and fix the ticking time bomb of Medicare have been met with hysteria about throwing old people on the street and leaving them to die. The issue was demagogued by the demagogic party in 1995. Do you favor any privatization of Social Security? If not, why not? If so, how can it be framed in terms that do not frighten seniors?

I believe that we should ensure that those currently receiving Social Security should continue to do so in its current form, but also give a new generation of workers the right to invest some of their money into accounts of their own. I understand the volatility of this issue, but it's another instance where we must put partisan rhetoric aside and take action for the benefit of our nation's future.

10) Many on the left preach compassion but you as a conservative actually live it. What made you begin to bring foster children into your life, and do you envision continuing to do so?

My husband and I have cared for twenty-three foster children, and I understand full well the struggles these children face on a daily basis. There are more than five hundred-thousand children in foster care nationwide, many of whom come from troubled homes and have been moved from family to family several times. These children are family, and I firmly believe that Americans should extend a helping hand to those in trouble. Taking in foster children was one of the most rewarding experiences of my life.

11) Without delving too deeply into your personal life, what would you want Americans to know about Michele Bachmann the person? One hundred years from now, what would you want people to remember about you, and what would you hope the history books say about you?

What keeps me fighting every day is my mission to leave a better and safer country to my children and future generations to come. More government is not the answer to the challenges facing our nation. Never was. Never will be. America's true stripes present themselves through personal liberty and entrepreneurship. We must do all we can to continue the proud history and heritage of our great nation.

12) Do you get bored with the marriage proposals that you get inundated with on a daily basis, and does your share of the 18-30-year-old male vote decrease when they find out you are happily married?

For as many enthusiastic supporters that I have cheering me on, there are probably just as many hoping for me to fall. The more success you have, the more persistent these antagonists become. I firmly believe that our opponents may shout the loudest, but we can tell the truth the longest and we have to, because there's too much at stake to cower away. I am so thankful to all my supporters.

I would like to thank Congresswoman Bachmann and her staff for their grace, class, and professionalism.

I suspect that her combination of charm and political intelligence will have her moving up the ranks rapidly. Minnesota Governor Tim Pawlenty running for president leaves a vacancy in the governor's mansion that she may be asked to fill. If Senator Norm Coleman fills the seat, then she would be a solid choice to fill his former Senate seat and fire the liberal currently defiling it.

Then again, the 2012 nominee could shock the world and select Congresswoman Bachmann to be the next vice president. Perhaps she as the presidential nominee might shock us and pick one of them to be her VP.

Whatever her next position, America is lucky to have such a talented woman give her prime earning years to public service. I took part in a conservative radio blogger group that met her at the GOP convention. Thanking her again was my pleasure.

eric

Chapter 18:
American Violence

America was founded by taking our enemies and beating the ever-loving daylights out of them. For those who want to complain about American aggression, immediately sell your home and give it to an American Indian family. Cash out your stock portfolio and give it to any minority with a sob story of oppression that occurred one hundred years ago. Better yet, take your finest pair of shoes, and give them to some angry Middle Easterners living in Iraq. After all, they will use the shoes to throw at conservative liberators, which is what liberals only wish they could do. Violence runs this world. It would be nice if liberals for once in their lives were capable of directing their hostility outward, rather than at their fellow Americans. Despite them, there are enough conservatives to make sure that when we engage in violence, it will be just, necessary, and victorious.

233 Years and Beautiful–America Remains Great in 2009

Happy 233 America!

On Independence Day of 2009 in Sacramento, I visited the beautiful island of Rio Linda where Mt. Rush Limbaugh got his start. There were fireworks displays from downtown San Diego to the Washington State northern border, and out Eastward to Maine and Key West, Florida. The spirit of America was alive with tea parties all across the nation.

I know what July 4th means to me. Independence Day is special. Before offering my own wistfulness, I would rather let some of the finest people associated with the finest military in the world offer their heartfelt sentiments. Without these brave heroes, the miracle that began in 1776 would pale by comparison. Here are their July 4th memories, and what Independence Day means to them.

ADMIRAL LEIGHTON "SNUFFY" SMITH

A simple answer: I think of what our forefathers sacrificed so that we could be free to work, pray and socialize as we wished. I think of Bosnia, and how I saw many people die for those very same things. I think of Iraq and Afghanistan and the number of people doing the same. We are so very lucky to have what we have yet we seldom seem to understand just what we do have in comparison to the rest of the world.

SS

RETIRED SOLDIER AND CONSERVATIVE BLOGGER SNOOPER

What does the 4th of July mean to me?

It means the spirit of American freedom reigns supreme throughout the world and that the vast majority of Americans, when the chips are down, will do whatever it takes to remain free.

It reminds me that when facing odds seemingly stacked against us, we as a nation will always rise to the top.

Currently, I reside in the GREAT Republic of Texas as does my son who has recently returned from the War in Iraq. I am a retired DAV and have served my nation since 1976.

As Francis Scott Key was writing our national anthem, I can only imagine the sight of which he beheld. Every time I myself returned across The Wire and caught a glimpse of our Flag flying, chills traveled up and down my spine and that experience remains with me to this day. The American flag represents that which millions of others wish they had. Why else is it that millions try to get to the United States and millions are not trying to leave?

July 4ᵗʰ, to me, represents that which no other country in the world has…True Freedom. I and millions like me are more than willing to give the ultimate sacrifice for our way of life, politics be damned.

COLONEL AL FRACKER

Our family vacation was always spent "up north" in a one-room cabin in the woods on the 4ᵗʰ of July. So, when someone mentions the 4ᵗʰ of July, my very first thought is standing next to a bonfire by Nichols Lake in mid-Michigan, the smoky scent of hot dogs tantalizing my nose and irritating my eyes. The words "freedom" and "independence" were thrown around as my Dad and relatives drank beer, ate, and retreated from long days working in a factory or climbing poles for Consumer Power Company, but those words meant little to me, as I was born free.

Ten years later, and the 4ᵗʰ of July meant so much more. I thought of my older brother who was born on July 2ⁿᵈ, the day the Declaration of Independence was signed, and how proud he was at seventeen to be a marine. Some say he died a needless death attacking the city of Hue. Three days after learning of his death, we received a letter from him describing a huge beetle he found that he wanted to add to our insect collection, and as a side note, he said not to worry because he was happy promoting freedom in a different land. Naïve? Maybe so, but poignant nonetheless.

My first official day in the army was July 2ⁿᵈ, 1972, and following a two day bus trip, I remember vividly the physical pain of push-ups, gorilla stomps, inverted crawls, and grass drills executed on the 4ᵗʰ of July. The utter frustration of being powerless on the receiving end of verbal and physical abuse highlighted the paradox, "one must lose freedom to gain freedom"… in other words, much like the song, "You don't know what you've got 'til it's gone".[133]

Fast forward another thirty-five years, and I'm part cynic and part optimist. The cynic laments our public's concept of freedom on this special day and latches onto cautionary excerpts sent from a friend. A Scottish History professor from University of Edinburgh in 1787 cites: "A democracy will continue to exist up until the time that voters discover they can vote themselves generous gifts from the public treasury. From that moment on the majority always vote for the candidates who promise the most benefits from the public treasury with the result that every democracy will finally collapse due to loose fiscal policy, which is always followed by dictatorship." He describes the cycle as, "from bondage to spiritual faith…from spiritual faith to great courage…from great courage to liberty…from liberty to abundance…from abundance to complacency…from complacency to apathy… from apathy to dependence…from dependence back into bondage".[134]

The optimist in me suggests this 4ᵗʰ of July will mean the same to me now as it did almost fifty years ago. We'll build a fire and scrounge up some hot dogs.

I'll remember the coolness of the lake, my Dad's strong laugh, and Uncle Joe losing his false teeth while water skiing...not once, but two years running. And these innocent memories will be accompanied kindly by a depth of convictions, experience, and reality...convictions of faith and service to my God, family, and country... experience of seeing what the lack of hope and freedom does to people, and the reality that each person can and must make a difference. Being free is a daily commitment, whether home, on the road, or in some foreign country. I didn't choose to be free – I was born free, and I am committed to die that way. I will be surrounded by soldiers who wrote a blank check to the American people, a check payable with their lives, who are living JFK's aged yet appropriate appeal to the public: "Ask not what your country can do for you, but what you can do for your country."[35] With these men on the 4th of July, I will be hopeful for a free Iraq, and more importantly, a continued freedom within the United States, and we'll pretend there's a lake, Uncle Joe's false teeth, and beer on the other side of the berm.

Al Fracker

COL, IN

16th Iraqi MITT

Team Chief

LANCE CORPORAL JOHN BIVONA

For me, the Fourth of July is not just about sparklers (but man, they're fun) and corn on the cob (no one can eat just one). Nor is it about hot dogs, although tofu pops and smart dogs make delicious meat-free ones. Please look for them at your local retail food store. I like Whole Foods. It's my source for all the vegan organic goodness that plumps the one hundred-forty pound community of cells I call moi.

Having served as a marine in Operation Desert Storm/Shield, Independence Day takes on an even greater symbolism, as is the case for most U.S. servicemen and women. Pride, honor, tradition, heritage, corn on the cob (Sorry, I guess I am hungry)...The tenacious and bold spirit that was necessary to overcome our old world oppressors is still very much alive today. The fireworks serve as a visual reminder of the beauty in finding independence from those who put unnecessary burdens on us.

The universe rewards bold action coupled with intelligence. We had a plan. We put it into effect. Fast forward two hundred years. Wal-Marts and America Idol. It sure beats Little House on the Prairie. Well, not really. Laura Ingalls, you go girl!

My mission this 4th...my plan...seek and destroy all organic corn on their cobs. Eliminate all kernels from their oppressive cobs. I will provide them independence. Fear not America. Meat-free hot dogs eaten with an independent spirit and my newly straightened chompers. Oohrah! Hey, where's the relish? Go vegan. Break your chains. See what lies beyond.

LEE SORENSEN

The 4th of July always means to me one thing: The flag.

We all know the history of our founders and their role in building our country. We even know the history of our flag. But when I see our Flag, I stop and give thanks to all the things this country has given me and done for me. It makes me want to give back to America all I can in the spirit of the last line of our Declaration of Independence,

"We mutually pledge to each other our Lives, our Fortunes and our sacred Honor." 136

Most of us cannot even begin to imagine the horrors our military saw in Vietnam, World War II or the U.S. Civil War. The only thing I can do to honor those who fought for the people that could not help themselves is by serving my country in the military. To a lot of us it makes no matter if the war is in Iraq or Iowa, we just give to our country. Sometimes with our life.

One day in the far future I hope, a flag will drape my coffin. It will be the proudest day of my life and I wish all who see that flag know, it is the same exact flag that draped my father's coffin as a WW II vet, and my grandfathers as a WW I vet. Although I will be there I wish I could see it, but you can bet I will be smiling.

So when you see our flag anywhere think of all the people that would defend you with their life, just because you are an American.

Lee S.

Balad, Iraq

As for me, I love the little things that are uniquely American.

For those wanting to see the glory of America, I take you to Coney Island in Brooklyn. The year is 2007, although the glory was repeated in 2008 and 2009.

On July 4th, American supremacy continues, especially in Brooklyn. Lady Liberty is shining her beacon of freedom all over the world, but primarily in the greatest city in the world, Brooklyn, New York.

The rest seems unimportant.

What is relevant is the real story in the news coming out of Brooklyn, in a small area called Coney Island. Coney Island is the home of the Brooklyn Cyclones, the Boardwalk, and the original Nathan's hot dog stand from 1916. Nathan's hot dogs are not only the greatest hot dogs in the world, but also the home of the world famous Hot Dog Eating Contest. For the last six years, Japanese winner Takeru Kobayashi reigned like the Lance Armstrong of competitive eating. Not today! Not in 2007.

"NEW YORK — American Joey Chestnut broke the world hot-dog eating record Wednesday at the annual Nathan's Famous International Hot Dog Eating Contest, downing 66 franks to beat six-time defending champ Takeru Kobayashi." (story courtesy of Fox News)[137]

In the 1980s, there was a growing fear that America was no longer number one. The Japanese were replacing us. They bought Rockefeller Center. The American decline was premature, until the twenty-first century. Six straight Japanese wins at Coney Island left Americans questioning their greatness. Were we becoming a nation of tofu vegetarians, unable to compete? Not since the disastrous 1983 America's Cup sailing loss have we been so low. Today, supremacy has returned. Joey Chestnut has brought the yellow hot dog belt back to the United States of America.

"The two gustatory gladiators quickly distanced themselves from the rest of the seventeen competitors, processing more beef than a slaughterhouse within the first few minutes. The two had each downed 60 hot dogs with 60 seconds to go when Chestnut — the veins on his forehead extended — put away the final franks to end Kobayashi's reign."

First the British thought that they were better than us. If memory serves, it was Pete Sampras who kept winning the British Open in tennis. Tiger Woods did the same in golf. What about the Germans? Did Detlef Schrempf win anything? What about Dirk Nowitzki? The Russians have not been the same since the 1980 Olympic hockey game, which led to the Berlin Wall crashing down. Canada? Are you kidding me? The Mighty Ducks brought the might of America another victory.

Japan was not going to beat us in World War II, which lasted six years. Their dominance of the Nathan's Hot Dog Eating Contest lasted six years. This is no coincidence.

There are ultra-serious issues concerning July 4th. It is a day about freedom, liberty, democracy, and all things red, white and blue. I have repeatedly emphasized the pride I feel being American. I wish I could shake every soldier's hand for allowing me to focus on hot dog eating contests while they handle trivial matters such as saving my life. I well up with emotion when I hear Lee Greenwood sing "God Bless the USA."[138] I get fired up when Toby Keith sings about putting a "boot up the @ss"[139] of the bad guys who wish America harm. John Fogerty reminds us that not everybody is a "Fortunate Son."[140] Bruce Springsteen does sing about "Born in the USA," but I think "Glory Days,"[141] is a greater metaphor. Ours are continuing. I even find solace in the American dream expressed in John Mellencamp's "Pink Houses,"[142] although not everyone gets that pink house. At least they have a shot.

Some will try to paint July 4th as a day for fat, lazy, stupid American slobs to overindulge in food. If we are such awful people, why does everybody worldwide want to live here? Americans are good people. We have been blessed. Our indulgences are our way of expressing our blessings. We give generously to other nations, and are generous with ourselves, as we should be.

I am not Joey Chestnut. I will not be eating sixty-three hot dogs, although if I could, I would. I vacation twice a year in Coney Island, where my grandparents reside, along with other family members. When I see my friends, we take that magical trip to the Boardwalk, where the fireworks go off every weekend during the summer, and the Nathan's hot dogs taste fantastic.

Whether it is sports heroes such as Michael Jordan, Babe Ruth or Joey Chestnut, captains of industry such as Jack Welch or Donald Trump, or the fine heroes of our military, just remember what truly defines America. We are high achievers. We strive to be the best. We work hard, play by the rules, and truly believe in the noble greatness of the individual. America is sometimes down. We have repeatedly been counted out. Those doubters have been repeatedly wrong.

To explain American success, I turn to one of my favorite Brooklyn people, Oakland Raiders owner Al Davis. After winning another Super Bowl in 1983, he held the Lombardi Trophy. He was asked about what it took to achieve success. "First, you start out with great coaches. Then you get great players. Then you have a great organization. You go out and tell them one thing… Just Win Baby!"[143]

Americans are winners. Other nations talk trash. We go about our business. When you are the best, the results speak for themselves.

July 4th is a celebration of b*tchslapping those who tried to harm us. While I pray for the safety of our soldiers, I also pray that they b*tchslap some terrorists off the face of the Earth. They do that job brilliantly.

As we light Roman candles, and wave those American flags sky-high, let's be thankful and grateful that we truly do live in the land of the free, and the home of the brave.

May God bless America, Brooklyn, and soldiers everywhere defending our freedom. Nice job Joey Chestnut. Way to bring home the yellow belt.

July 4th is about even more than the glory of that Brooklyn day. July 4th is about America the Beautiful. Nobody sings that better than the late Ray Charles.

"America…I'm talkin' 'bout America…God done shed his grace on thee…"[144]

I would end this by saying God bless the USA, but based on the last two hundred-thirty-three years, he already has.

I wish a happy and peaceful July 4th to you all. May your fireworks shine bright, your flags wave sky-high, and your loved ones be close, happy, and safe on this day and every day thereafter.

eric

Violent Conclusions

My experiences are based on a simple premise: force works. Nobody in this world respects weakness.

In football, bodies collide, go down hard, get back up, and fight to the very end. The Super Bowl trophy is earned by surviving thousands of brutal collisions.

Love is not something that happens. It is hard work, and must be fought for. Feminists who publicly speak about chivalry privately long for Tarzan to swing from the vine, flip them over, slap them on the (redacted), maybe take a bite of the apple, and let them know that they are strong and able to take care of them. Women match the assertiveness by slapping the guy in the face when he crosses the line.

Love and sports are pleasures. Real life is about trying to keep a small brush fire known as life from being consumed by the literal global conflagration. Our choices are to bend over and take it like a liberal, or support the people who get paid to kick down doors, bust furniture, find the bad guys, and knock skulls. No, I do not mean Dennis Farina, although he is one of the better ones.

We need to support our troops, not through platitudes, but by actually getting involved. Send a care package. Shake a soldier's hand. Go to the voting booth and fire anybody that dishonors and slanders them.

God created me. If ever there was an entity about violence, it was God. God smacked around a ton of people centuries ago for not living right. God is not on our side. We have to be on his. My moral compass does not always point true north, but my logic meter does. If it takes violence to bring about peace and justice, then break out as much violence as necessary to get the job done. I just pray to God that I am right. I am prepared to be judged.

As for me, my battle cry remains the same. *Hineni*. Here I am. I am Jewish, proud, politically conservative, and morally liberal.

So what happen next?

I'll be flying down the highway headed west …

In a streak of black lightning, called the Tygrrrr Express.

On to the next adventure. God bless.

eric

Acknowledgements

My grandparents are gone, but with me always. Being a parent is the toughest job in the world. My parents tried their best. I was fed, clothed, and sheltered every day of my life.

Without love, there is no life. The current sexual administration is quite fulfilling.

My friendships are lifelong friendships. They are listed in alphabetical order by last name to avoid any possible (insert nightmare scenarios here).

Leeor Alpern, Gary Aminoff, Seth Arkin, Brian Arnold, Rachael Aron, Richard Baehr, Jane Barnett, Jeff Barry, Billy Beene, Michael and Ann Benayoun, Lara Berman, Arno Berry, Leo Bletnitsky, David Blumberg, Shane Borgess, Peter Bylsma, Sherry Caiozzo, Johnny Ceng, Ligang Chen, Lisa and Bob Cohen, Nim Cohen, Chaim and Tova Cunin, Val Cymbal, Toni Anne Dashiell, Ari and Fini David, Aaron Deutsch, Chuck and Diane DeVore, Susan Duclos, Seth Edelman, Brian Elfand, Jason Elman, Sharon Elias, Chad Everson, Uri Filiba, Ken Flickstein, Deron Freatis, Eric and Jennifer Goldberg, Steve Goldberg, Eugene Grayver, Molly and Leonard Grayver, Meri Green, Elyse and Aaron Greenberg, Larry Greenfield, Celeste Greig, Steve Grill, Moira Gruss, Danny Halperin, John Heller, Micky Himell, Julia and Marc Jaffe, Jason Kenniston, Tarik Khan, Jonathan Klein, Jamie Krasnoo, Jerry Krautman, Jeff Kuhns, Amy and Gene Laff, Elana Landau, Esther Levine, Isaac Lieberman, Lisa Macizo, David Marcus, Jason Margolies, Jersey McJones, Margie and Tom Mergen, Carl Merino, Mike Monatlik, Andrew Nelson, Izzy Newman, Greg Neyman, Erica Nurnberg, Doris Ohayon, Terry Okura, Mare Ouellette, Brian Ozkan, Mike Patton, Stevie Rivenbark, Harold and Sharon Rosenthal, Jeanie and Bernie Rosenthal, Ron Rothstain, Michael Rubinfeld, Peggy Sadler, Beverly Sandler, Pat Saraceno,

Daniel Savitt, Evan Sayet, Alan Schechter, Steven Slade, Alicia and Josh Stone, Ryan Szackas, Ruth and David Tobin, Borah Van Dormolen, Dov and Runya Wagner, Adam Wasserman, Doug Welch, Hilarie Wolf, Laura Wolfe, Woody Woodrum, Nate and Janna Wyckoff, Oliver Young, Marc Zoolman.

My extended family includes the Arzillos, the Diels, the Katzs, David Malakoff, the Mouradians, the Rossis, and the Weitzs.

Lara Berman convinced me to start a blog. Jamie Krasnoo provided the technological advice. Eliot Yamini of *Hotweazel* developed it. Hugh Hewitt, Armstrong Williams, Ward Connerly, Ralph Peters, Evan Sayet, and Larry Greenfield all have helped my blog expand. Celeste Greig, Peggy Sadler, Patricia Saraceno, Borah Van Dormolen, and Toni Anne Dashiell all helped my speaking career. Chabad, USC Hillel, the Republican Jewish Coalition, and the Zionist Crusader Alliance have all nourished and inspired me.

Thank you Ronald Reagan, George W. Bush, and Dick Cheney for your leadership.

Almighty God, thank you for keeping the lightning bolt from my rumpus.

eric, aka the Tygrrrr Express http://www.tygrrrrexpress.com

ENDNOTES

I am not Keith Olbermann or Arthur Sulzberger Jr. Unverified, angrily delivered stories are for liberals. Many of my sources are from liberal sites. While I detest acknowledging leftists in any way, listing established conservative sites would just open me up to liberal charges of less thorough research. I want the world to witness vicious left-wing ideological violence, and determine that the hatred emanates from leftist "sources."

(1) Burke, Edmund. *http://www.wikiquote.org*

(2) Limbaugh, Rush. Anatomy of a Smear. *www.rushlimbaugh.com*, September 26, 2007

(3) Reid, Harry. Speech on Senate Floor, October 1, 2007

(4) Clinton, Hillary. Speech on Senate Floor, April 8, 2008

(5) Moveon.org. General Petraeus or General Betray Us? September 10, 2007

(6) Boxer, Barbara. Barbara Boxer. *www.wikipedia.org*, 1991

(7) Thomas, Clarence. Senate Judiciary Testimony, October, 1991

(8) Fagen, Cynthia R. Anger at WTC Suicide. *New York Post*, November 8, 2004

(9) Cobain, Kurt. I Hate Myself and Want to Die. 1994

(10) Krauthammer, Charles. Charles Krauthammer. *www.wikipedia.org*, 2003

(11) Balleza, Maureen. Memos on Bush Are Fake but Accurate. *New York Times*, September 15, 2004

(12) Reagan, Ronald. Tear Down This Wall. *ReaganLibrary.com*, June 12, 1987

(13) Grayson, Alan. *Ed Schultz Radio Show.* October 21, 2009

(14) Seeleye, Katherine Q. Gore says Bush Betrayed the U.S. *New York Times*, February 9, 2004

(15) Pelosi, Nancy. *www.msnbc.com*, September 17, 2009

(16) Dean, Howard. Speech to Association of Democratic State Chairs, January 29, 2005

(17) Barron, David H. *Days of Wine, Women, and Wrong*, 1990

(18) Roberts, Julia. www.brainyquote.com.

(19) Markay, Lachlan. Media Amnesiacs Suddenly Appalled at Hitler Comparisons. www.newsbusters.org, November 30, 2009

(20) Ice-T. New Jack Hustler. *New Jack City Soundtrack*, 1991

(21) Diament, Nathan. How the GOP Won the Orthodox Vote. *The Forward*, November 11, 2004

(22) Kampeas, Ron. Conservative Supreme Court Rulings Vex Jewish Leaders. *Jewish Journal*, July 5, 2007

(23) Valley Beth Shalom. Hanukkah Sermon, December, 2008

(24) *PCU*, 1994

(25) Waxman, Henry. Speech at the Luxe Hotel, August 27, 2009

(26) Eban, Abba. Speech After Geneva Peace Talks, 1973.

(27) Meir, Golda. Speech to the National Press Club, 1957

(28) Richardson, Bill. President-elect Barack Obama announces Governor Bill Richardson as Secretary of Commerce. *www.change.gov*, December 3, 2008

(29) Greenfield, Daniel. Whatever You Do, Don't Upset the Muslims. www.sultanknish.blogspot.com, January 13, 2009

(30) Giuliani, Rudy. Speech to Orthodox Jewish Group in Brooklyn, October 18, 2009 (31) Goldberg, Jeffrey. Netanyahu to Obama: Stop Iran—Or I Will. The Atltantic, March 31, 2009

(32) Cohen, Roger. Israel Cries Wolf. *New York Times*, April 8, 2009

(33) Herbert, Bob. 'Drop Dead' is not an Option. *New York Times*, November 17, 2008

(34) Ruehl, Mercedes. *Frasier*, 1995

(35) Emanuel, Ari. The Curious Math of Hillary's "35 Years of Experience." *The Huffington Post*, January 17, 2008

(36) The Clovers. Love Potion No. 9. *Love Potion No. 9*, 1959

(37) Ice-T. *New Jack City*, 1991

(38) Guns 'n' Roses. Welcome to the Jungle. *Appetite For Destruction*, 1987

(39) Lord Acton. Letter to Mandell Creighton, April, 1887

(40) Al Gore's Son Busted For Drugs in Hybrid Car. *Reuters*, July 4, 2007

(41) Schwartz, Stuart. Maureen Dowd's Descent Into Fury. *American Thinker*, September 17, 2009

(42) Dowd, Maureen. Visceral Has its Value. *New York Times*, November 21, 2009

(43) Cher. If I could Turn Back Time. *Heart of Stone*, 1989

(44) Klein, Amy. Gays Get Married and I'm Still Single. *Jewish Journal*, June 26, 2008

(45) Strasser, Theresa. Performance at The University of Judaism, 2004

(46) Cimbalo, Guy. So Wrong It's Right. *Playboy*, June, 2009

(47) Gundy, Mike. Post-game Press Conference, September 22, 2007

(48) Ex-Official at Disney Free in a Sex Case. *New York Times*, December 23, 1999

(49) Berman, Chris. *NFL Primetime*, Debuted 1987

(50) Pelosi, Nancy. Interview on KTVU, April 15, 2009

(51) Jehl, Douglas. A Mustang and a Boy Named Bill. *New York Times*, April 18, 1994

(52) Cowan, Bill. Speech to David Horowitz Freedom Center. May 30, 2007

(53) Nicholson, Jack. *A Few Good Men*, 1992

(54) Reagan, Ronald. Speech at Marine Corps Air Ground Combat Center, 1985

(55) Rumsfeld, Donald. Briefing at the Foreign Press Center. January 22, 2003

(56) Pear, Robert. GOP Submits New Bill to Revamp Welfare and Medicaid. *New York Times*, May 23, 1996

(57) Reagan, Ronald. Campaign Speeches for Barry Goldwater, 1964

(58) Caine, Michael. *Batman: The Dark Knight*, 2008

(59) Thorogood, George. Bad to the Bone. *Bad to the Bone*, 1982

(60) Thorogood, George. Born to be Bad. *Born to be Bad*, 1988

(61) Sutton, Willie. *Where the Money Was*, 1976

(62) Krauthammer, Charles. Speech to Republican Jewish Coalition, May, 2008

(63) King, Larry. Interview With Ahmedinejad. *Larry King Live*, September 23, 2008

(64) Lasky, Ed. John Bolton. *American Thinker*, November 11, 2006.

(65) Bolton, John. Interview with Sean Hannity. Hannity & Colmes, September 23, 2008

(66) Firehouse. Reach For the Sky. *Hold your Fire*, 1992

(67) Lynyrd Skynyrd. That Smell. *Street Survivors*, 1977

(68) Stanley, Paul. Live to Win. *Live to Win*, 2006

(69) Hagar, Sammy. Winner Takes it All. *Over the Top Soundtrack*, 1987

(70) The Animals. Don't Let Me Be Misunderstood. *The Animals*, 1965

(71) Bobby Fuller Four. I Fought the Law. *I Fought the Law*, 1965

(72) Bon Jovi. It's My Life, *Crush*, 2000

(73) AC/DC. Moneytalks. *The Razors Edge*, 1990

(74) 1 Hostage Killed In Daring Peru Rescue, *Reuters*, April 22, 1997

(75) Asia. Heat of the Moment, *Asia*, 1982

(76) Europe. The Final Countdown. *The Final Countdown*, 1986

(77) Def Leppard. Rocket. *Hysteria*, 1987

(78) Guns 'n' Roses. Welcome to the Jungle. *Appetite For Destruction*, 1987

(79) Aerosmith. The Other Side. *Pump*, 1989

(80) Golden Earring. Twilight Zone. *Cut*, 1982

(81) Metallica. Enter Sandman. *Metallica*, 1991

(82) Rolling Stones. Sympathy For the Devil. *Beggars Banquet*, 1968

(83) Rolling Stones. Paint it Black. *Aftermath*, 1966

(84) Twisted Sister. I Wanna Rock. *Stay Hungry*, 1984

(85) Bush, George W. Speaking From Ground Zero, September 14, 2001

(86) Adkins, Trace. Honkytonk Badonkadonk. *Songs About Me*, 2005

(87) Adkins, Trace. *A Personal Stand*, 2007

(88) Adkins, Trace. *Politically Incorrect*, October 11, 2001

(89) Christensen, Jay. College Sports Dying a Slow Death. *The Wiz of Odds*, November 24, 2009

(90) Buckley, William Jr. *Meet the Press*, October 17, 1965

(91) Jan, Tracy. Harvard Professor Gates Arrested at Cambridge Home. *Boston Globe*, July 20, 2009

(92) Nisimov, Danielle. College GOP Will Ban Some From Horowitz. *Daily Trojan*, November 4, 2009

(93) Shams, Alex. *USC Students For Justice in Palestine*, November 3, 2009

(94) Horowitz, David. Speech to USC College Republicans, November 4, 2009

(95) Coolio. 1, 2, 3, 4 (Sumpin' New). *Gangsta's Paradise*, 1995

(96) McNerney, Georgina. Major to Close Due to Budget. *Campus Watch*, February 3, 2009

(97) Unplanned Parenthood. *South Park*, 1998

(98) Louis, E. The Voters Got It Right. *New York Daily News*, September 20, 2007

(99) Friedman, Neil S. Only Thing Special About Recent Election Was How It Evolved. Canarsie Courier, March 16, 2006

(100) Long Island's Wonderful Political Climate. *www.attaboy.tommydoc.net*, July 22, 2005

(101) O'Neill, Tip. On the Campaign Trail, 1935

(102) Bash, Dana. Alexander is on Message. *CNN Political Ticker*, December 1, 2009

(103) Green, Dennis. *No Room For Crybabies*, November, 1997

(104) Timberlake, Justin. Cry Me a River. *Justified*, 2002

(105) Clinton, Hillary. Kentucky Victory Speech. May 21, 2008

(106) Malkin, Michelle. Hillary's 'Iron My Shirts' Hecklers. www.michellemalkin.com, January 7, 2008

(107) Bush, George W. Speaking from Ground Zero. September 14, 2001

(108) Bush, George W. Speech to Congress. September 20, 2001

(109) Simon, Paul. You Can Call Me Al. *Graceland*, 1986

(110) Osama Bin Laden Has Fartypants. *South Park*, 2001

(111) ManBearPig. *South Park*, 2006

(112) Al Gore vs. Al Yankovic. MTV Celebrity Deathmatch, 2006

(113) Fox, Michael J. Here We Go Again. *Family Ties*, September 27, 1984

(114) Adams, Mason. Here We Go Again. *Family Ties*, September 27, 1984

(115) Lefevre, Edwin, *Reminiscence of a Stock Operator*, 1923

(116) Bray, Thom, *Riptide*, Debuted 1983

(117) Leary, Dennis. *No Cure For Cancer*, 1993

(118) The Animals. Don't Let Me Be Misunderstood. *The Animals*, 1965

(119) The Scorpions. Wind of Change. *Crazy World*, 1990

(120) Reagan, Ronald. Tear Down This Wall. *ReaganLibrary.com*, June 12, 1987

(121) Kennedy, John F. Inaugural Address. January 20, 1961

(122) Reagan, Ronald. Inaugural Address. January 20, 1981

(123) Kael, Pauline. Lecture to Modern Language Association. *New York Times*, December 28, 1972

(124) Kudlow, Larry. Free Markets Work. *RealClearPolitics.com*, April 26, 2006

(125) Bush, George W. Farewell Address, January 15, 2009

(126) Bush, George W. Live From Ground Zero. September 14, 2001

(127) Bush, George W. State of the Union. January 29, 2002

(128) Reid, Harry. *CBS News*, September 19, 2007

(129) Bush, George W. Speech to Congress, September 20, 2001

(130) Churchill, Winston. Winston Churchill as Historian. www.wikipedia.org, 1939

(131) Noah, Timothy. Adam Clymer Blows His Moment. *Slate*, September 5, 2000

(132) Letterman, David. *The Late Show*, June 9, 2009

(133) Cinderella. Don't Know What You Got (Till It's Gone). *Long Cold Winter*, 1988

(134) Tytler, Alexander. Tytler's Circle. *www.wikipedia.org*, 1790

(135) Kennedy, John. Inaugural Address. January 20, 1961

(136) Jefferson, Thomas. *Declaration of Independence*, 1776

(137) American Joey Chestnut Wins Hot Dog Eating Contest, Shattering World Record. *Fox News*, July 4, 2007

(138) Greenwood, Lee. God Bless the U.S.A., *You've Got a Good Love Comin'*, 1984

(139) (Keith, Toby. Angry American. *Unleashed*, 2002

(140) Creedence Clearwater Revival. Fortunate Son. *Willy and the Poor Boys*, 1969

(141) Springsteen, Bruce. Glory Days. *Born in the U.S.A.*, 1984

(142) Mellencamp, John Cougar. Pink Houses. *Lonesome Jubilee*, 1987

(143) Davis, Al. Super Bowl VXIII Post-game Interview. *CBS*, January 22, 1984

(144) Charles, Ray. America the Beautiful. *America the Beautiful*, 1976